Process and Structure in
Human Decision Making

Process and Structure in Human Decision Making

Edited by

HENRY MONTGOMERY
University of Göteborg, Sweden

and

OLA SVENSON
Lund University, Sweden

JOHN WILEY & SONS
Chichester · New York · Brisbane · Toronto · Singapore

Library of Congress Cataloging-in-Publication Data

Process and structure in human decision making.

   Bibliography: p.
   Includes index.
   1. Decision-making—Case studies. 2. Decision-making—Research. I. Montgomery, Henry.
II. Svenson, Ola.
BF448.P76   1989   153.8′3   88–33788
ISBN 0-471-91977-2

British Library Cataloguing in Publication Data

Process and structure in human decision making.
   1. Decision making. Psychological aspects
   I. Montgomery, Henry   II. Svenson, Ola
   153.8′3

ISBN 0-471-91977-2

Typeset by Associated Publishing Services Ltd, Petersfield and Salisbury.
Printed in Great Britain by St Edmundsbury Press, Bury St Edmunds, Suffolk

List of contributors

Anders Biel, *Department of Psychology, University of Göteborg, Box 14158, S-400 20 Göteborg, Sweden*

Ray Crozier, *School of Psychology, Lancashire Polytechnic, Preston PR1 2TQ, England*

Ulf Dahlstrand, *Department of Psychology, University of Göteborg, Box 14158, S-400 20 Göteborg, Sweden*

Anne Edland *Department of Psychology, University of Stockholm, S-10691 Stockholm, Sweden*

Irmtraud Gallhofer, *Sociometric Research Foundation, Blauburgwal 20, 1015 AT Amsterdam, The Netherlands*

Oswald Huber, *Universität Salzburg, Institut für Psychologie, Hellbrunner Strasse 34, A-5020 Salzburg, Austria*

Gunnar Karlsson, *Department of Psychology, University of Stockholm, S-10691 Stockholm, Sweden*

John Maule, *Department of Behavioural Sciences, Huddersfield Polytechnic, Queensgate, Huddersfield HD1 3DH, England*

Henry Montgomery, *Department of Psychology, University of Göteborg, Box 14158, S-400 20 Göteborg, Sweden*

Göran Nilsson, *Department of Psychology, University of Stockholm, S-10691 Stockholm, Sweden*

Rob Ranyard, *Department of Science, Bolton Institute of Technology, Deane Road, Bolton BL3 5AB, England*

Willem Saris, *Sociometric Research Foundation, Blauburgwal 20, 1015 AT Amsterdam, The Netherlands*

Gunilla Sundstroem, *Laboratory for Man–Machine Studies, University of Kassel, Mönchebergstrasse 7, 3500 Kassel, West Germany*

Ola Svenson, *Department of Psychology, Lund University, Paradisgatan 5, 223 50 Lund, Sweden*

Tadeusz Tyszka, *Department of Psychology, Polish Academy of Sciences, Plac Malachwskiego 1, 00-063 Warsaw, Poland*

Contents

Part III: Experimental studies

Part IV: Societal decision making

Contents

Introduction

Psychological studies of human decision making started out from normative models formulated outside psychology. The main issue in this early research was: how well do people's choices or judgements agree with normative requirements? However, in recent years there has been a growing interest in the cognitive and evaluative processes behind a particular choice or judgement. In addition, several studies have focused on how decision makers represent and structure information about the choice alternatives. Hence, recent research has been conducted on *process* and *structure* in human decision making.

The increasing focus on processes and structures in decision-making research has been paralleled by methodological advances. Decision-making processes are studied by a number of process-tracing techniques such as think-aloud reports and registration of eye movements. Decision structures are studied by the same techniques as well as by methods for analysing written documents and other accounts in which decisions are described or justified.

The present volume reports European research on process and structure in decision making. All the contributors to this volume are members of the European Group for Process Tracing Studies of Decision Making. The group has met once or twice a year since 1982. The editors of this volume have the feeling that the research conducted by the members of the group follows a particular European style. This style is characterized by (a) an ambition to develop broad integrative theories rather than mini-theories for very specific domains, (b) usage of verbal protocol data (primarily think-aloud reports and verbal documents) to study processes and structures, which does not preclude, however, that other data types are used and combined with verbal data, (c) an explorative research style, i.e. a wish to find out what really is in the data rather than just finding out whether a certain hypothesis is right or wrong, and (d) a growing interest in psychological processes and structures in societal decision making.

The book is organized to articulate the interplay between theory, method, and data. The first part of the book presents three theoretical perspectives which highlight the role of process and structure in decision making. Inspired by Newell and Simon's theory of human problem solving, Huber describes in his chapter how the application of different information-processing operators (process) changes the representation of a decision situation (structure). Montgomery discusses in his chapter a model for how the cognitive representation changes during a decision-making process. He assumes that decision making may be seen as the search for a dominance structure, i.e. a cognitive representation in which one alternative dominates the others. Both Huber and Montgomery anchor their ideas in cognitive psychology. Karlsson's chapter starts out from a rather different perspective, viz. phenomenological psychology. He criticizes researchers with a cognitive orientation who fail to take the subject's perspective and how they, too easily, take for granted that the subject perceives an experimental task (e.g. a decision task) in the same way as the researcher does. More specifically, Karlsson is critical to the idea that people deliberately *use* or *apply* certain strategies in order to make their decisions. The editors of this book think that cognitively oriented researchers in decision making have something to learn from phenomenological psychology, although we are aware that a perfectly happy marriage between the two approaches may not be possible.

The second part of the book presents methods for studying process and structure of decision making. Two chapters authored by Svenson discuss and exemplify how think-aloud data on decision processes may be collected and analysed. In the third chapter of this part Gallhofer and Saris compare a number of methods used with written documents as data for inferring decision rules and cognitive structures of actors in decision situations (particularly political decision situations).

The third and fourth parts of the book are devoted to data and report a number of empirical studies of decision making. Each part begins with an introductory chapter discussing theoretical and methodological aspects of the data to be presented. The third part presents process-tracing studies carried out in the psychological laboratory. By contrast, the fourth part, which deals with societal decision making, exemplifies how 'real' decisions (in politics) may be studied from written documents and by means of interview data. However, this part also includes one chapter written by Nilsson showing how experimental techniques may be used for pin-pointing cognitive structures of economic variables of great political relevance.

The editors hope that this book will make a contribution to the psychology of decision making. We think that not very much is yet known, actually, about the mental processes and structures leading to a decision. Hopefully, this volume sheds some light on these aspects of decision making. In any case, we expect that the ambition of this book to articulate the interplay between theory, methods, and data will inspire further research in the psychology of decision making. However, we also believe that the perspectives discussed in this volume are broad enough to attract interest from scientists and laymen outside the psychological discipline. For example, the book may be of value for persons who are interested in societal decision making or methods for analysing verbal accounts of important decisions. In addition, we also wish to find readers among all those who in their private lives have wondered what is going on in their own and other people's minds when they are engaged in a decision-making process.

HENRY MONTGOMERY
OLA SVENSON

Part I
Theory

1

Information-processing operators in decision making

OSWALD HUBER

Decision making is modelled as an (adaptive) process which can be partitioned into subprocesses (phases, stages) (see, for example, Biasio, 1969; Bettman, 1979; Hollnagel, 1977; Janis and Mann, 1977; Kahnemann and Tversky, 1979; and Montgomery, 1983). Examples of such subprocesses are: the generation of alternatives, the identification of consequences of actions, the selection of dimensions, the test as to whether an alternative satisfies one or more levels of acceptance (filtering), the selection of one alternative out of a set of alternatives, and so on. However, there is no general agreement on a specific phase model. Different theorists distinguish a different number of phases or stages and group subprocesses differently.

In my chapter I concentrate on two of these subprocesses: selection of one alternative out of a set of alternatives and filtering of alternatives according to one or several levels of acceptance. These subprocesses—especially the selection of one alternative out of a set of alternatives—have been the central topic for decision theory for a long time; consider, for example, models like the Additive Utility model and the Subjective Expected Utility (SEU) model, or heuristics like elimination by aspects or the lexicographic heuristic.

I shall discuss the interpretation of the process of decision making as a problem-solving process. Decision making, in my opinion, is one specific type out of the many types of problems. I believe this interpretation to be fruitful for decision theory, as the theoretical and empirical results of problem solving may improve our models about the decision process and may give us ideas for empirical investigations. However, I want to emphasize that I do *not* believe that the psychology of problem solving presents ready-made solutions to us.

Process and Structure in Human Decision Making
Edited by H. Montgomery and O. Svenson. © 1989 John Wiley & Sons Ltd

The interpretation of the decision process as a problem-solving process is suggested by the similarities between these processes (for a characterization of problem-solving processes see, for example, Newell and Simon, 1972). The decision process starts with an (undesired) initial situation (*initial state*) in which, for example, the decision maker is confronted with a set of alternatives to choose from. There is a desired goal situation (*goal state*), in which exactly one alternative has been chosen (in a competent manner). The problem solver does not know in advance how to transform the initial state into the goal state (provided the specific decision is not a routine task).

The problem solver transforms the initial state into the goal state by applying one or more operators. Without going too much into details an *operator* can be defined as an activity to alter states. If my car does not move when I want it to, the set of operators to change this initial state may include, for example, checking whether there is petrol in the tank or calling my garage. Usually the application of *one* operator does not suffice to transform the initial state (the car does not move) into the goal state (the car is running). Although diagnosing an empty petrol tank is an important operator, it does not solve the problem as such. Another operator (putting petrol into the tank) has to be employed to reach the goal state. Therefore a sequence of several operators (not necessarily distinct ones) is applied. The application of each operator generates an *intermediate state* (provided the achieved state is not the goal state). If the operators are already available the problem solver's task is to construct *a* or *the* sequence of operators leading to the goal state. In other problems the search for or the invention of operators may constitute a major part of the problem.

The problem-solving states and the operators together define the *problem space*, in which the operators can be conceived as paths for moving from one state to another. In a specific state not all of the operators may be applicable. This knowledge about the constraints is incorporated in the problem space. In most cases the subjective problem space is only a subset of the one objectively possible. Reasons for this are capacity limitations on information processing and restricted knowledge. One and the same problem may be represented by different problem solvers in considerably different problem spaces. As has been shown in different problem domains (see, for example, Simon, 1979), one variable affecting the subjective representation is expertise, other relevant variables being, for instance, the formulation of the problem or characteristics of the task.

Within this theoretical framework problem solving may be viewed as a journey through the problem space. It is important to distinguish clearly between the merely mental simulation of the application of an operator in the problem space and the actual application of this operator. The cognitive representation enables us to test the consequences of an operator (e.g. a specific move in a game of chess) without performing irreversible actions in the real world.

In most states several operators could be applied. Therefore the problem solver has to select one of them in some way. Among the strategies employed for operator selection are, for example, general problem-solving strategies like means–end analysis and progressive deepening, or more task-specific ones like the recursive subgoal strategy and the pattern-following strategy used in the 'Towers of Hanoi' puzzle (Simon, 1979). Evaluation processes play an important role in these strategies (e.g. the evaluation of the similarity between the attempted state and the goal state). Thus *one* common theme for decision theory and problem solving is the choice among operators. However, within the limitations of this chapter I shall not pursue this specific topic further. Whereas strategies like those mentioned above seem to be sufficient for explaining the behaviour in well-defined problems of low complexity (e.g. Towers of Hanoi), other control processes seem to be necessary in more complex and/or ill-defined problems (e.g. planning the construction of a house). Different dimensions of complexity are discussed at present, e.g. by Funke (1986) and Mackinnon and Wearing (1980).

There are various possibilities of defining types of problems (e.g. Reitman, 1965; and Greeno, 1978). The distinction between problems with a well-defined and an ill-defined goal state is most relevant for decision making. In a problem with a well-defined goal state there are clear-cut rules defining for any state within the problem space whether it is a (or the) goal state or not. Examples of such problems are chess or the Towers of Hanoi. No such rules exist in problems with ill-defined goal states. For example, when writing a comedy the playwright does not have a detailed concept of the goal state, at least at the beginning. There is no objective rule telling him/her if and when the comedy is perfect. Another example relevant for our discussion is decision making. If I want to buy a new computer, the goal state is very vague at the beginning of the decision process. Of course I want to buy the best computer for my purposes, and I may even have some ideas about the criteria the best computer should fulfil, but I have no clear goal state. The goal state may become clearer and more specific in the course of the process or it may undergo changes. The standards of evaluation of the distance to the goal state may also vary considerably in different stages of the decision process. Thus an ill-defined problem like decision making seems to require more complex control processes than a well-defined one like the Towers of Hanoi. Most research in problem solving has been done with well-defined problems.

In the following sections I shall go into greater detail regarding the operator approach of problem-solving theory to decision making. The first section presents some general ideas on the operator approach in decision making and defines those types of decisions for which the operator model is developed. The operator model is described in the next two sections. The first of these contains the list of elementary operators and their description while the second presents complex operators as sequences of elementary operators. The fourth section reports some empirical results concerning hypotheses about the application of operators dependent on task variables.

THE OPERATOR APPROACH

In the operator approach a set of operators for altering states in the problem space is defined explicitly, and the decision process is modelled as a sequence of such cognitive operators. The operator approach has been reviewed by Posner and McLeod (1982). On a very general level the development of an operator model may be divided into two phases; (a) the identification and definition of the set of operators which are going to be used in the process; (b) the development and empirical test of hypotheses regarding operators. Defining a set of operators does not simply mean to divide the process into consecutive stages. Operators may be components of serial as well as parallel processes. According to Neisser (1983) an operator is a cognitive unit, which is well defined and stable, and does much the same thing in every context.

Some developments in decision research may be interpreted as being similar to the operator approach. The aforementioned distinction of phases or stages of the decision process may be viewed as a definition of very coarse operators.

A variety of decision heuristics (like Lexicographic-ordering, Majority and Weighted-pros heuristics) have been formulated and investigated; for reviews see Aschenbrenner (1981), Huber (1982), and Svenson (1979). These heuristics may be interpreted as operators, on a more fine-grained level than decision phases. However, even these heuristics appear to be too coarse as units of analysis. Decision makers use parts of such heuristics and combine them constructively in the decision process. This combining seems to be influenced by the decision maker as well as by the specific decision task (see also Bettman, 1979). Another problem with these simple heuristics seems to be the lack of a common theoretical base.

To overcome these disadvantages an operator model was developed (Huber, 1979, 1982, and see also 1986). The model concentrates on the problem of choosing one alternative out of a given set of alternatives. Other partial problems of the decision process, such as the search for alternatives, criteria, and information have been excluded (so far). Engemann *et al.* (1988) have utilized this operator model in the construction of their programming language HEURISCO, which permits simulations of decision processes in a very user-friendly manner.

The model is designed for the types of decisions in which the decision heuristics mentioned above are applicable: multidimensional decisions or simple decisions under risk. Throughout the chapter I am employing the following notation:

$A = \{x, y, z, \ldots\}$ is a set of alternatives.

$D = \{D_1, D_2, \ldots, D_i, \ldots\}$ is a set of dimensions (or a set of events in decisions under uncertainty and risk).

Each alternative x is a vector of aspects (or outcomes in decisions under uncertainty and risk):

$$x = \langle x_1, x_2, \ldots, x_i, \ldots \rangle, \quad \text{with } x_i \in D_i.$$

The set A/D_i contains the aspects of the alternatives on dimension D_i:

$$A/D_i = \langle x_i, y_i, z_i, \ldots \rangle.$$

Values, subjective probabilities, and weights are introduced with specific elementary operators (see the next section).

ELEMENTARY OPERATORS

The repertoire of elementary operators constitutes the vocabulary for the construction of complex operators and individual paths through the problem space. The term 'elementary' is always used relative to the present analysis; further decomposition of these operators is not excluded (see the conclusion section). Two types of elementary operators are distinguished: elementary operators specific for decision problems and unspecific ones.

Unspecific elementary operators

These operators belong to the general operator repertoire of the decision maker. They are also applied in the solution process of other problems, such as concept formation, solving of anagrams, and so on; see, for example, Newell and Simon (1972).

For our purpose a few examples of such operators will be sufficient:

$X = :Y$ This operator sets X equal to Y, where X and Y are sets or elements of sets

$X \& Y$ Output of this operator is the pair $\langle X, Y \rangle$, X and Y being sets or elements of sets.

$X \in M$?   This operator tests whether X is an element or a subset of M. Output is the corresponding element of $\langle$true, false$\rangle$.

SELECT(M)   Output is one element of the set M. The operator does not specify how this element is selected.

COUNT(M)   Output is the number of elements in the set M.

FOR ONE (m) FROM (M) AFTER THE OTHER $\rightarrow \alpha$ The sequence α of operators is performed in turn with all elements from M.

IF (condition) TRUE: α
                FALSE: β If the tested condition (e.g. $X \in M$?) is true, the process goes to the sequence α; if false to sequence β.

Specific elementary operators

These operators are specific for decision making (and presumably for similar tasks).

EVAL, EVAL+, EVAL—

These three operators evaluate one element m of the set M on the subjective scale E_M, where $E_M = \langle e1_M, e2_M, \ldots \rangle$ is a vector of different evaluation codes for the set M.

EVAL(m, E_M) attaches one element of the subjective evaluation scale E_M to m. For example, if E_D is the scale for weights of dimensions and D_i is a specific dimension, EVAL(D_i, E_D) evaluates the weight of this dimension. The subjective evaluation scale may be fine graded or very coarse in comparison with the information available. For example, a decision maker may evaluate the probability of winning in a gamble only as 'high' or 'low', even if the exact probability is presented. The scale may use a verbal, numerical, or analogue code.

The operator EVAL is a judgement process. An abundance of knowledge is available in psychology about such processes. One example is context effects (e.g. anchors, contrast effect, etc.); see, for example, the general review of Weintraub (1975) and Kahnemann, Slovic, and Tversky (1982) for context effects in probability judgements. In the course of the decision process the context for the evaluation of a specific element m may change, which may lead to different results of the operator EVAL(m, E_M).

EVAL+ and EVAL— are like EVAL, but produce a positively or negatively biased evaluation. The evaluations produced by the operator EVAL with the subjective evaluation scale E_M are the decision maker's standard evaluations. One way to produce a biased evaluation is to move scale E_M up or down. For example, a decision maker may evaluate one and the same numerical aspect of an attribute as 'not acceptable' usually but as 'acceptable' when it occurs in an alternative which is favoured in the final stage of the process (Huber, 1982).

MAX(M; $\succ$), MIN(M; $\succ$), EQUAL(M; $\succ$)

M is a set and $\succ$ is an ordering relation defined over M (e.g. preference, subjective probability, subjective weight). The operator MAX selects that (those) element(s) which is (are) at the top of the ordering. For example, the output of MAX(D; weight) consists of the most important dimension(s).

MIN(M; $\succ$) is the counterpart to MAX; it selects that (those) element(s) which is (are) at the bottom of the ordering (e.g. the least probable event).

EQUAL(M; $\succ$) produces as output one element of the vector $\langle$true, false$\rangle$. The output 'true' results if the elements of the set M are 'equal' in respect to the ordering relation $\succ$, e.g. if two (or more) events are equally probable, if two or more aspects are equally preferred, and so on. Formally this operator could be defined with the help of MAX or MIN, but I presume that a test of equality activates other cognitive processes than the selection of the maximal or the minimal element.

CONCATENATE and DIFF

CONCATENATE(M) concatenates the elements of the set M somehow. In fact this operator is a whole bundle of different concatenation operations. If, for example, the information is presented numerically in terms of cost, CON-CATENATE may perform an arithmetical summation. If the information is available in analogue form (e.g. the winnings in a gamble as a stack of coins) an analogue concatenation operation may be applied (e.g. piling one stack of coins upon the other mentally). Some forms of representation of information may inhibit the application of the CONCATENATE operator. For example, in choosing among job offers, the decision maker may not be able to concatenate directly the following two aspects; six weeks of vacation per annum, 24 km distance to home (see Experiment 2 in Huber, 1982). However, CONCATENA-TION can be administered easily if these aspects are evaluated with one of the EVAL operators beforehand.

DIFF(X,Y) is the counterpart to CONCATENATE and produces as output the subjective difference between X and Y. DIFF(x_i, y_i), for example, generates the difference between the alternatives x and y on dimension D_i.

CRITERION, CRITERION↑, CRITERION↓

CRITERION defines a level of acceptance for one of several dimensions (e.g., a maximum price). Output of CRITERION(D_i) is a true subset of D_i, e.g. the subset {red, yellow, black} of the set of all colours. Conditional levels of acceptance can also be defined. The test as to whether an alternative satisfies a defined level of acceptance is realized with the operator $X \in M$? CRITERION↑ and CRITERION↓ raise and lower the level of acceptance respectively.

DISARMABLE(x_i)?

This operator tests whether the aspect x_i can be transformed into a more fitting aspect x_i'. This operator is in fact a combination of several others. One tests, for example, whether a change of x_i can be assumed in due time; another is whether the credibility of the information can be questioned. When the answer is 'yes', the negative aspect x_i can be eliminated or replaced by a better aspect x_i'.

COMPLEX OPERATORS

A complex operator is an ordered sequence of elementary operators. For our discussion the distinction between three types of complex operators is sufficient; subheuristics, structuring plans, and decision heuristics.

Subheuristics

Subheuristics select from the set of alternatives A a subset of (one or more) alternatives $S(A)$. Both $S(A) = A$ and $S(A) = \emptyset$ are possible extreme cases. Some of the subheuristics have resemblance to well-known heuristics, but they do not lead to a decision in the present model. The limited space allows for only two examples of the many possible subheuristics.

Repeated applications of the subheuristic LEX are similar to the Lexicographic-ordering heuristic. LEX includes the possibility that there is not *one* single most important dimension, but several. I assume that in this case the decision maker tests whether one or more alternatives dominate on the most important dimensions. The dominant alternatives(s)—if there are any—is (are) selected with the subheuristic DOMINANCE.

In the following sequence each operator is listed with its input and output, in the general form of OPERATOR (input) → output:

LEX(A,D)
1   Max(D; weight) → D_{max}
    COUNT(D_{max}) → n(D_{max})
    IF (n(D_{max}) > 1) TRUE: 2
    MAX(A/D_{max}; preference) → best alternative(s)
    output =: best alternative(s)
2   DOMINANCE(A, D_{max}) → dominant alternative(s)
    output =: dominant alternative(s)

Another example for a subheuristic is the + BIASED TEST. There is not enough room to go beyond a verbal description; for a formalization see Huber (1982). This subheuristic includes some aspects of Montgomery's dominance-structuring model (Montgomery, 1983; see also Dahlstrand and Montgomery, 1984).

+ BIASED TEST tests whether a vector of aspects of one alternative—$x' = \langle x_i, \ldots, x_m \rangle$ (with $x' \subseteq x$) — is acceptable or not. This test is biased because the decision maker wants a positive result and for this reason is willing to 'cheat' a little. A situation where this subheuristic seems to be activated is the following. In a task with several alternatives and many dimensions the decision maker first concentrates on the important dimensions and (pre)selects one alternative. Then he/she looks to see whether this alternative is also acceptable on the other dimensions. If this is the case the decision process is finished, so that a little bias does not have much effect. Only if significant negative aspects come to light is this alternative questioned again.

There are several ways to bias the test:

(a) Using EVAL+ an aspect is evaluated as positively as possible.
(b) A negative aspect can be compensated by a positive one. Formally this implies the evaluation of two (or three etc.) aspects, instead of a single one. Again EVAL+ may be activated.
(c) The decision maker may compute the subjective difference between an aspect and some standard on the same dimension (using DIFF). He/she may do this for a negative and a positive aspect. Then he/she compares the differences for the positive and the negative aspects (with EQUAL and MAX). If the difference for the positive aspect is equal to or greater than that for the negative one, the negative aspect is compensated.
(d) The decision maker can re-evaluate the dimension with a negative aspect, making the weight as small as possible with EVAL−.
(e) The decision maker can try to eliminate the negative aspect with the help of DISARMABLE(x_i)?.

Another biasing technique is bolstering, i.e. the selective search for and introduction of information supporting the actual evaluation of an alternative (see, for example, Montgomery, 1983). Bolstering behaviour cannot be incorporated into the present operator model, because the model contains no operators for information aquisition.

Structuring plans

In many decision situations the decision maker is confronted with an overwhelming amount of information; e.g. with several alternatives described on several dimensions. In such situations decision makers seem to employ plans for structuring the task; see, for example, Payne (1982) and Svenson (1979). In the present formalism a structuring plan is a complex operator where some details are left open. These details are filled in when necessary in the course of executing the process. A structuring plan is a plan to structure the *process* of decision making. There are several possibilities to do this. One, for instance, is the separation of relevent from irrelevant information, as in the pre-editing phase in Montgomery's model (Montgomery, 1983). Another example is the plan to compare many alternatives pairwise. I assume that the (procedural) long-term memory, at least of adult decision makers, contains such structuring plans and that the decision maker is able to develop new ones in new task situations.

The following example of flexible adaptation of the number of dimensions was used by several subjects as described in Huber (1982), when there were several alternatives and more than ten dimensions. For the sake of brevity I shall describe the structuring plan only verbally:

(a) The decision maker partitions the set of dimensions into three groups: very important ones, important ones, less important ones (with EVAL and an evaluation scale E_D with three levels).
(b) The decision maker then concentrates on the very important dimensions only and reduces the number of alternatives quickly, using any subheuristic(s) he/she wants.
(c) If the number of remaining alternatives is small enough (two or three) the decision maker expands the set of dimensions and selects the best alternative by using information on the very important and important dimensions and activating any subheuristic.
(d) Finally, the decision maker tests whether this selected alternative is also acceptable on the less important dimensions. Here + BIASED TEST may come into action.

Decision heuristics

As output a decision heuristic produces one—the best—alternative. A decision heuristic consists of the following components:

(a) It contains *at least* one subheuristic, but may also contain other—simple or complex—operations.
(b) It contains *at least one* evaluation of the difference between the present problem solving state and the goal state. I shall come back to this issue later.
(c) It *may* contain one or more structuring plans.

The evaluation of the difference between the goal state and the present problem-solving state (see component (a)) is—in other words—the problem, when the decision maker terminates the decision process. Everyday decisions usually do not have a 'natural' end. For example, there is always further information to be gathered (e.g. by asking experts or by ordering brochures from further producers), the information can be processed by another sub-heuristic, or the evaluations (preferences, probabilities, weights) could be readjusted. However, even if some 'pathological' decision processes go on and on, usually the decision maker comes to an end in time. As far as I know decision theory has not investigated the question of when the decision process is terminated—with some exceptions. Ölander (1975) goes into this topic in the context of the satisficing principle. Wendt (1975) defines the goal state as one where the decision maker has reduced the number alternatives to one, i.e. when $S(A)$ contains exactly one alternative: $n(S(A)) = 1$. $S(A)$ is a subset of the set A of alternatives, selected by a subheuristic. In Montgomery's dominance-structuring model (Montgomery, 1983) the decision process is terminated when a dominance structure has been found and the relevant information has been evaluated.

$n(S(A)) = 1$ is, of course, *one* characteristic of the goal state, because the decision maker's explicit task is to select one alternative. However, $n(S(A)) = 1$ is only a necessary, not a sufficient, condition for a state to be the goal state. If $n(S(A))$ were the sole condition the decision maker could solve the decision problem very quickly; simply selecting one alternative (e.g. randomly) would be sufficient.

I assume that any state is characterized (at least) by the triplet

$$\text{state}(i) = \langle n(S(A)) = 1, \langle \text{aspects} \rangle, \langle \text{op} \rangle \rangle$$

$\langle \text{aspects} \rangle$ is the set of aspects the decision maker has used so far. It refers to the amount of information about the alternatives processed up to state(i). I assume that the decision maker attempts to process all the relevant aspects of the alternatives, especially of the alternatives in the final choice. This assumption is based on the results of several experiments: see Dahlstrand and Montgomery (1984), Huber (1982), and Payne (1982).

$\langle \text{op} \rangle$ is the sequence of operators the decision maker has employed up to now. Different operators (e.g. subheuristics) may have different values, i.e. if the decision maker evaluates subheuristic H1 as better (more rational, etc.) than H2, a choice made with H1 would give the decision maker more confidence in the correctness of the decision than a choice made with H2 (other things being equal). A remarkable common result of the experiments of Adelbratt and Montgomery (1980) and Huber (1983) seems to be that subjects prefer more complex heuristics (processing more information, requiring more memory space) to simple ones.

Both $\langle \text{aspects} \rangle$ and $\langle \text{op} \rangle$ are stored in the decision maker's memory. Therefore these vectors do not constitute an objective record of the decision process.

The initial state is the triple:

$$\text{Initial state} = \langle n(S(A)) = n(A), \langle \text{aspects} \rangle = \varnothing, \langle \text{op} \rangle = \varnothing \rangle$$

The goal state is characterized by the vector:

$$\text{Goal state} = \langle n(S(A)) = 1, \langle \text{aspects} \rangle^*, \langle \text{op} \rangle^* \rangle$$

where $\langle \text{aspects} \rangle^*$ and $\langle \text{op} \rangle^*$ are an acceptable vector of aspects and operators respectively.

The decision maker terminates the decision process when the distance between the present state and the goal state is zero or at least smaller than a fixed threshold, in other words, when the characteristics of the present and the goal state are similar enough. Which vectors of aspects and of operators are acceptable is usually not clear at the beginning of the process (decision making being a problem with an ill-defined goal state). The criteria for acceptance may change considerably in the course of the decision process. I assume that at least the following variables influence the acceptance of the vectors of aspects and of operators (for other variables see, for example, Beach and Mitchell, 1978):

(a) The specific information available about the alternatives and the quality of that information. Consider, for example, a decision maker who is confronted with two alternatives, neither of them dominating. If this decision maker evaluates a subheuristic resembling the dominance heuristic as best, he/she nevertheless would have to readjust the level of acceptance, because this subheuristic does not lead to a decision in the present situation.
(b) Characteristics of the decision task that influence directly the processing of information. Examples are time–pressure or the presentation mode of the alternatives (simulataneous or sequential).
(c) The amount of time and effort already invested in the decision task.
(d) The importance of the decision, e.g. the amount of utility involved, the number of people affected, etc.

In the next section I shall report some results of an experiment that tests some hypotheses concerning the question as to which task variables should affect the level of acceptance of a state as being a goal state and which should not.

A decision heuristic provides a complete path through the problem space. An infinite variation of decision heuristics can be composed from the vocabulary of elementary and complex operators. In very simple cases a decision heuristic consists of only one subheuristic and the evaluation of the goal distance. If the first subheuristic does not lead to the goal state the decision maker applies another subheuristic and/or structuring plan. This sequence may be repeated, which results in a long and complicated path through the problem space. Examples of simple and complex decision heuristics in different decision tasks can be found in Huber (1982). For example, one subject, who had to choose one out of six simple gambles, employed three subheuristics until he was satisfied. One subheuristic computed the total sum of winnings for each alternative using the CONCATENATE operator (ignoring probabilities) and selected the alternative with the highest sum. The second subheuristic was similar to the majority rule, and finally he used a subheuristic corresponding to the maximum strategy. As it happened, the same (non-dominant) gamble was selected with each subheuristic, thus in the end the decision maker chose that gamble.

The way through the problem space seems to depend on the individual as well as on the characteristics of the task. I shall present some relevant empirical results in the next section. The task variables affecting the decision process that are reviewed, for example, in Payne (1982) and Pitz and Sachs (1984) can be incorporated in the operator model. In Beach and Mitchell's (1978) contingency model the dependency of the choice of a decision strategy from the type of the problem, the task environment, and characteristics of the decision maker is modelled explicitly.

SOME EMPIRICAL RESULTS CONCERNING TASK VARIABLES

As mentioned before, the definition of elementary operators and the construction of complex ones is merely a first step in the development of an operator model. The next step is the test of empirical hypotheses concerning operators. In the experiments reported in Huber (1982) several have been tested. Because these results are not available in English I am giving a brief account of some of the findings of one of these experiments concerning operators (Chapter 6 in Huber, 1982).

Twenty-eight paid subjects participated in this experiment. Subjects were students from various scientific disciplines; every one of them was at the time of the experiment looking for a student job during summer vacations. The following six independent variables were varied:

(a) Familiarity of the task. In the familiar condition the alternatives were student jobs, in the unfamiliar condition research projects in various scientific fields.

(b) Presentation mode. In the simultaneous presentation mode all information about all alternatives to choose from was presented to the subject at the same time. In the sequential presentation mode information for only one of the alternatives was available at one time but the subject could look at each alternative as often as he or she wanted.

(c) Description mode. In the matrix mode information was presented in the form of the common alternative s dimensions matrix. In the text mode alternatives were described in the form of a prose text.

(d) Order of dimensions (within one set of alternatives). In the same-order condition the dimensions for all alternatives in a set were ordered in the same way. In the different-order condition the order of dimensions was different for all alternatives (the rank correlation among the orderings within one set of alternatives was zero).

(e) Number of dimensions: 4 or 14.

(f) Number of alternatives: 2 or 6.

A split-plot factorial design was constructed, with presentation mode, description mode, and order of dimensions as between-block treatments; and familiarity of the task, number of alternatives, and number of dimensions as within-block treatments. Each subject performed at least eight decisions, besides one warming-up decision for each type of task. A concurrent thinking-aloud procedure was employed. After each choice the subject rated his or her confidence of having made the best decision. At the end of the experiment the subject was confronted in sequence with the 'names' of two alternatives of the student jobs and two of the research projects. One of the alternatives in each pair had been chosen in one of the decisions made by the subject, the other one had not. One pair was selected from the two-alternatives condition, the other from the six-alternatives condition. In the latter case the non-chosen alternative presented to the subject was selected randomly from the five non-chosen alternatives. All alternatives had been described on fourteen dimensions previously. The subject was asked to recall as many aspects of each alternative as possible.

One set of hypotheses concerns the relative use of comparative operators and evaluative operators. Comparative operators are those where two (or more) aspects are compared directly or combined (MAX, MIN, EQUAL, CONCATENATE, DIFF); evaluative operators evaluate a single aspect against an internal or external standard (EVAL, CRITERION). Let $n(C)$ be the number of verbal statements indicating the application of one of the comparative operators and $n(E)$ the number of verbal statements indicating the use of an evaluative operator. An index of relative comparativity RC was estimated by

$$RC = \frac{n(C) + 1}{n(C) + n(E) + 2}$$

The RC scores were subjected to a split-plot analysis of variance (presentation mode × description mode × order of dimensions × familiarity of the task × number of alternatives × number of dimensions), and the following hypotheses were tested.

Comparative operators should be used more often in the unfamiliar task, because in the familiar task the decision maker has already established evaluation standards more likely. This hypotheses was confirmed: mean $RC = 0.27$ with student jobs and 0.35 with research projects; $F(1, 13) = 14.81$, $p < 0.005$. Similar results have been found by Tyszka (1986).

Comparative operators should be applied more often in the simultaneous presentation mode. In the sequential presentation mode the decision maker would have to store more information temporarily if he or she uses a heuristic employing comparative operators, this would put more stress upon the cognitive capacity. This hypothesis was confirmed: mean $RC = 0.35$ in the simultaneous presentation mode and 0.28 in the sequential mode; $F(1, 13) = 6.03$, $p < 0.05$.

Comparative operators should occur more often in the matrix mode, because the text mode makes a separation into aspects and a comparison of aspects more difficult and should therefore lead to a more alternative-wise processing. This hypothesis was disconfirmed (barely), although the difference between scores was in the predicted direction: mean $RC = 0.32$ in the matrix mode and 0.28 in the text mode; $F(1, 13) = 4.29$, $p < 0.06$.

Comparative operators should be employed more often in the same-order condition, because the task of comparing aspects is more difficult in the different-order condition. This hypothesis was falsified; there is no interpretable difference between the same-order and the different-order conditions ($F = 0.01$). It is remarkable that the order of dimensions also did not reveal any differences in mean decision time (185.3 s in the same-order condition and 182.3 s in the different-order one), whereas in the other independent variables differences in decision time were at least 65 s. Decision makers seem to gather relevant information in a very systematic manner irrespective of how the information is ordered.

Comparative operators should be applied more often in the two-alternatives condition. This is to be expected from the well-known fact that with more than two alternatives decision makers usually first reduce the number of alternatives (using evaluative operators with very few dimensions). This well-established hypothesis was tested as a kind of control. If it were falsified, the quality of the verbal protocols in my experiment would be very doubtful. The hypothesis was confirmed: mean $RC = 0.40$ with two alternatives and 0.22 with six; $F(1, 13) = 30.13$, $p < 0.0001$.

Recall data were analysed to investigate the hypothesis that decision makers test whether the selected alternative is acceptable also on the less important dimensions (see the preceding section).

If this hypothesis is true, the decision maker should recall more aspects of a chosen alternative than of an alternative that was not chosen. This should be the case especially in choices between two alternatives. The numbers of correctly recalled aspects per alternative were subjected to an analysis of variance (number of alternatives × chosen/not-chosen alternative). The hypothesis was confirmed: mean number of correctly recalled aspects was 3.63 with a chosen and 1.5 with a not-chosen alternative ($F(1, 60) = 22.13$, $p < 0.001$); in choices between two alternatives the mean number was 3.76 with the chosen alternative and 1.71 with the not-chosen one ($p < 0.001$). This result is in agreement with results showing that decision makers pay less attention to non-chosen alternatives (Montgomery and Svenson, 1983; Dahlstrand and Montgomery, 1984).

Confidence ratings (confidence of having made the best decision) are interpreted as an indicator of the threshold or level of acceptance for the distance between the present state of the decision process and the goal state (see the preceding section). If the threshold is surpassed, the decision process is terminated. I assume that the confidence rating of a decision is higher if the threshold is higher (and vice versa). The threshold (and therefore the decision maker's confidence) should *not* be affected by the following task variables: presentation mode, order of dimensions, and number of alternatives. This hypothesis follows from the interpretation of the decision process as an adaptive problem-solving process. I assume that the decision maker attempts to adjust the decision heuristic to the specifications of the decision task in such a manner that the quality of the decision is maintained. This can be done with the three task variables listed above. For example, a sequential presentation mode can be compensated by applying different operators. Such compensation is not possible to the same extent if the quality of available information about the alternatives is insufficient. Therefore the number of dimensions and the familiarity of the decision task may very well influence the confidence ratings. The confidence ratings were subjected to a split-plot analysis of variance (presentation mode × description mode × order of dimensions × familiarity × number of alternatives × number of dimensions). The hypothesis was confirmed: neither the presentation mode, nor the order of dimensions, nor the number of alternatives, nor an interaction involving any of these factors had a significant effect (smallest $p = 0.11$). Confidence was higher in the familiar task ($F(1, 13) = 11.24$, $p < 0.01$) and—surprisingly—higher in the four-dimensions condition ($F(1, 13) = 11.02$, $p < 0.01$). There is not enough room to present and discuss the quite interesting interactions.

Confidence ratings were used also in studies of two other authors. Kühberger (1986) investigates the effect of missing information on the decision process. Confidence was not affected by the number of dimensions missing (the information of at least one dimension was missing in any case), by the weight(s) of the missing dimension(s), and by a negative or positive task formulation. The finding that confidence is not affected by the number of missing dimensions seems quite counterintuitive. Maybe one possible explanation for this result lies in the fact that the information of at least one dimension was missing in any case and that it does not matter so much whether one or more dimensions are missing. In the study of Emig (1986) confidence in decisions made under time–pressure was lower than in decisions performed without time–pressure. Both results are in agreement with the hypothesis formulated above.

The results reported in this section are examples for hypotheses about the application of operators dependent on characteristics of the task situation.

CONCLUSION

One aim of empirical investigation of an operator model is to detect operators which are not included in the model but used by the decision makers. The analysis of thinking-aloud protocols of Huber (1982, 1983) and Kühberger (1986) revealed two (types of) elementary operators which have to be incorporated in the operator model:

(a) An operator that combines dimensions which were related semantically. For example, a subject may combine the following attributes of cars into the more abstract attribute 'beauty': colour, design of the car body, type of rims, design of the cockpit. This operator was observed several times. It helps to reduce the number of dimensions and is about the same as the collapsing operation in the dominance-structure model (Montgomery, 1983).

(b) An operator that introduces information from the decision maker's memory. This operator was used often in those experiments where information for one of the alternatives was missing explicitly. However it was observed also in decision tasks where the experimenter presented all relevant information (or at least intended to do so), especially in familiar tasks. Several variations of this operator may be distinguished. One example is an operator that substitutes a missing aspect using as base a high subjective covariation of the dimension with the missing aspect and a dimension for which information is available (e.g. 'if that person possesses such high intelligence, he will also have high professional qualifications').

An incorporation of these two types of elementary operators requires also at least some basic assumptions about the semantic memory and the representation of alternatives.

Elementary operators should of course be analysed further whenever possible. They may link decision theory to general psychology. In some cases one can fall back upon already existing theories: e.g. theories about linear orderings (see, for example, Potts *et al.*, 1978) model the cognitive processes in connection with selecting the maximal (or minimal) element out of a set. These theories may help to analyse the operators MAX and MIN in greater detail. Specific instances of the operators DIFF and CONCATENATE are addition and subtraction. Theories of mental arithmetic are transferable directly to these instances. Posner and McLeod (1982) review the research on elementary operators in several areas.

The aim of this chapter was to present some preliminary ideas and results of an information-processing model of decision making and to demonstrate that an operator system is a very flexible adaptable tool to model individual decision behaviour on different levels of detail, without abandoning the aim of developing generalized theories.

REFERENCES

Adelbratt, T., and Montgomery, H. (1980). Attractiveness of decision rules, *Acta Psychologica*, **45**, 177–85.

Aschenbrenner, K. M. (1981). Efficient sets, decision heuristics, and single-peaked preferences, *Journal of Mathematical Psychology*, **23**, 227–56.

Beach, L. R., and Mitchell, T. R. (1978). A contingency model for the selection of decision strategies, *Academy of Management Review*, **3**, 439–49.

Bettman, J. R. (1979). *An Information Processing Theory of Consumer Choice*, Addison-Wesley, Reading, Mass.

Biasio, S. (1969). *Entscheiden als Prozess*, Hans Huber, Bern.

Dahlstrand, U., and Montgomery, H. (1980). Information search and evaluative processes in decision making: a computer based process tracing study, *Acta Psychologica*, **56**, 113–23.

Emig, W. (1986) *Der Einfluss von Zeitdruck auf die Informationsverarbeitung bei komplexen Entscheidungen*, Unpublished doctoral dissertation, Universität Salzburg, Salzburg, Austria.

Engemann, A., Radtke, M., Sachs, S. and Schreter, Z. (1988). A computer simulation system for individual decision processes. In A. Upmeyer (Ed.), *Attitudes and Behavioral Decisions*, Springer, New York (in press).

Funke, J. (1986). *Komplexes Problemlösen*, Springer, Berlin.

Greeno, J. G. (1978). Nature of problem-solving abilities. In W. K. Estes (Ed.), *Handbook of Learning and Cognitive Processes*: Vol.5, *Human Information Processing*, Erlbaum, Hillsdale, N. J., pp. 239–70.

Hollnagel, E. (1977). Cognitive functions in decision making. In H. Jungermann and G. DeZeeuw (Eds), *Decision Making and Change in Human Affairs*, Reidel, Dordrecht, pp. 431–44.

Huber, O. (1979). Kognitive Strategien für multidimensionale Entscheidungen als Hierarchien von elementaren Strategien. In H. Ueckert and D. Rhenius (Eds), *Komplexe menschliche Informationsverarbeitung*, Hans Huber, Bern, pp. 401–10.

Huber, O. (1982). *Entscheiden als Problemlösen*, Hans Huber, Bern.

Huber, O. (1983). The information presented and actually processed in a decision task. In P. C. Humphreys, O. Svenson, and A. Vari (Eds), *Analysing and Aiding Decision Processes*, North-Holland, Amsterdam, pp. 441–54.

Huber, O. (1986). Decision making as a problem solving process. In B. Brehmer, H. Jungermann, P. Lourens, and G. Sevon (Eds), *New Directions in Research on Decision Making*, North-Holland, Amsterdam, pp. 109–38.

Janis, I. L., and Mann, L. (1977). *Decision Making*, The Free Press, Collier-Macmillan, New York.

Kahnemann, D., Slovic, P. and Tversky, A. (Eds) (1982). *Judgement under uncertainty: Heuristics and Biases*, Cambridge University Press, New York.

Kahnemann, D., and Tversky, A. (1979). Prospect theory: an analysis of decisions under risk, *Econometrica*, **47**, 263–91.

Kühberger, A. (1986). *Entscheiden bei unvollständiger Information unter besonderer Berücksichtigung der Formulierung des Entscheidungsproblems*, Unpublished doctoral dissertation, Universität Salzburg, Salzburg, Austria.

Mackinnon, A. J., and Wearing, A. J. (1980). Complexity and decision making, *Behavioral Science*, **25**, 285–96.

Montgomery, H. (1983). Decision rules and the search for a dominance structure: towards a process model of decision making. In P. C. Humphreys, O. Svenson, and A. Vari (Eds), *Analysing and Aiding Decision Processes*, North-Holland, Amsterdam, pp. 343–69.

Montgomery, H., and Svenson, O. (1983). A think aloud study of dominance structuring. In R. Tietz (Ed.), *Aspiration Levels in Bargaining and Economic Decision Making*, Springer, Berlin.

Neisser, U. (1983). Components of intelligence or steps in routine procedures, *Cognition*, **15**, 189–97.

Newell, A., and Simon, H. A. (1972). *Human Problem Solving*, Prentice-Hall, Englewood Cliffs, N. J.

Ölander, F. (1975). Search behavior in non-simultaneous choice situations: satisficing or maximizing? In D. Wendt and C. Vlek (Eds), *Utility, Probability and Human Decision Making*, Reidel, Dordrecht, pp. 292–306.

Payne, J. W. (1982). Contingent decision behavior, *Psychological Bulletin*, **92**, 382–402.

Pitz, G. F., and Sachs, N. J. (1984). Judgment and decision: theory and application, *Annual Review of Psychology*, **35**, 139–63.

Posner, M. I., and McLeod, P. (1982). Information processing models—in search of elementary operations, *Annual Review of Psychology*, **33**, 477–514.

Potts, G. R., Banks, W. P., Kosslyn, S. M., Moyer, R. S., Riley, C. A. and Smith, K. A. (1978). Encoding and retrieval in comparative judgments. In N. J. Castellan Jr. and F. Restle (Eds), *Cognitive Theory*, Vol.3, Erlbaum, Hillsdale, N.J., pp. 273–308.

Reitman, W. (1965). *Cognition and Thought*, Wiley, New York.
Simon, H. A. (1979). Information processing models of cognition, *Annual Review of Psychology*, **30**, 363–96.
Svenson, O. (1979). Process descriptions of decision making, *Organizational Behavior and Human Performance*, **23**, 86–112.
Tyszka, T. (1986). Information and evaluation processes in decision making: the role of familiarity. In B. Brehmer, H. Jungermann, P. Lourens, and G. Sevon (Eds), *New Directions in Research on Decision Making*, North-Holland, Amsterdam, pp. 151–61.
Weintraub, D. J. (1975). Perception, *Annual Review of Psychology*, **26**, 363–89.
Wendt, D. (1975). Decision making and cognition: comments. In H. Jungermann and G. DeZeeuw (Eds), *Decision Making and Change in Human Affairs*, Reidel, Dordrecht, pp. 425–30.

2

From cognition to action: The search for dominance in decision making

HENRY MONTGOMERY

The current theorizing on human decision making is pervaded by an ambition to view the decision process as a part of a larger psychological picture. Hence decision making is related to and contrasted with action (Kuhl, 1986; Sjöberg, 1980), it is seen as a problem-solving process (Huber, 1986), it is related to emotion (Simon, 1983; Toda, 1980), it is related to the structure of human memory (Grunert, 1986; Kuhl, 1986; Thüring and Jungermann, 1986) and to capacity limitations of human information processing (Simon, 1983), and, finally, it is related to general judgemental mechanisms (Anderson, 1986; Lopes, 1987).

The present chapter is meant as a contribution to this ambition to view human decision making as included in a larger psychological system. In a previous paper (Montgomery, 1983), I took a few steps in line with such an ambition. A model of decision making was presented in which the decision process is seen as a search for good arguments and not only as governed by a number of decision rules, as has been traditionally assumed in research on human decision making. More precisely, the decision-making process is seen as a search for a dominance structure, i.e. a cognitive structure in which one alternative can be seen as dominant over the others. In such a structure, the drawbacks, if any, of the to-be-chosen alternative are neutralized or counterbalanced in one way or another and because of this the final choice will follow in a self-evident way from the given structure. In the previous paper, the dominance-search model was discussed mainly in relation to current research on decision making and judgement. In the present chapter we will widen the perspective. We will examine how a dominance structure helps the decision

Process and Structure in Human Decision Making
Edited by H. Montgomery and O. Svenson. © 1989 John Wiley & Sons Ltd

maker to act and how the search for dominance is facilitated by a number of fundamental properties of human cognition. Before discussing these ideas I will present the dominance-search model in its original version.

THE DOMINANCE-SEARCH MODEL

In line with previous decision-making research it is assumed that a decision situation involves a number of *alternatives* (e.g. flats) which could be described on subjectively defined dimensions or *attributes* (e.g. rent, size). The values of each attribute are referred to as *aspects* (e.g. a certain rent or a certain size). The aspects on a given attribute are experienced as more or less *attractive* by the decision maker. The attractiveness levels of aspects within a given attribute are comparable with each other, but attractiveness levels across attributes are not necessarily commensurable. For example, it may be difficult to compare the attractiveness of a certain rent with the attractiveness of a certain size of a flat.

The search for a dominance structure is assumed to go through four phases, viz. pre-editing, finding a promising alternative, dominance testing, and dominance structuring. Each of these phases has particular goals, the fulfillment of which helps the individual in his/her search for a dominance structure. Figure 1 gives an overview of how the decision process is organized in terms of the four phases.

In the *pre-editing phase*, which primarily occurs in the beginning of a decision process, the decision maker selects those alternatives and attributes that should be included in the decision maker's representation of the decision problem. Attributes are discarded/selected depending on how important they are experienced to be. Alternatives are discarded if they are seen as having a very small chance to become dominant. In particular, alternatives that are very unattractive on an attribute are eliminated.

The activities associated with *finding a promising alternative* aim at finding an alternative that has a reasonable chance to be seen as dominant over the others. An alternative that is more attractive than the other alternatives on an important attribute may be selected as a promising alternative. In this way, one requirement of dominance will be more or less fulfilled, i.e. the requirement that the chosen alternative is more attractive than the other alternatives on at least one attribute.

In the *dominance-testing phase*, the decision maker tests whether a promising alternative is dominant over the other alternatives. Primarily, he/she checks whether the promising alternative has any disadvantages as compared to other alternatives or as compared to some absolute criterion values on different attributes. These tests could be more or less systematic and exhaustive. If the promising alternative is found to be dominant it is chosen and the decision process is terminated.

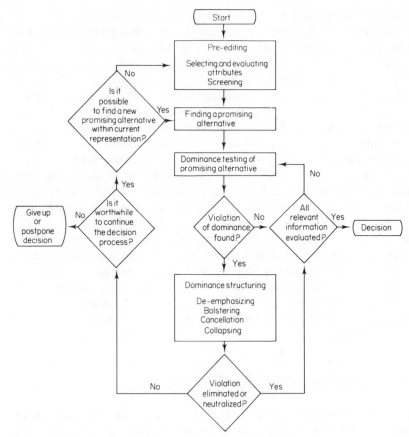

Fig. 1   A dominance search model of decision making.

If the decision maker finds that a promising alternative violates a dominance structure he/she continues to the *dominance-structuring phase*. The goal of this phase is to restructure the given information in such a way that a dominance structure is obtained. To achieve this end, the decision maker attempts to neutralize or counterbalance the disadvantage(s) found for the promising alternative. A number of operations are used in these attempts. The decision maker may *de-emphasize* a given disadvantage. He may argue that the probability of the disadvantage is very low and that it could be controlled or avoided in some way or another. He could also argue that a disadvantage on a given attribute is not very large, after all, as compared to how other alternatives are located on the same attribute or as compared to some criterion value.

Another possibility is to *bolster* the advantages of the promising alternative or the disadvantages of non-promising alternatives. Bolstering implies that the decision maker enhances the importance of an aspect, e.g. by creating vivid images of what the aspect stands for. The results of bolstering may be that disadvantages of the promising alternative are experienced as less important as compared to the very attractive advantages of the promising alternative. De-emphasizing and bolstering could be seen as irrational ways of constructing a dominance structure. A seemingly more rational operation is *cancellation*, which implies that the decision maker counter-balances a disadvantage by relating it to an advantage that has some natural connection to the disadvantage in question (e.g. in terms of a natural trade-off relationship, such as the trade-off between quality and prize, or in terms of similarity). Another more 'rational' dominance-structuring operation is *collapsing*, which implies that two or more attributes are collapsed into a new more comprehensive attribute (e.g. different types of monetary costs may be collapsed into total cost).

If the decision maker fails in his/her attempts to find a dominance structure for a promising alternative he/she may go back to a previous phase and make a new start in the search for dominance. He/she may try to find a new promising alternative or may go back to the pre-editing phase and redefine the representation of the decision problem. Alternatively, he/she may postpone the decision, if this is possible.

WHY DOMINANCE SEARCH?

Numerous empirical findings suggest that people do not make decisions in line with normative models of decision making, like the subjective expected utility model (for a review see Svenson, 1979). Instead, it is commonly assumed that human decision making could be described in terms of 'bounded rationality' (Simon, 1955, 1983); i.e. people are fairly rational within their cognitive limits. They use heuristics instead of algorithms; they satisfice instead of optimize; they do not use all given information but only the most important pieces of information, etc. There are also authors who emphasize clearly irrational aspects of human judgement and decision making (e.g. Janis and Mann, 1977; for a review of different views of the extent to which decision making is seen as rational, see Sjöberg, 1982a). The dominance search model is compatible with both more or less 'rational' and 'irrational' decision making (with rationality defined in terms of the decision maker's contact with reality). A dominance structure constructed on the basis of cancellation and collapsing operations could be in good contact with reality, whereas this is less true for a dominance structure based on de-emphasizing or bolstering operations. Dominance search is also compatible with the view of man as a limited information processor. In fact, this model can be seen as a principle for *facilitating* the information processing in a decision situation. Dominance search implies that difficult interattribute compensatory judgements are kept to a minimum and it implies that given information becomes structured in such a way that it can easily be seen which alternative is the best one (Montgomery, 1983).

It seems safe to conclude that the dominance-search model is *compatible* with current knowledge about man as an information processor. However, in order to find theoretical arguments which more directly support the model we will first consider what it means to make a decision. A common view is that decision making is a problem-solving process, the goal of which is to find the best option (or an acceptable option) among a set of given options (see Huber, 1986, and Chapter 1 of this volume). It could hardly be denied that a decision maker normally wants to find the best possible option. Still, this statement omits a fundamental feature of decision making, viz. the link between decision and action. By making a decision the individual commits him/herself to act in a certain way; i.e. a decision-making process does not only result in a problem solution (the finding of an eligible option) but also in an intention to perform certain actions (and to give up other actions). For example, by choosing a certain flat the individual acquires the intention to move into the flat, to live there for a certain time, to pay the rent, etc. In general, a decision implies that the individual intends to stick to the chosen alternative and, hence, not to give it up (unless, of course, a possibility of giving up the chosen alternative is part of the decision).

Several researchers have pointed out that it may be problematic for a decision maker to maintain the intention to act in line with a previous decision (Kuhl, 1986; Sjöberg, 1980). In order to maintain the intention it may be necessary for the decision maker to actively defend his/her decision against competing wishes or temptations. Kuhl (1985, 1986) has suggested a number of 'action-control' mechanisms which support the intention to maintain behavioural decisions. Sjöberg and Samsonowitz have highlighted the very moment when a person is tempted to give up a previous decision (e.g. a decision to quit smoking) and they have shown how people use various more or less successful strategies to fight against these temptations (Sjöberg, 1980; Samsonowitz and Sjöberg, 1981; Sjöberg and Samsonowitz, 1985). In general, it seems that people tend to process information in such a way that they protect ongoing activities from competing action tendencies (Kuhl, 1985; Lewicka, 1985; Shallice, 1978). To do so, people engage in a confirmatory search for sufficient conditions to make it possible to initiate and stick to a certain line of action (Lewicka, 1985). Below, I will assert that dominance structures provide conditions that serve such functions for the individual.

If we accept that decision making results in an intention to act in a certain way and that the maintenance of such an intention may be problematic for the individual, what does this mean for the process of making a decision? It will be assumed in the present chapter that the answer to this question is that a decision-making process should be seen as a preparation for action. More precisely, I assume that during the decision process the individual attempts to build up an intention to act in line with a promising alternative. It will be important for the individual that this intention acquires such a stability that it is possible for him/her to stick to the decision. When the individual experiences that he/she has managed to build up a stable enough intention he/she will make the decision.

The above view of a decision process raises a number of questions, which, however, all could be answered in line with the dominance-search model. First, does the use of the term 'promising alternative' imply that it is taken for granted that *before* making a decision the individual knows which alternative to choose? My answer to this question is that before making a choice the decision maker has a *hypothesis* about the choice ('the promising alternative'). However, earlier in the decision process there may have been other hypotheses about what to choose (i.e. other promising alternatives) which have been rejected. The hypothesis testing concerns whether it is possible to build up a stable enough intention to act in line with the promising alternative. Hence the decision process is seen as a hypothesis-testing activity, where each tested hypothesis is a tentative or a preliminary decision to choose a certain alternative—the promising alternative (cf. Montgomery and Svenson, 1983; Dahlstrand and Montgomery, 1984)—and where the tests aim at checking whether it is possible to form a stable enough intention to act in line with a promising alternative.

Second, what does it mean to build up an intention? I assume that an intention is backed up by beliefs about the implications of acting in line with the intention. These beliefs may be seen as the individual's expectations with respect to aspects of different choice alternatives. That intentions indeed are related to beliefs about the implications of acting in line with the intentions has been demonstrated in Ajzen and Fishbein's (1980) research on the relationship between attitudes and behaviour. This research has shown that the intention to perform a certain behaviour is closely related to the individual's attitude to that behaviour which in turn, to a large extent, is dependent on the individual's beliefs related to the behaviour in question. In the present context we will likewise assume that the intention to act in line with a certain alternative is backed up by the individual's beliefs. Accordingly, it is assumed that during the decision process the individual after having selected a promising alternative investigates whether he/she has access to a system of beliefs that supports that alternative (or whether he/she can form such a system, cf. the dominance-structuring phase in the dominance-search model). The structure of this belief system determines whether the individual will acquire a stable enough intention to act in line with the alternative.

Third, why is it assumed that intentions should be *stable* enough rather than, say, *strong* enough in order to make action possible? By using the term 'stable' I want to emphasize that before choosing an alternative the decision maker checks more or less thoroughly whether he/she could maintain an intention to act in line with that alternative regardless of what aspects of the pertinent alternative, or of its competitors, are considered (cf. the dominance-testing phase). When these checks are performed the decision maker experiences a more or less strong intention to act in line with the promising alternative depending on how attractive or unattractive are the aspects that are attended to in a given moment. (The experienced attractiveness of previously attended-to aspects may also affect the strength of the intention.) These variations in the momentary strength of an intention determine how stable the intention is experienced to be. A large number of studies have shown that the attractiveness of an object changes continuously as new information is focused (e.g. Anderson, 1986; Lopes, 1982). In other words, the attractiveness of the object changes as a function of the attractiveness of the aspects which the individual attends to at a given moment. Let us now assume, in line with Ajzen and Fishbein's findings, referred to above, that there is a close link between intention to act in line with a given option and the experienced attractiveness of that option (i.e. the individual's attitude to the option). It will then follow that the strength of the intention indeed will vary as the decision maker considers different aspects of varying attractiveness.

Fourth, what is meant by a stable *enough* intention? The answer is simply that regardless of what aspect is considered in relation to a promising alternative the decision maker should be able to maintain an intention to choose the alternative, i.e. to act in line with the alternative. This stability is normally attained, I assume, when the information considered by the decision maker follows a dominance structure. Such a structure implies that regardless of the aspect that is considered by the decision maker there is no risk that a favourable aspect associated with the promising alternative could be outweighed by a less favourable aspect. Hence an initial (preliminary) intention to choose a promising alternative could be maintained when there is a dominance structure at hand. In this way, a dominance structure will help the individual to fight wishes to give up a decision, wishes that may occur if the individual is confronted with disadvantages of the chosen alternative. However, a dominance structure is no guarantee for stable behavioural intentions. Depending on how the dominance structure is related to reality, it will be more or less helpful for the individual to have access to the dominance structure when confronted with the actual disadvantages of the chosen alternative. In general it may be assumed that the usefulness of a dominance structure for maintaining a decision is related to the extent to which the individual has incorporated the actual disadvantages of the chosen alternative in his/her dominance structure.

DO WE ALWAYS FIND DOMINANCE?

Do people always construct a dominance structure before making a decision? I will not answer this question with a clear-cut 'yes' or 'no'. Rather, I assume that the construction of a dominance structure is a desirable *goal* for the decision maker and that the decision maker could be more or less successful in his/her attempts to attain this goal. As indicated above, there are good dominance structures and not so good ones inasmuch as the real world may be more or less adequately represented in a dominance structure. A representation of a decision situation may also be more or less close to a fully developed dominance structure. In a fully developed dominance structure there are either no disadvantages of the chosen alternatives on any of the attributes that have been considered by the decision maker or the disadvantages have been completely neutralized by means of cancellation or collapsing. In a less developed dominance structure the disadvantages are dismissed by declaring them to be small or negligible (de-emphasizing) or the decision maker simply restricts his attention to those combinations of attributes and alternative (i.e. aspects) that do not violate a dominance structure.

Sometimes the decision maker has not the time available for constructing a fully developed dominance structure or will not pursue attempts to find a dominance structure because the decision is experienced as unimportant. In such cases the decision maker to some extent may base his/her decision on the momentary impressions of the alternatives or his/her decision may follow some decision rule which does not require dominance in a strict sense (e.g. the conjunctive rule, the disjunctive rule, or a lexicographic rule; cf. Montgomery and Svenson, 1976; Svenson, 1979). It should be noted, however, that many decision rules can be seen as means for providing an approximative dominance structure (i.e. a less developed dominance structure). On the one hand these rules imply that the decision maker simplifies his/her representation of the decision situation (e.g. by using crude attractiveness evaluations or by not considering all combinations of alternatives and attributes). On the other hand, in the resulting representation the chosen alternative has no disadvantages as compared to the other alternatives. Consider, for example, the conjunctive and disjunctive rules. The conjunctive rule implies that the chosen alternative exceeds a certain criterion value on all attributes whereas this is not the case for other alternatives if only one alternative is to be chosen according to this rule. The disjunctive rule implies that only the chosen alternative exceeds a certain criterion on an attribute. Both rules imply that the attractiveness of aspects are reduced to two attractiveness levels, viz. attractiveness below and above the criterion. It is easily realized that in terms of this two-valued attractiveness representation the chosen alternative will dominate the others when the rules are applicable. Consider, finally, the lexicographic rule which implies that the decision maker searches for the most important attribute on which one, and only one, alternative is better than all the other alternatives. This alternative is then chosen. Obviously, when the lexicographic rule is relevant the chosen alternative will dominate the other alternatives in terms of those attributes that are used for the decision.

The decision maker may also approach a dominance structure by simply increasing the attractiveness of these aspects that support the decision and by decreasing the attractiveness of those aspects that go against the decision. It is clear from previous studies that such processes actually occur even in hypothetical decisions made by subjects in laboratory situations (Montgomery and Svenson, Chapter 7 in this volume; Dahlstrand and Montgomery, Chapter 8 in this volume). Hence, even if a decision is not based on a fully developed dominance structure it may be true that the decision maker's representation of the choice alternative is closer to dominance when the decision is made as compared to the beginning of the decision process.

It may be asked how the dominance-search model could be falsified. Is it at all possible to falsify the model? The idea that a dominance structure could be more or less fully developed indeed makes it difficult to falsify the model in a clear-cut way. However, it is possible to imagine a decision process that clearly is at odds with the model. Imagine, for example, a decision maker who (a) evaluates the attractiveness of each alternative on each relevant attribute with no tendencies to de-emphasizing or bolstering, (b) computes the sum of the attractiveness values for each alternative, and then (c) directly chooses the alternative with the highest sum of attractiveness values. Decision makers certainly add advantages and disadvantages in order to find the best option (Adelbratt and Montgomery, 1980; Huber, 1983). However, it may be the case that adding of advantages and disadvantages is done primarily in connection with dominance structuring, i.e. in line with the cancellation and collapsing operations (see Montgomery, 1983). Moreover, the fact that decisions are only moderately predictable from (weighted) sums of subjective attractiveness values (e.g. Beach, Campbell, and Townes, 1979; Humphreys and McFadden, 1980; Lindberg, Gärling, and Montgomery, 1986) suggest that the hypothetical decision process described above is usually only a partially valid description of what in fact is going on in the process.

The dominance-search model would also be inapplicable if the decision maker just follows his/her momentary impression of the alternatives and chooses the alternative that appears to be best without any search for dominance. As suggested above, decisions may be made in this way in certain situations. However, I think that people are quite talented at finding dominance structures and they indeed also do so in order to uphold a sufficient stability in their intentions. In the following section, I will present evidence for the assumption that people have a mental readiness for dominance structuring.

ARE WE PREPARED FOR SEEING DOMINANCE?

The question, whether we have a mental readiness for dominance structuring, may be specified as follows. Do we have access to mental procedures or structures that help us to see dominance in decision situations? I will propose that people in their search for dominance use three mental procedures, which in turn are more or less clearly related to fundamental structural properties of the human mental apparatus. These procedures are anchoring, semantic network search, and the use of causal schemata. Below I relate these procedures to dominance search and give examples from empirical research as to how each of these mental procedures facilitate the construction of a dominance structure.

Anchoring

A massive amount of data has shown that judgements of a given stimulus are made in relation to one or more anchors or reference points (e.g. Helson, 1964; Hellström, 1984; Lopes, 1982; Rosch, 1975; Tversky and Kahneman, 1974). For example, if an object is judged as big this judgement may reflect the fact that the object is *bigger* than a certain anchor stimulus or that it is *equally big* as an anchor labelled as 'big'. In their prospect theory, Kahneman and Tversky (1979) advocated that value judgements in a decision situation should be seen as judgements of gains or losses in relation to a reference point. Hence according to this theory there are no absolute value judgements but only relative judgements. The positive or negative evaluations that result from these judgements reflect how the individual experiences that a given aspect of an alternative will improve or worsen a situation in relation to some reference point. Kahneman and Tversky (1984) demonstrated how the same objective decision situation may be framed in different ways (i.e. based on different reference points) by different individuals and dependent on the wording of the description of the situation. Below I will discuss how selecting appropriate anchors may help the decision maker to find a dominance structure. It will be assumed that the decision maker evaluates aspects on an attribute in relation to an anchor (or anchors) which is (are) specific for that attribute. Each anchor is assumed to correspond to a valued aspect (or set of aspects) on a given attribute (e.g. a bad location or acceptable communications for a flat). It is furthermore assumed that the decision maker will try to select the anchors in such a way that the resulting evaluations will form a dominance structure.

Although the present theory has in common with Kahneman and Tversky's prospect theory that anchoring and the resulting framing is important for how decisions are made, there are a number of differences between the present theory and prospect theory. First, anchors will be seen as a very broad concept. In prospect theory the anchor is a neutral value, but here it is assumed that anchors could have several different values. Moreover, the attribute, with which an anchor is associated, is not necessarily equivalent to outcomes (e.g. gains or losses of money), as is the case in prospect theory, but could correspond to the probability of a given outcome (e.g. the probability to win much money). Second, the evaluations made in relation to an anchor are assumed to be expressed in broad categorical terms, such as 'good', 'acceptable', or 'not-acceptable'. For example, aspects that are evaluated as 'acceptable' could be any aspect that is not on the other side of an anchor that corresponds to an acceptable aspect. Think-aloud data from decision processes give ample evidence for the assumption that aspects are evaluated in such broad categorical terms (e.g. Montgomery, 1977; Svenson, 1974). The usage of broad evaluative categories facilitates the construction of a dominance structure. This is because alternatives which are evaluated in terms of the same category on a given attribute will be equal on that attribute in the decision maker's cognitive structure regardless of the size of the objective difference between the alternatives on the attribute in question. Third, it is assumed that a decision is made when the individual in relation to a given set of anchors finds that one alternative dominates over the others. This is in marked contrast to prospect theory, which assumes that the decision follows from an estimate of the total value of a prospect (i.e. an alternative) which is obtained by integrating probabilities and evaluations of outcomes according to a multiplicative rule. Dominance structuring implies that no information integration is required for making the decision. The decision is just a question of deciding for the dominant alternative.

Anchoring plays a key role in several theories about judgements in general, and hence not only judgements in decision situations (e.g. Tversky and Kahneman, 1974; Lopes, 1982; Sjöberg, 1984). In the present context, Lopes's (1982) 'procedural theory of judgement' is of some interest. According to the procedural theory, judgement is seen as a serial 'anchoring and adjustment' process. Consider an individual who judges how likeable a person is from a given list of adjectives. He/she may start by evaluating the first adjective on the list. This evaluation gives an initial impression of the stimulus person which will serve as an anchor for the following judgement process. Hence when the judge considers a second adjective on the list he/she will adjust the initial impression upwards or downwards depending on how the adjective is evaluated, and so on for each new adjective that is considered by the judge. The process ends when the judge deems that sufficient information has been integrated. The judge will then output the current value of the adjusted quantity as his/her evaluation of the stimulus person. The procedural theory is similar to the present theory in as much as the anchor could have any value and in that there are no particular restrictions on what type of aspects could be anchors. However, the procedural theory differs from the present approach in that anchoring and adjustment process operates *across* attributes whereas the present approach concerns the role of anchoring for evaluations *within* a given attribute.

There is ample empirical evidence for the validity of the procedural theory (Lopes, 1982; Anderson, 1986). However, I only know of one experiment in which the theory has been tested for decision-making data (Lopes and Ekberg, 1980). The subjects in that study were given only one type of task, which was of a rather special character (choices between a sure thing and a gamble), and it is therefore difficult to generalize the results of the study to decision making in general.

My own view of the role of anchoring and adjustment across attributes in a decision process is as follows. Anchoring and adjustment operations certainly are performed in a decision process and they lead to a more or less favourable impression of an alternative. However, this impression may be unstable depending on what aspects the decision maker is paying attention to at a particular moment. As discussed above, the decision makers tend to ask for a more stable basis for choice than the current impression of the given alternatives and such a stability will be obtained through a dominance structuring. Anchoring and adjustment may operate in screening (as a part of the pre-editing phase) and finding a promising alternative phase of a decision process; i.e. by means of anchoring and adjustment some alternatives are experienced as more or less probable candidates for the final choice. However, to make a choice the decision maker attempts to confirm these impressions by looking for a dominance structure that supports the promising alternative.

In a recent paper Lopes (1987) presented a theory on decision making under risk which appears to be unrelated to the procedural theory. As will be shown below, the theory may be used to illustrate the role of anchors in dominance structuring. The theory is applied to choice situations where each alternative may lead to a number of more or less attractive outcomes (i.e. gains or losses) and where each outcome has a certain probability. The theory assumes that risk taking is dependent on two factors, viz. (a) motivation for security versus potential (minimizing risks of bad outcomes versus maximizing possibilities of good outcomes) and (b) current level of aspiration, which reflects immediate needs and opportunities. With respect to factor (a) Lopes (1987) assumes that personality factors are largely responsible for which of the two motives will be prevalent in a decision situation. Factor (b) implies that due to various situational features people sometimes will play it safe (security) and at other times take chances (potential). Thus, both factors deal with security and potential, but differ with respect to whether the subject's priorities are due to personality or situational characteristics.

In the present paper, judgements of security or potential are seen as related to anchors. In both cases the anchor may be expressed as a probability or as an outcome. For gain lotteries security judgements could be anchored to a high probability of winning a reasonable amount or to a reasonable level of the lowest amount to win. Similarly, in judgements of potential, the anchors could be a reasonable probability of winning a lot or a high level of the largest amount to win. Each type of anchor will function as a valued aspect on an attribute with the attractiveness levels + (positive value) and − (negative value). For example, if the anchor is a high probability of winning a lot the attribute will be probability to win a lot and the attractiveness levels will be + (= aspect close to the anchor, i.e. a high probability to win a lot) and − (= aspect far from the anchor, i.e. not a high probability to win a lot).

Lopes (1987) backs up her two-factor theory by a number of quotations from protocols that subjects wrote to explain their preferences in a risky choice task (pairwise choices between gain or loss lotteries). In the following, I will use the same protocols to show how the two-factor theory may be interpreted in terms of anchoring and dominance structuring. Table 1 presents a number of these quotations and how they have been interpreted. The table shows for gain lotteries all quotations in the Lopes paper illustrating both factors in her theory. It should be noted that the quotations show how subjects justified their choice *after* they have made their choice. Hence the quotations do not show how subjects' decision processes developed over time and we cannot use the quotations to validate the process model in Figure 1. Rather, the quotations could be used for getting ideas about the final dominance structure, if any, that supports a decision.

To make the present ideas of anchoring and dominance structuring more concrete let us consider the third quotation in Table 1. The quotation concerns a choice between a riskless gamble (i.e. no risk to win less than $70, a high probability to win $70, and then decreasing probabilities to win higher amounts) and a short shot (high probability to win $130 and decreasing probabilities to win less). The subject associates the riskless lottery with both security ('I am assured of winning $70') and with potential ('a better than even chance of winning more than $70'). The sure winning of $70 is assumed to correspond to a security anchor (SEC in Table 1) and a high potential of winning more than $70 is assumed to correspond to a potential anchor (POT in Table 1). Each of these anchors yield a definition of an attribute on which the lotteries could be evaluated, viz. probability of winning $70 (denoted as p(70) in Table 1) and probability of winning more than $70 (denoted as p(>70) in Table 1). On both attributes the subject makes a positive evaluation (denoted as + in Table 1) of the riskless lottery. The short-shot lottery is not explicitly evaluated by the subject. However, it is obvious that the riskless lottery is seen as superior to the short-shot lottery with respect to security ('It is the assurance of winning $70 that appeals to me'). Because of this it is assumed that the subject makes an implicit negative evaluation (denoted as {−} in Table 1) of the short-shot lottery with respect to security. As for potential, it is assumed that the subject implicitly makes a positive evaluation of the short-shot lottery. This is because it is obvious that also for the short-shot lottery there is 'a better than even chance of winning more than $70'. It can now be seen that in terms of the evaluations made the two lotteries are equal with respect to potential (+, +

Process and structure in human decision making

Table 1 Analysis of protocol statements (Lopes, 1987) from choices between gain lotteries

Statement	Attribute	Evaluation of alternative		Type of anchor
The chances are in the (peaked) lottery that I will get something close to $100, and I might get much more. I don't know why (I should) let $130 be the top limit when there's a reasonable chance of nearing $100 and a possibility for more. (Subject 3)		P	SS	
	p(100)	+	{+}	?
	p(>100)	+	{−}	POT
	$(max)	+	−	POT
Since I am assured of winning something I am willing to risk a moderate amount for the possibility of a substantially greater amount. (Subject 4)		RL	ST	
	p(some)	+	{+}	SEC
	$(min)	−	} +	SEC
	$(max)	+		POT
I chose the (riskless lottery) because I am assured of winning at least $70. In addition, I have a better than even chance of winning more than $70. It is the assurance of winning $70 that appeals to me. (Subject 7)		RL	SS	
	p(70)	+	{−}	SEC
	p(>70)	+	{+}	POT
I chose the (sure thing) because I would rather take the $100 as a sure thing than risk winning less. The other lottery also offers a sure thing ($70 at the least), but the chances of winning less than $100 are about 50–50 in that lottery, so I opt for the safe bet of $100, a sure thing. (Subject 7)		ST	RL	
	p(100)	+	−	SEC
	p(70)		+	SEC

Note. Alternatives are P (peaked lottery: approximately normal probability distribution, peak around $100, maximum at $200, and minimum at zero), ST (sure thing: winning $100 for sure), SS (short shot: highest and most probable prize $130, decreasing probabilities to win less, minimum at zero), RL (riskless: lowest and most probable prize $70, decreasing probabilities to win more, maximum at $200). Attributes are denoted by the probability (p) of winning amount within parentheses or by amount ($) for type of prize given within parentheses. Evaluations within brackets are implicit evaluations inferred from the protocol statements and from the structure of the pertinent lotteries. A bracket uniting two evaluations denotes a comparison between the evaluated aspects. The resulting evaluation is shown to the right of the bracket. Types of anchors are potential (POT) and security (SEC).

in Table 1) whereas the riskless lottery is superior to the short-shot lottery with respect to security (+, − in Table 1). Hence, in this representation of the decision situation the riskless lottery dominates the short-shot lottery.

If we now inspect all four quotations in Table 1, the following observations can be made.

First, with one exception all value judgements in the protocols can be seen to be related to one of the two types of anchors described above. However, each type of anchor could be specified in different ways, i.e. in terms of different probabilities or gains. For example, the amount to win specified for security anchors could be 'winning something' (subject 3), '$70' (subject 4, first and second quotation) or '$100' (subject 4, second quotation).

Second, all justifications can be described as dominance structures. Note, however, that in one case the subject (4) finds a violation of dominance but neutralizes it by making a comparison with a corresponding advantage of the chosen alternative. 'Corresponding' implies that the comparisons are made with respect to the levels of the outcomes associated with the anchors involved in the comparison. In this way the comparison can be seen as an example of the cancellation operation in the dominance-search model since this operation requires some common basis for a comparison of aspects across attributes.

Third, it seems sufficient to distinguish only between positive (+) and negative (−) evaluations in order to explain subjects' choices. As noted above, using broad evaluative categories facilitates the construction of a dominance structure since violations of dominance, in a strict sense, may be masked by the fact that the same evaluative category is used for different aspects.

In all, there are 23 quotations in Lopes's paper from how subjects justified their choices. All 23 quotations were coded in line with the principles exemplified in Table 1. Only in one case was there a violation of dominance in the coded pattern of positive and negative evaluations.

The anchoring theory discussed above is easily generalized to decision situations in which outcome probabilities are not in focus. In such a situation, potential may correspond to a maximax orientation (favouring alternatives with maximally attractive aspects) and security to a minimax orientation (avoiding alternatives with minimally attractive aspects). A maximax orientation may imply that evaluations of aspects on a given attribute are anchored at a 'maximal' anchor, i.e. at a maximally attractive aspect on the attribute, whereas a minimax orientation may imply that the evaluations are anchored at a 'minimal' anchor, i.e. at minimally attractive aspects.

If we assume again that decision makers use broad evaluative categories to judge how aspects relate to an anchor it follows that the above orientations easily result in a dominance structure. Consider, for example, a maximax-oriented person who chooses between two alternatives, A and B, where A is very attractive on one attribute and very unattractive on another attribute whereas B is mediocre on all attributes. This person will form a dominance structure in favour of A if he/she represents the very attractive aspect as 'positive' (+) and all other aspects, i.e., mediocre as well as very unattractive aspects, as 'non-positive' (−).

To conclude, anchoring creates many possibilities for representing a given situation and it gives the individual a freedom to concentrate on those features that he/she experiences as essential. These two characteristics of anchoring— flexibility and selectivity—explain why anchoring helps the individual to represent given information in line with a dominance structure. However, besides anchoring there is another important basis for evaluative judgements in a decision situation as well as for the construction of a dominance structure. This basis is the decision maker's conceptions of the outcomes of different alternatives. Below I will assert that people have belief systems which help them to believe in outcomes that are in line with a dominance structure.

Semantic network search

It is widely believed among cognitive psychologists that human knowledge to a large extent can be represented as a network of interrelated concepts and words — a so-called semantic network. Network theorists typically assume that performance results from activating certain paths in the network (e.g. Anderson, 1983; Collins and Loftus, 1975). For example, the verification of a sentence is seen as resulting from activating paths starting out from the concepts referred to in the sentence. The network view implies that when explaining performance the importance of storage is stressed as opposed to computation (Smith, 1978). In decision making, this means that how we make decisions is largely determined by the structure of the knowledge used for making the decision rather than on computational processes (e.g. calculations of probabilities or utilities). More precisely, a decision process is seen as resulting from activating certain paths in a semantic network (Grunert, 1986). Although the output of this process is determined by the structure of the activated regions of the network, the direction of the process may be controlled by the decision maker; i.e. he/she may decide which regions should be activated in order to attain a current goal (cf. Anderson, 1983). For this reason, I would prefer to regard the activation of paths in a semantic network as a more or less active *search* process.

The following discussion is based on three assumptions concerning semantic networks that commonly are made. First, it is assumed that the structure of a semantic network is rather 'messy' (Collins and Loftus, 1975) and not in line with a neat hierarchical structure as was assumed in early network theories

(Collins and Quillian, 1969). Second, the links between the 'nodes' (concepts or words) in the network are of different types. For example, they may be causal (e.g. frustration leads to aggression) or they may be conceptual (e.g. a canary is a bird) (cf. Lindsay and Norman, 1977; Grunert, 1986). Third, activation of paths in the network is assumed to follow 'the spreading activation' principle (Collins and Loftus, 1975; Anderson, 1983). According to this principle, as concepts become activated in memory, this activation spreads out along the network. As soon as attention shifts, the activation of the concept begins to decay. Hence according to spreading activation principle only a limited region of the semantic network is active at a given moment. Below I will take for granted that these three assumptions are relevant for understanding how a dominance structure may be found in a decision situation. I will begin by discussing the structure of the knowledge utilized by the decision maker.

The attributes involved in a decision situation could be on different levels of generality. For example, the attribute 'cost' is more general than the attribute 'investment costs'. In multiattribute utility theory it is assumed that attributes are organized in a strict hierarchy, i.e. in terms of a 'value tree' (von Winterfeldt and Keeney, 1983). A strict hierarchy implies that there should be no overlap among branches of the tree; i.e. each lower level attribute is directly related to only one higher level attribute. In a pilot study, Pitz and Riedel (1984) found that attributes generated by subjects were strongly inconsistent with a strictly hierarchical value tree. Below, I will refer to more data which show that the value tree hypothesis is grossly inadequate for describing how people represent attributes on different levels of generality. I will show that people view relationships between attributes on different levels in a more 'messy', network-like fashion.

In line with multiattribute theory, I will assume that higher level attributes correspond to 'values' (Pitz and Riedel, 1984) or, more specific-ally, to 'life values' or 'personal values' (cf. Montgomery, 1984; Lindberg *et al.*, 1988). Lower level attributes will simply be denoted as attributes. How do people view the relationships between attributes and values? Table 2 presents data from subjects who were instructed to rate the extent to which different levels of a number of housing attributes lead to the attainment of different life values (Lindberg, Gärling, and Montgomery, 1986). It can be seen that the general structure of the data in Table 2 is clearly inconsistent with a strict hierarchy. Rather, most attributes are clearly related to *several* life values (see, for example, the attributes cost, friends, recreation, and transportation). It should be noted that an attribute could be related to very different values. For example, the attribute access to transportation is related to comfort, excitement (presumably the possibility of experiencing amusements in the downtown area), and freedom.

The relationship between attributes and values obviously are of a causal rather than a conceptual nature. For example, from a conceptual analysis it does not follow that good transportation leads to excitement, but there

Table 2 Index of perceived effects of housing attributes on the attainment of life values (Lindberg, Gärling, and Montgomery, 1986)

Housing attributes	Life values												
	Com-fort	Ex-cite-ment	Fami-ly	Free-dom	Happi-ness	Health	Inner har-mony	Lei-sure	Money	Plea-sure	Secu-rity	Toge-ther-ness	M
Intrinsic													
Cost	2.36	4.81	3.19	4.50	2.64	0.81	3.28	3.22	10.08	1.92	3.44	1.39	3.47
Size	5.67	2.69	4.97	5.08	2.14	1.19	2.97	2.00	−2.42	2.83	1.36	2.69	2.60
Standard	6.86	2.25	4.03	2.92	2.53	1.42	3.11	2.03	−1.94	3.11	2.53	1.94	2.56
Location													
Downtown	4.94	4.00	0.97	3.56	1.89	0.14	1.92	2.28	1.47	1.83	1.33	1.97	2.19
Friends	3.94	4.22	5.78	4.11	4.86	1.42	4.69	3.97	1.89	3.81	5.89	7.22	4.32
Recreation	4.03	5.25	3.56	4.56	3.47	5.42	4.11	6.22	1.50	3.69	1.94	4.11	3.99
Schools	3.42	1.42	3.22	2.92	1.47	0.56	1.83	1.56	2.33	1.25	3.14	1.75	2.07
Work	4.61	1.83	3.22	3.36	1.50	0.78	1.75	2.69	4.17	1.06	1.78	2.14	2.41
Neighbourhood													
Facilities	4.58	1.44	2.22	3.94	1.36	0.56	2.14	1.39	1.78	1.36	2.39	1.47	2.05
Noise	4.11	1.14	4.06	2.50	2.86	4.69	4.44	1.31	0.50	3.89	2.56	2.47	2.88
Reputation	3.19	2.28	3.50	2.94	3.39	1.78	4.28	2.00	0.19	2.53	5.69	3.78	2.96
Transport	6.42	5.03	3.31	6.50	2.39	1.03	2.92	5.03	2.58	2.33	4.14	4.33	3.83
M	4.51	3.03	3.50	3.91	2.54	1.65	3.12	2.81	1.84	2.47	3.02	2.94	2.94

Note. The entries of the table give the mean ratings of the effects of the 'best' level of each attribute on the attainment of each life value (maximum rating = +6) minus the same ratings for the 'worst' level (minimum rating = −6).

may be a causal relationship between transportation and excitement. The attributes are *means* which may or may not lead to certain values or ends. For this reason, attributes and values could be related to each other in a 'messy', non-hierarchical way. It should be noted, however, that even purely conceptual relationships between more or less general concepts are not necessarily organized in a hierarchical fashion in a semantic network (cf. Collins and Loftus, 1975).

It is important to note that there are very few negative relationships between the attributes and values in Table 2. In other words, it seldom happens that the attainment of certain values via a certain attribute implies decreased possibilities of attaining other values. This fact, taken together with the fact that attributes can lead to many values, implies that dominance violations on the attribute level could be obviated on the value level. This will be true even if the conflicting attributes appear to have little in common. Consider, for example, two flats—A and B—with A having a high cost but being located close to friends and B having a low cost but being far from friends. Assume, furthermore, that the most important values are comfort, inner harmony, and togetherness. Assume, also, that attributes and values are related to each other as shown in Table 2. Comparing how cost and friends in Table 2 relate to the three life values, it can be seen that friends is more strongly related to each value than is the case for cost. This implies that alternative A probably will dominate over alternative B with respect to the three life values (i.e. A will be more attractive than B with respect to comfort, inner harmony, and togetherness), and this will be true despite the fact that dominance is violated on the attribute level. If dominance is not immediately found on the value level, it is possible to go one step further and consider relations between values. For example, the three life values mentioned above may in various ways be related to the life values security and enjoyment (cf. Montgomery, 1984). It may be found that one of the alternatives dominates with respect to the attainment of these two life values as a result of how they are related to the three values originally considered. In this way, the search for dominance could go on and, theoretically, the search could proceed endlessly or until dominance is found. This is because of the large number of relationships in various directions between different values (see Montgomery, 1984).

The above way of searching for dominance implies that a certain type of search is made in the semantic network. The search is made *forwards* by activating links that stand for implications or consequences of an activated node. Another type of search would be *backwards* search. With this I mean attempts to find alternative paths to a given node (e.g. a certain aspect of an attribute or value) which may change the activation of that node. In this way, a violation of dominance could be eliminated by deactivating an aspect that gave rise to the dominance violation. Assume, for example, that a certain investment alternative has been found to be non-dominant since the aspect 'bad economy' has been activated via the aspect 'high investment costs'. However, the former aspect could be deactivated if it is found that the alternative in question has low running costs (assumed to be negatively related to the aspect 'bad economy'). It may be noted that this process corresponds to the cancellation operation in the dominance-search model.

Ample evidence for the possibilities of finding or rescuing dominance through backwards search is to be found in Biel and Montgomery's studies of decision making in energy politics (Biel and Montgomery, 1986, Chapter 14 in this volume; Montgomery and Biel, 1984). The data show how objections made against possibilities of attaining a certain goal may be countered by considering new ways of specifying the goal (subattributes) or new means (instrumental attributes) or different ways of looking at a given means. It seems that within a given domain a decision maker may have access to a semantic network which almost guarantees that a dominance structure could be defended against any objections which are made against a favoured alternative.

It seems safe to conclude that the structure of the knowledge typically used in a decision situation gives many possibilities for finding a dominance structure. Particularly this may be the case when the decision maker is thinking in causal terms, i.e. when he/she considers the consequences or chains of consequences that may follow from the implementation of a given alternative. Therefore it is perhaps not surprising that practically all data that I have found on how people justify decisions in which causal chains have been considered show the same pattern: chains starting out from the chosen alternative lead to consequences which are evaluated as better than or at least as good as the consequences of non-chosen alternatives (Axelrod, 1976; Crozier, Chapter 16 in this volume; Biel and Montgomery, 1986, Chapter 14 in this volume; Gallhofer and Saris, Chapter 17 in this volume; Montgomery and Biel, 1984). In other words, there is a dominance structure. In his book on the cognitive maps of political decision makers Axelrod (1976) notes that cognitive maps tend to be balanced (i.e. to include a dominant alternative). Gallhofer and Saris examined a total of 235 Dutch foreign policy decisions. The data were documents in which the decision makers explained their choices. According to the classifications made by Gallhofer and Saris a minimum of 179 decisions (76 per cent) were structured in such a way that no value conflicts between chosen and non-chosen alternatives were noted (i.e. no violations of dominance were noted). In the remaining 56 cases value trade-offs occurred in 19 cases, inasmuch as the adoption of utility rules apparently were used in 13 cases and lexicographic rules in 6 cases (Gallhofer, personal communication, 18 May 1987). These results should not be taken to imply that a given decision situation has certain objective characteristics that invite construction of a certain dominance structure. On the contrary, different dominance structures are often found by different actors in a given situation. Sometimes, different actors even may have diametrically opposed dominance structures in their cognitive maps for a given situation (see, for example, Biel and Montgomery, Chapter 14 in this volume). In other words, if alternative X dominates over alternative Y for person A, Y could dominate over X for person B.

Although there are many possibilities of finding a dominance structure in a given situation it may still be asked how does a decision maker proceed to find dominance among all the possible paths in his/her semantic network. It may also be asked how it is possible for different actors to have firm beliefs in their own dominance structures also when these structures are diametrically opposed to the dominance structures of other actors. Obviously, in such a situation all the actors cannot be right in an objective sense. Still, each actor often believes that his dominance structure is the right one (cf. Sjöberg, 1982b). In the following section, we will discuss how decision makers find and defend a particular dominance structure among all the possible dominance structures that may be found in a given situation.

Causal schemata

In cognitive psychology schemata refer to 'organized structures of stereotypic knowledge' (Eysenck, 1984). Schemata (or frames or scripts) guide our actions and how we process information in specific situations. As soon as a certain schema is adopted by an individual he/she will behave or function in a manner that is consistent with the schema (cf. for example, Abelson, 1981; Bransford and Johnson, 1972; Schank and Abelson, 1977). Schemata may be of a causal nature inasmuch as they specify chains of causally related events (e.g. the chain of events associated with a restaurant visit). Such schemata are often called scripts (Abelson, 1981), but I prefer the term *causal schemata* which seems to be a more general (and looser) term than scripts. A causal schema then means a set of stereotyped preconceptions about the structure of causal relations within a given domain.

In decision making a causal schema may be used as a guideline for the generation of causal chains that will support the choice of a certain alternative. Once a certain schema is adopted by a decision maker it will be possible to predict a large proportion of the causal chains he/she will use for justifying a certain alternative. In many areas it is evident that actors are guided by causal schemata when they make and justify decisions. In energy politics, one may distinguish between a large-scale schema and a small-scale schema with respect to the scale of energy systems. This is to say that all those who see advantages with a certain type of scale (and disadvantages with the opposite type of scale) tend to organize their line of reasoning in a very similar way (Biel and Montgomery, Chapter 14 in this volume). Another example of schematic causal thinking in politics is given by Carbonell (1979) in his computer simulations of lines of reasoning in American foreign policy. Using a limited number of assumptions about the belief systems of 'hawks' and 'doves' in American foreign policy Carbonell (1979) was able to predict in a convincing way how politicians from a certain camp would reason in a specific situation. A non-political example of schematic causal thinking in decision making is to be found in a recent study of how jurors interpret available evidence in a story-like fashion when deciding about the verdict (Pennington and Hastie, 1986).

The causal schemata that I have found evidence for (mostly in political decision making) have all been organized in a black-and-white fashion; i.e. either the schema will predict only good consequences (for a favoured alternative) or it will predict only bad consequences (for a non-favoured alternative) in a given situation. Believers in a large-scale schema only see advantages with a large scale whereas the situation is totally reversed for believers in a small scale. The same black-and-white patterns could be found in Carbonell's (1979) study. Obviously, if decision makers reason in line with schemata of that sort they will easily find a dominance structure that supports a certain alternative.

A schema may be represented in a semantic network as a cluster of closely interconnected nodes (cf. Anderson, 1983). Hence, when one of these nodes is activated the activation spreads to the other nodes in the schema and in this way the entire schema becomes activated. Schema theory is thus compatible with network theory. However, it may be asked why certain concepts (or nodes) happen to form a schema. It may also be asked why schemata are organized in line with a dominance structure. Sjöberg (1982b) suggested that tendencies to think in a black-and-white fashion is due to the fact that our beliefs and values are guided by images. For examples, the beliefs and values of a teetotaler may be guided by an image of a drunken father beating his child. The opponent of nuclear power may have an image of the disasters associated with a core meltdown. It is not difficult to imagine how images of that type may inspire a person to form a causal schema of the black-and-white type which in turn will support a dominance structure. It may be the case that it is difficult, or even impossible, to represent a value conflict (i.e. a violation of dominance) in the same image. For example, it seems to be impossible to form an image which captures both the joys and the misery that may be associated with drinking alcohol. Perhaps the activation of one type of image may suppress the activation of opposite types of images and in this way a dominance structure may continue to survive. These ideas are speculations. We know very little of how and how much images guide action, but I think that these issues are a promising starting point for research on the mechanisms behind dominance structuring.

DISCUSSION

In the present chapter the dominance-search model has been scrutinized in the light of theories and empirical findings within and outside decision-making research. It has been shown that the model generally is consistent with ideas about action control in motivational psychology and with a number of theories and constructs in judgemental and cognitive psychology (anchoring, semantic network theory, and schema theory). Moreover, it has been demonstrated that a number of empirical findings directly support the model. However, the findings considered in the present chapter imply that compared to the original presentation of the model (Montgomery, 1983) more could be said about the nature of mental processes associated with the search for dominance. I would like to stress that the search for dominance in many situations is probably a very fast and more or less automatic process. The evidence presented above implies that in several respects we are 'prewired' to see dominance and hence that a dominance structure can be found with a minimum of effort in many situations. Anchoring plus the usage of broad evaluative categories implies that a decision maker quickly may find a subset of aspects which could be used for forming a dominance structure. Search in a semantic network is often a matter of approximately a second (Loftus and Suppes, 1972). Such a short processing time may be unrealistic for forming a dominance structure in a typical decision situation since it may be impossible to consider all relevant alternatives and attributes in one search process. On the other hand, if the decision maker in his/her search process finds that he/she could adopt a causal schema of the black-and-white type then he/she immediately has access to a dominance structure.

How do the above assumptions relate to the different phases and operations in the search for dominance (see Figure 1)? Anchoring obviously is related to the pre-editing phase. It may be seen as a procedure for finding relevant attributes in a decision situation. Anchoring could also be used to de-emphasize or bolster particular aspects; i.e. by using different anchors or by changing the definition of an anchor it is possible to change the evaluation of an aspect into a more or less extreme direction (bolstering and de-emphasizing respectively). The adoption of a causal schema could lead to the finding of a promising alternative. As noted above, a causal schema may immediately give access to a dominance structure. Thus, in this case the finding of a promising alternative and dominance testing are merged into one process. However, the two phases will be separate from each other if the decision maker tests the adequacy of a dominance structure suggested by a certain causal schema. Backwards search in the semantic network is related to the cancellation operation since it may result in the cancellation of a disadvantage or advantage related to a more general value (e.g. the disadvantage of high investment costs, which may be related to the more general value of costs, may be cancelled by another advantageous cost aspect, say low running costs). Forwards search is primarily related to the collapsing operation since it may lead to a more comprehensive representation of the choice alternatives.

We have now explored a number of possibilities to form and defend dominance structures. On the other hand, it is certainly true that the world we live in is full of trade-offs and hence dominance in a strict sense is not to be expected in a decision situation. Is then our talent to find dominance structures a purely psychological phenomenon? Do we live in a world of dreams with a lacking awareness of the dangers and drawbacks associated with our actions? It may be true that we often are biased in our perception of possible drawbacks with our actions (cf. Janis and Mann, 1977). Still, I do not think that dominance structuring mainly reflects a talent for dreaming. Rather, what we do is to exploit certain characteristics in the structure of our life situation, as we experience it. Hence although life is full of trade-offs it is also full of possibilities to find and defend dominance structures. Sometimes these possibilities actually become real and at other times people will never get a negative feedback from actions that in fact were non-optimal (Brehmer, 1980; Einhorn and Hogarth, 1978). The trade-offs in our life situation often are not visible and in this way we can maintain our dominance structures without any obvious lack of contact with the reality around us. In addition, as pointed out above, there are possibilities to incorporate trade-offs in a dominance structure, although these possibilities certainly are not exploited as often as would be possible. Occasionally, of course, after a decision has been implemented the decision maker discovers that the decision was based on an erroneous dominance structure. In such cases, we may revise our belief systems, but often nothing prevents us from constructing new types of dominance structures for future decisions in similar situations. Reality sometimes teaches us hard lessons but we could still go on to construct and defend more or less reality-oriented dominance structures in order to facilitate consistent and efficient action.

REFERENCES

Abelson, R. P. (1981). Psychological status of the script concept, *American Psychologist,* **36,** 715–29.
Adelbratt, T., and Montgomery, H. (1980). Attractiveness of decision rules, *Acta Psychologica,* **45,** 177–85.
Ajzen, I., and Fishbein, M. (1980). *Understanding Attitudes and Predicting Social Behavior,* Prentice-Hall, Englewood Cliffs, N.J.
Anderson, J. R. (1983). *The Architecture of Cognition,* Harvard University Press, Cambridge, Mass.
Anderson, N. H. (1986). A cognitive theory of judgment and decision. In B. Brehmer, H. Jungermann, P. Lourens, and G. Sevón (Eds), *New Directions in Research on Decision Making,* North-Holland, Amsterdam, pp. 63–108.
Axelrod, P. (Ed.) (1976). *Structure of Decision: The Cognitive Maps of Political Elites,* Princeton University Press, Princeton, N.J.
Beach, L. R., Campbell, F. L., and Townes, B. D. (1979). Subjective expected utility and the prediction of birth-planning decisions, *Organizational Behavior and Human Performance,* **24,** 18–28.
Biel, A., and Montgomery, H. (1986). Scenarios in energy planning. In B. Brehmer, H. Jungermann, P. Lourens, and G. Sevón (Eds), *New Directions in Research on Decision Making,* North-Holland, Amsterdam, pp. 205–18.

Bransford, J. D., and Johnson, M. K. (1972). Contextual prerequisites for understanding: some investigations of comprehension and recall, *Journal of Verbal Learning and Verbal Behavior*, **11**, 717–26.

Brehmer, B. (1980). In one word: not from experience, *Acta Psychologica*, **45**, 223–41.

Carbonell, J. (1979). Politics. In R. C. Schank and K. C. Riesbeck (Eds), *Inside Computer Understanding*, Hillsdale, Erlbaum, Hillsdale, N.J., pp. 259–307.

Collins, A. M., and Loftus, E. F. (1975). A spreading-activation theory of semantic processing, *Psychological Review*, **82**, 407–28.

Collins, A. M., and Quillian, M. R. (1969). Retrieval time for semantic memory, *Journal of Verbal Learning and Verbal Behavior*, **8**, 230–47.

Dahlstrand, U., and Montgomery, H. (1984). Information search and evaluative processes in decision making: a computer based process tracing study, *Acta Psychologica*, **56**, 113–23.

Einhorn, H. J., and Hogarth, R. M. (1978). Confidence in judgment: persistence in the illusion of validity, *Psychological Review*, **85**, 395–416.

Eysenck, M. W. (1984). *A Handbook of Cognitive Psychology*, Erlbaum, Hillsdale, N.J.

Grunert, K. G. (1986). Cognitive determinants of attribute information usage, *Journal of Economic Psychology*, **7**, 95–124.

Hellström, Å. (1984). The time-order error and its relatives: mirrors of cognitive processes in comparing, *Psychological Bulletin*, **97**, 35–61.

Helson, H. (1964). *Adaptation-level Theory*, Harper and Row, New York.

Huber, O. (1983). The information presented and actually processed in a decision task. In P. C. Humphreys, O. Svenson, and A. Vari (Eds), *Analyzing and Aiding Decisions*, North-Holland and Hungarian Academic Press, Amsterdam/Budapest, pp. 441–54.

Huber, O. (1986). Decision making as a problem solving process. In B. Brehmer, H. Jungermann, P. Lourens, and G. Sevón (Eds), *New Directions in Research on Decision Making*, North-Holland, Amsterdam, pp. 109–138.

Humphreys, P., and McFadden, W. (1980). Experiences with MAUD: aiding decision structuring versus bootstrapping the decision maker, *Acta Psychologica*, **45**, 51–69.

Janis, I. L., and Mann, L. (1977). *Decision Making*, The Free Press, New York.

Kahneman, D., and Tversky, A. (1979). Prospect theory: an analysis of decisions under risk, *Econometrica*, **47**, 263–91.

Kahneman, D., and Tversky, A. (1984). Choices, values, and frames, *American Psychologist*, **39**, 341–50.

Kuhl, J. (1985). Volitional mediators of cognition-behavior consistency: self-regulatory process and action versus state orientation. In J. Kuhl and J. Beckman (Eds), *Action Control: From Cognition to Behavior*, Springer, New York, pp. 101–28.

Kuhl, J. (1986). Human motivation: from decision making to action control. In B. Brehmer, H. Jungermann, P. Lourens, and G. Sevón (Eds), *New Directions in Research on Decision Making*, North-Holland, Amsterdam, pp. 5–28.

Lewicka, M. (September 1985). *Towards a Motivational Account of Human Cognitive Biases*, Paper presented at the Tenth Research Conference on Subjective Probability, Utility, and Decision Making, Helsinki.

Lindberg, E., Gärling, T., and Montgomery, H. (1986). *Beliefs and Values and Determinants of Residential Preferences and Choices*, Umeå Psychological Report 188, Department of Psychology, University of Umeå, Umeå.

Lindberg, E., Gärling, T., Montgomery, H., and Waara, R. (1988). People's evaluation of housing attributes: a study of underlying beliefs and values, *Scandinavian Housing and Planning Research* (in press).

Lindsay, P. H., and Norman, D. A. (1977). *Human Information Processing*, Academic Press, New York.

Loftus, E., and Suppes, P. (1972). Structural variables that determine the speed of retrieving words from long-term memory, *Journal of Verbal Learning and Verbal Behavior*, **11**, 770–7.

Lopes, L. L. (1982). *Toward a Procedural Theory of Judgment*, Report WHIPP 17, Department of Psychology, University of Wisconsin, Wisconsin.

Lopes, L. L. (1987). Between hope and fear: the psychology of risk, *Advances in Experimental Social Psychology*, **20**, 255–95.

Lopes, L. L., and Ekberg, P. H. S. (1980). Test of an ordering hypothesis in risky decision making, *Acta Psychologica*, **45**, 161–8.

Montgomery, H. (1977). A study of intransitive preferences using a think-aloud procedure. In H. Jungermann and G. de Zeeuw (Eds), *Decision Making and Change in Human Affairs*, Reidel, Dordrecht, pp. 347–62.

Montgomery, H. (1983). Decision rules and the search for a dominance structure: towards a process model of decision making. In P. Humphreys, O. Svenson, and A. Vari (Eds), *Analyzing and Aiding Decision Processes*, North-Holland and Hungarian Academic Press, Amsterdam/Budapest, pp. 343–69.

Montgomery, H. (1984). *Cognitive and Affective Aspects of Life Values as Determinants of Well-being: A Pilot Study*, Göteborg Psychological Report 14, No. 3, Department of Psychology, University of Göteborg, Göteborg.

Montgomery, H., and Biel, A. (April 1984). *Scenarios and Causal Models in Political Decision Making*, Paper presented at the Annual Conference of the British Psychological Society, Warwick.

Montgomery, H., and Svenson, O. (1976). On decision rules and information processing strategies for choices among multiattribute alternatives, *Scandinavian Journal of Psychology*, **17**, 283–91.

Montgomery, H., and Svenson, O. (1983). A think aloud study of dominance structuring. In R. Tietz (Ed.), *Aspiration Levels in Bargaining and Economic Decision Making*, Springer, Berlin.

Pennington, N., and Hastie, R. (1986). Evidence evaluation in complex decision making, *Journal of Personality and Social Psychology*, **51**, 242–56.

Pitz, G. P., and Riedel, S. (1984). The content and structure of value tree representations, *Acta Psychologica*, **56**, 71–80.

Rosch, E. (1975). Cognitive reference points, *Cognitive Psychology*, **7**, 532–47.

Samsonowitz, V., and Sjöberg, L. (1981). Volitional problems of socially adjusted alcoholics, *Addictive Behaviors*, **6**, 385–98.

Schank, R. C., and Abelson, R. P. (1977). *Scripts, Plans, Goals and Understanding*, Erlbaum, Hillsdale, N.J.

Shallice, T. (1978). The dominant action system: an information-processing approach to consciousness. In K. Pope and J. E. Singer (Eds), *The Flow of Conscious Experience*, Plenum, New York, pp. 117–57.

Simon, H. A. (1955). A behavioral model of rational choice, *Quarterly Journal of Economics*, **68**, 99–118.

Simon, H. A. (1983). *Reason in Human Affairs*, Blackwell, Oxford.

Sjöberg, L. (1980). Volitional problems in carrying through a difficult decision, *Acta Psychologica*, **12**, 123–32.

Sjöberg, L. (1982a). Aided and unaided decision making: improving intuitive judgment, *Journal of Forecasting*, **1**, 349–63.

Sjöberg, L. (1982b). Beliefs and values as attitude components. In B. Wegener (Ed.), *Social Attitudes and Psychophysical Measurement*, Erlbaum, Hillsdale, N.J.

Sjöberg, L. (1984). The problem of subjective intensity. In K.M.J. Lagerspetz and P. Niemi (Eds), *Psychology in the 1990s*, Elsevier, Amsterdam, pp. 333–66.

Sjöberg, L. and Samsonowitz, V. (1985). Coping strategies and relapse in alcohol abuse, *Drug and Alcohol Dependance,* **15,** 283–301.
Smith, E. E. (1978). Theories of semantic memory. In K.W. Estes (Ed.), *Handbook of Learning and Cognitive Processes,* Vol. 6, Erlbaum, Hillsdale, N.J. pp. 1–56.
Svenson, O. (1974). *A Note on Think-aloud Protocols Obtained During a Choice of a Home,* Reports from the Psychological Laboratories, University of Stockholm, No. 421.
Svenson, O. (1979). Process descriptions of decisions, *Organizational Behavior and Human Performance,* **23,** 86–112.
Thüring, M., and Jungermann, H. (1986). Constructing and running mental models for inferences about the future. In B. Brehmer, H. Jungermann, P. Lourens, and G. Sevón (Eds), *New Directions in Research on Decision Making,* North-Holland, Amsterdam.
Toda, M. (1980). Emotion and decision making, *Acta Psychologica,* **45,** 133–55.
Tversky, A., and Kahneman, D. (1974). Judgment under uncertainty: heuristics and biases, *Science,* **185,** 1124–31.
von Winterfeldt, D., and Keeney, R. L. (September 1983) *Value Tree Analysis as a Tool for Analyzing Conflicting Objectives,* Paper presented at the Ninth Research Conference on Subjective, Probability, Utility, and Decision Making, Groningen.

ACKNOWLEDGEMENTS

Preparation of this chapter was supported by The Swedish Council for Research in the Humanities and Social Sciences.

I am grateful to Anders Biel, Hannes Eisler, Lola Lopes, Ola Svenson, and an anonymous reviewer for their comments on previous versions of the chapter.

3

Rules and strategies in decision making: A critical analysis from a phenomenological perspective

GUNNAR KARLSSON

One important part of scientific work is to define and clarify the concepts that science deals with. Therefore, in this chapter I have chosen to address an issue which, unfortunately, has been very neglected in decision-making research. The issue concerns the notions of 'rule' and 'strategy' in decision making. These terms are often used interchangeably and treated as if they have the same meaning. 'Strategy' is sometimes defined as 'composed of one or several rules' (Svenson, Chapter 4 in this volume). A discussion of these terms is important, since one of the aims in the information-processing tradition in decision-making research is to find the rules or strategies that are used by the subject or decision maker.

My task will be to examine the terms 'rule' and 'strategy' and see how they are used in decision-making research. I will suggest that the term 'strategy' is a more appropriate term than 'rule', considering the aim of decision-making research. Thereafter, I will argue that abstract rules or strategies can hardly be considered to be *applied* by subjects. This brings me to the psychologist's fallacy, in which I think that one can find the origin of this mistake. I will thereafter present a different view within which strategies can be understood. A phenomenological approach will be presented, which stresses the fidelity to the phenomenon being studied. Such an approach to decision making attempts to study decision making without any pre-fixed hypothetical constructions or

Process and Structure in Human Decision Making
Edited by H. Montgomery and O. Svenson. © 1989 John Wiley & Sons Ltd

definitions. I will thereafter present how strategies can be understood from a phenomenological perspective, as well as show that the choice process is not exhausted by enumerating the applied strategies.

The first point to discuss is the interchangeable use of the terms 'rule' and 'strategy'. To show the interchangeable use of the two terms, consider the following notation from Payne (1982, pp. 382–3):

> One possible reason that a decision maker decides to use a particular *decision strategy* in a specific task environment is that *rule selection* is the result of cost/benefit analysis. The idea is that any *decision strategy* has certain benefits associated with its use and also certain costs .... *Decision rule* selection would then involve consideration of both the costs and benefits associated with each possible *strategy* (my underlinings).

By looking at ordinary language, one can determine the different meanings of the two terms. 'Rule' is usually understood to be a prescribed guide for conduct or action. A rule is some kind of criterion or regulating principle. Rules determine how activities can be carried out. Rules cannot be changed without changing the situation. Rules are followed or obeyed. Some typical examples of rules are the grammatical rules used to enable a language to be spoken or the rules defining the game of chess. The term 'strategy', on the other hand, has quite a different connotation, which is why it is unfortunate to use these terms interchangeably. Strategy has the connotation of a plan or method applied in order to reach a goal. Strategies do not define the parameters of a situation in the same way that rules do. To take a concrete example, in order to play a game of chess, one needs to obey the rules. However, one is free to choose between different chess-playing strategies.

I will raise the question: which one of these two terms is more appropriate for decision-making research? An important aim of decision-making research is to describe which rules or strategies subjects use in order to make a decision (e.g. 'the subject used to applied a lexicographic rule or strategy'). In accordance with the above characterization of the terms 'rule' and 'strategy', it would be more appropriate to use the expression 'lexicographic strategy' rather than 'lexicographic rule'. If, on the other hand, the aim of research is to find the *rules* one follows when one makes a decision, the researcher would look for the necessary conditions or parameters needed in order to make a decision. What could they be? To mention just a few examples, obviously, one necessary condition is that the person who makes the decision is the originator of the decision. That is to say, no one else can decide for that person, without changing the situation into something other than that person's decision. Another obvious condition is that all decision making posits a *realizable future*. A decision can never be about something past, nor about a phantasized future which is not realizable (such as a *wished* future, for example). Let me just say briefly that the aim of finding out the required rules or regulating principles for a phenomenon (such as, in this case, decision making) is quite in line with phenomenological philosophy and phenomenological psychology (although the term 'rule' is not usually used by phenomenologists), as well as more linguistic philosophy (cf. Wittgenstein, 1958). However, it is clear that this is not the aim of decision-making research today and that when decision-making researchers refer to rules they usually mean that which I have called 'strategy'. In line with the above discussion of rule versus strategy, I will hereafter use the term 'strategy' instead of 'rule'.

Another issue to discuss is the meaning of the terms 'use' or 'apply' which play an important role in decision-making research. As I have said, an important aim in research is to describe which strategies subjects use or apply in making decisions. The terms 'use' and 'application' are synonymous in the English language (cf. *Webster's Dictionary*, 1969), which is also how they are used in decision-making research. The issue here is the meaning of the terms 'use' or 'apply'. Consider the following examples: 'The man used a hammer in order to repair the table' or 'The person used a psychoanalytic theory in order to interpret the painting'. Perhaps the first thing that comes to our attention is that we have a subject who is confronted with a task: to repair a table, to interpret a painting. Insofar as I can see, the examples show that a *subject* uses or applies something. An object cannot use or apply anything. A further point, more subtle, yet important for this discussion, is that in order for a subject to use or apply something, this subject must be explicitly or implicitly aware of that which he/she uses. The person must be aware of the hammer and its function in order to use it. The person interpreting a painting must be aware of psychoanalytic theory in order to use it.

Now, let us try to answer the question: what does it mean to say that someone uses or applies a strategy? First, there is a subject (decision maker) who is the agent and originator of an action, in this case, using a strategy. Second, the subject, in order to use the strategy, must be aware of, or upon reflection be capable of becoming aware of, this strategy in order to use it.

Let us now look at the strategies found in decision-making research (see Svenson, 1979, for a review). Some of these strategies are very abstract (e.g. addition of utilities) and require quite complex processes on the part of the decision maker in order to be applied (cf. Montgomery, 1983). One may then wonder whether these strategies are to be understood to be *applied* by the subjects, given my characterization of 'applied'. Of course, we can never, in principle, deny that these abstract strategies can be applied by subjects. The issue cannot be addressed by a theoretical analysis: it is an empirical question. It would, however, be an easy task to ask the subjects which strategies they applied in making a decision. I think that it is quite unlikely that the subjects would reply by enumerating, for example, the addition of utility strategy. Such strategies are rarely applied by subjects, as very few subjects are aware of such strategies. Even among decision-making researchers, who are aware of the existence of these strategies, how often can we say that we apply these strategies when making decisions? Instead of assuming that subjects consciously apply or use these abstract strategies, I think that these strategies can be considered to be the researcher's theoretical constructions designed in order to understand the data obtained from the subjects. In other words, I think that there are many cases in which the researcher assumes the existence of abstract strategies, which from the point of view of the subject do not exist. Later I will argue that the decision-making process should be conceived of as entailing many other processes besides the use of strategies.

To sum up, I have tried to show that the term 'strategy' is a more appropriate word to use than 'rule' in describing that which decision-making research attempts to discover. In addition, I have argued that the abstract strategies found in decision-making research are incompatible with the notion of a subject *using* or *applying* a strategy. In order to use or apply a strategy one must be aware of it. The abstract strategies should rather be understood as theoretical constructions.

I would like to suggest that the source of the confusion described above can be found in what William James called 'the psychologist's fallacy' (James, 1890, pp. 196–7). The psychologist's fallacy is described as a confusion of standpoints between the subject and the researcher. The psychologist mistakes his/her knowledge about a situation (e.g. decision making) for the subject's experience of it; i.e. the researcher presupposes that his/her knowledge of the decision-making situation is automatically compatible with the subject's experience of the situation. The standpoint of the researcher may be theoretical and very elaborate, whereas the subject concretely lives through the situaton. The researcher often describes the decision-making situation from a perspective that requires abstract cognitive processes and knowledge which the subject does not have any access to and that do not in any way reflect the subject's lived experience. For instance, the researcher who describes the alternatives in terms of similarity or dissimilarity, number of dimensions, etc., must be aware that such characterizations or judgements of the situation are on an abstract cognitive level and not automatically an accurate description of the subject's experience.

One example of a widely discussed topic in decision-making research, which I think reveals an insensitivity to the subject's situation on the part of the researcher, is the discussion concerning the expected value (EV) and expected utility (EU) as well as the subjective expected utility (SEU) models. These models have been widely discussed. One popular way to invalidate them has been to show that the transitivity axiom does not hold; i.e. if alternative A is preferred to alternative B and B to C, then A must be preferred to C, otherwise transitivity is violated (cf. Tversky, 1969). The fact that decision makers do not always behave in accordance with the transitivity axiom has been taken as a sign of irrational behaviour on the part of the decision makers. My point is not to continue the discussion about the possible validity/invalidity of the above-mentioned models, nor to discuss the rationality/irrationality of decision makers. I mean that the whole discussion as to whether various models are valid or invalid indicates the presence of something that could be called 'the psychologist's fallacy'.

A typical experiment, which aims at verifying or disconfirming these models (EV, EU, SEU), is one in which the participating subjects choose between two different games. The subjects are usually allowed to play the chosen game once, or possible a few times. I would like to contrast the *subject's* situation here with the researcher's framework from which the subject's behaviour (or experience) is then interpreted. The researcher's framework is statistical objective, in the sense that the value or utility of the model is based on playing *an infinite series* of games. In reality, however, the subjects play the game a few times at most. Is there not a significant difference, then, between the standpoint of the subject and the standpoint of the researcher?

Let me give a further example of the psychologist's fallacy, this time within the field of perception. Hopefully, this will make my point concerning the psychologist's fallacy in decision making clearer. In the field of perception it is very common to postulate the existence of sense data as preceding (and in some theories causing) the perception of an object. However, there is nothing in the experience of perception itself to reveal or point to the existence of sense data. A faithful account of the experience of perception does not reveal the existence of sense data. Instead, the notion of sense data can be understood as a natural scientific description of the perceived object. In other words, the natural scientific *knowledge* of the perceived object has been inserted into the phenomenon of perception. However, such an account is not a faithful description of the experience of perception.

Before trying to formulate an alternative view of decision making, free from the psychologist's fallacy, within which our results (strategies and other processes) can be understood, I will try to characterize in a very general fashion the subject's experience of making a decision. The decision-making process is an experience for the subject which can be said to fluctuate between two levels. One level can be called the 'lived experience', the other level can be called 'the known' (cf. Merleau-Ponty, 1962). The lived experience is an experience which we live or go through without being thematically aware of it, like, for example, the lived position of my body at the moment. The lived experience can be thematically known if I reflect upon it and thereby focus my attention upon it. Much of the experience of making a decision is a lived experience for the subject. The known is what we are thematically aware of. For instance, I can decide thematically to use the 'elimination by aspect' strategy in order to reach a decision. Decision making is certainly often a fluctuating process between the lived and known experience.

The researcher's object of analysis is the subject's protocol (if we restrict ourselves to the process-tracing method). The protocol is not synonymous with the subject's experience *per se*. There is, in a certain sense, a gap between the subject's original experience and the protocol. In my understanding, this is necessarily the case, insofar as the researcher uses empirical data as his/her object of analysis. The only case where the researcher could have immediate access to experience is when the researcher examines his/her own stream of consciousness. The gap between the subject's original experience and the subject's protocol may be clearly illustrated in the case of a written retrospective protocol, where the time gap may have resulted in forgetfulness on the part of the subject or a re-figuration of the situation described in the protocol. In a similar way, a concurrent think-aloud protocol contains a gap between the thinking and the utterances of the thoughts. Not only is it impossible for the subject to pronounce aloud all thoughts, but thinking may have a different structure than speaking, which follows certain grammatical and syntactical rules. My point is that the object of analysis for the researcher is the subject's protocol and not the subject's original experience.[1]

THE FUNCTION OF THEORY IN PSYCHOLOGICAL RESEARCH

At this point I wish to introduce the notion of theory. The traditional view in psychological research is that the researcher must have a theory within which the researcher pursues the analysis of the protocol. The claim that one does not need to use theories in the attempt to understand protocols is met with much scepticism among most researchers. Therefore I would like to clarify the notion of 'theory' in order to subsequently answer the question: to what extent can one be a theory-free (pre-suppositionless) researcher? To begin with, however, I will discuss the expression 'theoretical attitude', since this attitude is common to any research. A theoretical attitude within a scientific endeavour is character- ized by the use of a systematic procedure in order to gain knowledge about the phenomenon being studied. This attitude entails the adoption of a method, which characterizes all scientific procedures. 'Theoretical attitude' refers then to a systematic, 'reflective' procedure. In a broad sense, it is important to realize that all scientific endeavour is 'theoretical' in that it demands a reflective stance taken towards the object of study. More specifically, the theoretical attitude always implies a certain perspective within which the object of study is understood. A protocol is open to many different sorts of analyses, e.g. sociological, psychoanalytic or whatever (cf. Giorgi, 1985, p. 11).

---

[1] It is beyond the scope of this article to further elaborate on the relationship between the subject's original experience and the protocol, as well as the researcher's different moments of understanding depending upon whether the focus of understanding is directed towards the original experience or towards the protocol. In Karlsson (1987) I discuss such issues within a hermeneutical framework.

One meaning of the term 'theory' is one that has been developed within the philosophy of science by the so-called 'Weltanschauungen' philosophers (Hanson, Kuhn, and Toulmin) in opposition to a positivistic view (cf. Suppe, 1977). The 'Weltanschauung' determines how one views and describes the world. One of the claims of the 'Weltanschauungen' philosophers is that observation and facts are imbued with conceptual organization, which means that all observation is culturally, historically, and linguistically influenced. There is no objective observation in the sense that it would be free from such an influence. For psychological research in decision making, this means that our understanding takes place within a cultural, linguistic framework. Our research is furthermore guided by certain 'metaphysical' views, which can be more or less thematic, but which are always there, no matter how unthematic. Psychological research often neglects the attempt to thematize its metaphysical position.

Finally, there is the meaning of theory as hypothetical construction. This meaning can be illustrated by Föllesdal and Walloe (1977, p. 53); namely, that a theory is a 'set of propositions whose interrelatedness is made explicit. It is therefore characteristic of a theory that it makes clear how the different propositions which are included in it depend upon each other' (my translation from Norwegian). The use of this type of theory is typical when the researcher seeks to verify an explicit hypothesis, i.e. the researcher has a pre-judged, explicit idea which he/she attempts to verify. It is especially this type of theorizing that I associate with the psychologist's fallacy.

AN ALTERNATIVE VIEW: THE PHENOMENOLOGICAL APPROACH

In the above section I claimed that all research partakes of a theoretical attitude. Furthermore, all psychological research takes place within an historical, cultural and linguistic understanding and is guided by certain metaphysical positions, which can be more or less explicit. Finally, I presented the notion of 'theory' as hypothetical construction. Different methods in psychological research can vary considerably with respect to their use of theoretrical constructions. There are methods that do not use constructed theories. Particularly, I am thinking of the empirical phenomenological psychological method, which is guided by phenomenological (philosophical) psychology.

There is not enough space in this article to adequately present phenomenological philosophy here (cf. Husserl, 1977). However, for my purpose it is important to briefly mention the fundamental aim of phenomenology (phenomenological philosophy as well as phenomenological psychology). Phenomenology began with the works of Edmund Husserl (1859–1938), and its aim was to disclose the essence of phenomena. Its motto was 'to go back to the things themselves', i.e. to describe the phenomena as faithfully as possible and avoid reducing them to systems of thought, which were not disclosed in the phenomena themselves. To reiterate the example about perception, there is nothing in perception itself that reveals anything like sense data. Thus from a pheno- menological point of view, one cannot postulate sense data as a part of perception. Instead, the aim of phenomenological analysis is to describe the phenomenon from within itself. As Heidegger (1980, p. 58) has put it: 'to let that which shows itself be seen from itself in the way in which it shows itself from itself'.

As was said above, empirical phenomenological psychology admits its commitment to a phenomenological philosophical analysis. The first and foremost consequence of this commitment is that consciousness is seen as characterized by intentionality. The fact that empirical phenomenological psychology is guided by a certain philosophical anthropology and world view is not the same thing as being guided by a theory in the second sense that I presented above, namely theory as hypothetical construction. Phenomenological methodology seeks to avoid the psychologist's fallacy.

A word should be said about the connection between hypothetical construc- tion and the psychologist's fallacy before continuing the presentation of the phenomenological method. Hypothetical construction is only one *possible* form of the psychologist's fallacy. This means that there may be hypotheses that are not examples of the psychologist's fallacy, e.g. if the hypothetical construction would coincide with the subject's perspective. Other forms of the psychologist's fallacy may also exist, apart from hypothetical constructions. Indeed, to be on guard against the psychologist's fallacy demands a constant self-critical scrutiniz- ing. I wish to emphasize in this article the close connection between hypothesis testing and the commitment of the psychologist's fallacy. Hypothesis testing demands constructed theory in advance, an understanding of the data *before* the researcher has even seen the data. One can see how this model of understanding necessarily diminishes the researcher's sensitivity to the data. In contrast to this, one can introduce the aim of openness on the part of the researcher vis-à-vis the data and a methodological attitude on the part of the researcher to encounter the data without any prior judgements or hypothetical constructions.

It is impossible here to describe satisfactorily the phenomenological method, whose function is to secure an open attitude on the part of the researcher (cf. Bullington and Karlsson, 1984; Giorgi, 1975, 1985; Karlsson, 1987; Wertz, 1983). Suffice to say, the core of the method is to abstain from pre-judgements, in order to be able — from a more critical, 'distanced' position — to understand the essence of the phenomenon being studied. The demand to be free from presuppositions comes not only from the phenomenological 'camp'. This is also emphasized by Carroll (1980, p. 70): 'we need methods that remain true to the performance of interest with minimal intrusion of the decision analysts' preconceptions'.

This brings me to another disputed question: what means of verification can be used for phenomenological inquiries? The traditional means of verification in psychological research is prediction, although it is clear that there is nothing in prediction as such that guarantees an understanding of the phenomenon in question. Instead, phenomenology relies on the human characteristic to understand, although (interpretive) understanding in empirical phenomenological psychological analyses is a more disciplined, systematic form of understanding.[2]

If this is rejected as being too 'unscientific' by someone brought up with the idea that prediction is the only means of verification, I would retort: how does the researcher verify that (his/her understanding of) the prediction is correct? At some point prediction comes to an end and the researcher must trust his/her understanding. Prediction cannot be the only means of verification, because prediction itself rests upon the prior 'unscientific' mode of understanding, without which no scientific project could be pursued.

A phenomenological study is limited to the aim of describing the phenomenon. It is quite another thing to have a technical interest, in the sense that one seeks to be able to control and predict the probability of a certain behaviour. In the latter case, the researcher's aim can be to find out the probability of a certain choice, given a specific situation as it has been defined by the researcher. However, if one is truly interested in descriptive accounts of phenomena, one must be careful to avoid such predefined research situations.

SOME EMPIRICAL EXAMPLES OF RESULTS FROM A PHENOMENOLOGICAL STUDY

Finally, I will briefly discuss some empirical results, relevant for this chapter, obtained in a phenomenological psychological study on choices among travel aims (see Karlsson, 1987, Chs. 10 and 11).[3] The aim of the study was to describe the process of making a choice. The study used a phenomenological psychological method, as well as some of the principles of the process-tracing method (cf. Svenson, 1974, 1979).

The empirical results showed that the choice process cannot be understood by merely describing the possible strategies that the subject applied. That a decision process would be exhausted by one strategy is rejected by several researchers. There are those who consider the decision process to contain

---

[2] A closer examination of the procedure of validating phenomenological results is beyond the scope of this article. In Karlsson (1987) it is argued that the validating procedure for the empirical phenomenological psychological method is of an argumentative kind (cf. Ricoeur, 1981) and there are certain specific criteria involved.

[3] I will here use the terms 'choice' and 'decision' synonymously, although it has been found in Karlsson (1987) that there are important differences between them.

different phases or subprocesses (cf. Einhorn and Hogarth, 1981; Kahneman and Tversky, 1979; Montgomery, 1983; Tversky and Kahneman, 1981). Indeed, there is much more involved in making a choice than applying one or several strategies. The application of strategy was only one among many processes and was, in fact, a very infrequent one. Further, the strategies that were applied were not at all as abstract as some of those that are tested and discussed in decision-making research today (like the addition of utilities). In order to say that a subject applied a strategy, the subject had to be thematically aware of the strategy. An example of such a strategy is: 'I won't look at hotel rooms yet, I'll see what it says about the place.' From this I conclude that when the researcher attempts to describe the decision-making process, without using any pre-formed hypothetical constructions, the strategies found are not very elaborate or abstract.[4]

Apart from applying strategies, there are a multiplicity of other processes going on when making a decision. I will mention below another process. As we said earlier, the decision-making process can be said to fluctuate between two levels. One level is the decision maker's concrete immersion in the situation, while the other level is the more reflective and 'self-conscious' level. According to my interpretation of subjects' protocols, the application of a strategy was an example of a process that belonged to the reflective, self-conscious level. Another example of a process on that level is when the subject explicates values (including preferences, desires, antipathies, and so on). The values may have been operating earlier on in the process of making the choice, but what is specific about this process is the subject's *explication* of them. In general, the reflective capability on the part of the decision maker is neglected in much decision-making research. If we want to be faithful to the decision maker's experience, this ability must be revealed and taken into account, otherwise we will end up with too mechanistic a description. There is much more research needed to be done in order to better understand the role of reflection in decision making.

There is yet another point that I would like to mention, which needs further elaboration in decision-making research. It is the importance of extraexperimental factors. Much too often in decision-making research, the laboratory is seen as a closed system. My study showed that the subjects often explicated pre-experimental experiences. An example of this occurred when one subject remembered that her friend had made a trip to one of the travel aims. Indeed,

---

[4] I would like to reiterate the standpoint that the results in my study do not in principle invalidate the possibility of a subject using abstract strategies (like the addition of utilities). Nevertheless, I take the results as a good indication of the possible correctness of my position in the previous theoretical discussion; namely, that very often the abstract strategies are not faithful descriptions of the subject's experience. Montgomery (Chapter 2 in this volume) presents a model in which such processes like the addition of utilities are not described in the traditional way (as strategies or rules). This is an exception from the common way of understanding/describing such processes.

decision making can never be understood without taking into account the decision maker's historical background.

As has been said, the described processes here are only a small selection of all those found. Instead of enumerating more of them, I will say a word about their function in decision making. Each psychological process plays a certain role in making the decision. The different psychological processes correspond or belong to different phases. Four different phases were found in the study: (a) mapping out of information, (b) preparatory, (c) the execution of the choice, as well as rejections of non-chosen alternatives, (d) the strengthening of the choice.[5] Many different processes correspond to each phase. For instance, the mapping-out phase includes first and foremost the search for and clarification of information. The preparatory phase includes, among other processes, evaluation and comparison of alternatives. The processes of choosing and rejecting alternatives are included in the third phase. Finally, the fourth phase (strengthening of the choice) includes, among other processes, the process of imaginary realization of the chosen alternative. The processes are 'closer' to the subject's experiences in that the processes describe the cognitive acts or experiences of the subjects as they go through the decision-making situation, according to the interpretation of the protocols, whereas the phases are more abstract in that they describe the *function* (meaning) of these processes seen in the light of the whole decision-making procedure. The phases can be seen in the light of the researcher's privileged position—the overview of the whole text or protocol with respect to the phenomenon being studied. The phases, ascertained through a phenomenological method, are not hypothetical constructions; nor are they directly experienced by subjects, although the subjects may have access to them through reflection.

This extremely brief and incomplete discussion concerning the results of my empirical study is only meant to exemplify some results obtained by a phenomenological psychological method. As I have argued earlier, the phenomenological method enables the researcher to obtain purely descriptive results, thus avoiding the psychologist's fallacy.

REFERENCES

Bullington, J., and Karlsson, G. (1984). Introduction to phenomenological psychological research, *Scandinavian Journal of Psychology*, **25**, 51–63.
Carroll, J. S. (1980). Analyzing decision behavior: the magician's audience. In T.S. Wallsten (Ed.), *Cognitive Processes in Choice and Decision Behavior*, Erlbaum, Hillsdale, N.J.

[5] Unfortunately, there is no possibility here to compare these four phases with those proposed by Montgomery (1983, Chapter 2 in this volume) in his dominance-search model for decision making. Undoubtedly there are some interesting overlaps between my phases and his.

62   *Process and structure in human decision making*

Einhorn, H. J., and Hogarth, R. M. (1981). Behavioral decision theory: process of judgment and choice, *Annual Review of Psychology*, **32**, 52–88.

Föllesdal, D., and Walloe I. (1977). *Argumentationsteori og vitenskapsfilosofi*, Universitetsforlaget, Bergen.

Giorgi, A. (1975). An application of phenomenological method in psychology. In A. Giorgi, C. Fischer, and E. Murray (Eds), *Duquesne Studies in Phenomenological Psychology*, Vol. 2, Duquesne University Press, Pittsburgh, pp. 82–103.

Giorgi, A. (1985). Sketch of a psychological phenomenological method. In A. Giorgi (Ed.), *Phenomenology and Psychological Research*, Duquesne University Press, Pittsburgh.

Heidegger, M. (1980). *Being and Time*, Basil Blackwell, Oxford.

Husserl, E. (1977). *Phenomenological Psychology*, Martinus Nijhoff, The Hague.

James, W. (1890). *The Principles of Psychology*, Macmillan, London.

Kahneman, D., and Tversky, A. (1979). Prospect theory: an analysis of decision under risk, *Econometrica*, **47**, 263–91.

Karlsson, G. (1987). *A Phenomenological Psychological Method: Theoretical Foundation and Empirical Application in the field of Decision Making and Choice*, Akademitryck, Stockholm.

Merleau-Ponty, M. (1962). *The Phenomenology of Perception*, The Humanities Press, New Jersey.

Montgomery, H. (1983). Decision rules and the search for dominance structure: towards a process model of decision making. In P. Humphreys, O. Svenson, and A. Vari (Eds), *Analyzing and Aiding Decision Processes*, North-Holland and Hungarian Academic Press, Amsterdam/Budapest.

Payne, W. (1982). Contingent decision behavior, *Psychological Bulletin*, **92**, 382–402.

Ricoeur, P. (1981). The model of the text: meaningful action considered as a text. In J. B. Thompson (Ed.), *Hermeneutics and the Human Sciences*, Cambridge University Press, Cambridge.

Suppe, F. (Ed.) (1977). *The Structure of Scientific Theories*, University of Illinois Press, Urbana.

Svenson, O. (1974). A note on think aloud protocols obtained during the choice of a home, Report 421, Psychological Laboratories, University of Stockholm.

Svenson, O. (1979). Process descriptions of decision making, *Organizational Behavior and Human Performance*, **23**, 86–112.

Tversky, A. (1969). Intransitivity of preferences, *Psychological Review*, **76**, 31–48.

Tversky, A., and Kahneman, D. (1981). The framing of decisions and the psychology of the choice, *Science*, **211**, 453–8.

Webster's Seventh New Collegiate Dictionary (1969). G.C. Merrican Company Publishers, Springfield, Mass.

Wertz, F. J. (1983). From everyday to psychological description: analyzing the moment of a qualitative data analysis, *Journal of Phenomenological Psychology*, **14**, 197–242.

Wittgenstein, L. (1958). *Philosophical Investigations*, Macmillan, New York.

ACKNOWLEDGEMENTS

I would like to express my gratitude to Jennifer Bullington, Henry Montgomery, and Göran Nilsson whose critical comments have been a great help to me.

This chapter was supported by a grant to Ola Svenson from the Swedish Council for Research in the Humanities and Social Sciences.

Part II
Method

4

Eliciting and analysing verbal protocols in process studies of judgement and decision making

OLA SVENSON

In the beginning of this century psychologists studying human cognition often collected and used verbal protocols in their data analyses. Even John Watson, one of the most influential behaviourists, wrote: 'a good deal more can be learned about the psychology of thinking by making subjects think aloud about definite problems than by trusting to the unscientific method of introspection' (Watson, 1920, p. 91).

Today, the distinction between introspection and the think-aloud method is not as well known as 60 years ago. In brief, introspection requires experienced subjects who through previous training know what in their thought processes they should attend to while engaged in a cognitive activity. The subjects are requested to report on their subjective experiences and avoid making the stimulus error (e.g. reporting physical facts). In contrast, the think-aloud technique uses unsophisticated subjects who are instructed 'to think-aloud' all their thoughts while doing a task. Hence, the think-aloud method does not require the subject to actively analyse his/her experiences as in the case of introspection. Related to the think-aloud method is the collection of retrospective verbal reports about a thought process just after a subject has completed a task.

The present paper will discuss the collection and analysis of simultaneous (think-aloud) and retrospective verbal protocols collected as tape recordings or as the judgement or a decision. Most of the illustrations will be from studies by the author.

Process and Structure in Human Decision Making
Edited by H. Montgomery and O. Svenson. © 1989 John Wiley & Sons Ltd

PURPOSE OF VERBAL PROTOCOL STUDY

The completeness, reliability, and validity of verbal protocols must be seen in relation to the purpose of an investigation—whether that be to test a single hypothesis or to obtain a detailed and complete view of a cognitive process.

Talk-aloud, think-aloud, and retrospective protocols

Ericsson and Simon (1980, 1984) presented a model for how different types of verbal data are generated. In this model think-aloud protocols are generated when subjects vocalize thoughts which are assumed to be 'inner speech'. Think-aloud protocols also cover other non-verbal thought processes. Such processes have to be attended to and interpreted verbally which may make the inferences from the protocols less obvious (cf. also Ericsson and Oliver, 1986).

In talk-aloud protocols there is no obvious split of attention, as in the case of other think-aloud situations where the subject has to divide his/her attention between the main focal task and the coding of his/her thoughts into a verbal form that can be vocalized. Ericsson and Simon (1984) found no differences between cognitive processes accompanied by think-aloud protocols and processes where no protocols were gathered except for situations where subjects used non-verbal codes in their thinking. In those cases the thought process was slowed down (cf. Payne, Braunstein, and Caroll, 1978).

Retrospective verbal protocols are unobtrusive with regard to the process covered but they are associated with shortcomings depending on memory failures and tendencies to reconstruct a trustworthy story even in the absence of one, as in the case of a fully automatized and unconscious process (cf. Nisbett and Wilson, 1977). Thus, retrospective protocols give the subject a chance to reconstruct the thought processes in a way that seems justifiable and that does not necessarily represent what actually happened.

Russo, Johnson, and Stephens (1986) differentiate between two forms of invalidity of verbal protocols. A protocol is *reactive* if the verbalization changes the primary process under study. Reactivity is indicated either as a disturbance of the primary process which may change the result of that process or it may lead only to a prolongation of the process. Of these effects the former is worse than the latter for the interpretation of the protocols. A protocol is *non-veridical* if it does not reflect the process under study. Errors of omission (of not reporting everything) are common and can be coped with up to a certain level, errors of comission (reporting things that did not occur) are harder to handle in analyses that are not based on a very rigorous theory (e.g. a psychoanalytic theory). Retrospective protocols seem particularily vulnerable to the non-veridicality bias, as mentioned above. Bainbridge (1985) has provided concrete descriptions of the process of collecting and analysing think-aloud protocols from process-control tasks in the process industry.

The degree of reactivity as a result of concurrent verbal protocols reported by Russo, Johnson, and Stephens (1986) did not follow what would be expected from the Ericsson and Simon (1984) model. Instead of slowing down and changing the process more for non-verbal processes than for inherently verbal problem-solving processes, the contrary was found for the problems and subjects generating the Russo, Johnson, and Stephens data. The authors present an interesting discussion attempting to explain these findings. This is a very interesting and important topic of research at the present time.

Explorative investigation versus hypothesis testing

If the verbal protocols are analysed for explorative reasons the experimenter may be more open ended in designing his/her experiment, ensuring only that the subjects generate as complete protocols as possible. The think-aloud technique is preferable to retrospective reports because it enables the researcher to observe simultaneous and spontaneous reactions to each situation. If, on the other hand, the aim of the investigation is to test a model or a hypothesis it is preferable to design an experiment where a lot of information is generated on a few basic aspects. This can be achieved by choosing the judgement or decision tasks carefully. Retrospective and simultaneous verbal protocols may both be well suited for hypothesis testing, but simultaneous protocols have advantages over retrospective protocols as mentioned above. However, if the problems are all similar, solved quickly, and presented in great numbers then retrospective protocols are more appropriate as there may not be enough time to generate simultaneous think-aloud protocols. On the other hand, such decision problems may be more or less automatic and unconscious which in turn makes all verbal reports difficult to inerpret.

Analysis in conjunction with analyses of judgements/decisions made versus independent analysis

Whenever possible, analyses in conjunction with conventional analyses of human behaviour (e.g. studies of final decisions or numerically scaled responses) are recommended. However, when there are only a few or a single important decision that interests the researcher, it is impossible to analyse the final decisions or judgements with conventional statistical techniques. In such cases process tracing data such as verbal protocols provide the only source of data on the cognitive processes of interest to the researcher.

THE TASK

A number of characteristics of the task the subject is going to perform are important for the quality of the verbal protocols.

Familiar versus unfamiliar task

In general, unfamiliar tasks have the advantage that they may generate protocols that provide information about the cognitive structuring of a problem and the creation of a solution process. Familiar tasks tend to be associated with already available cognitive strategies for solving them; these may be more stable than in unfamiliar tasks but the disadvantage is that they may also have become highly automatized, rapid, and less accessible to studies of verbal protocols. Shiffrin and Schneider (1977) have differentiated between automatic and controlled cognitive processing and their theory is highly relevant for the scholar attempting to analyse verbal protocols.

Many repeated versus one or a few tasks

Even if a decision problem is not familiar before the experiment, repeated exposures to a large set of similar problems make a subject familiar with the situation. In this case the subject gets the opportunity to develop a strategy for coping with the problem. This may lead to less dense verbal protocols as the subject becomes more familiar with the task. In other words, when a subject has found a strategy he/she is not any longer so keen on reporting what he/she is doing every time he/she solves a problem.

When a problem requires a longer time (a few minutes or more) the risk of running into an automated routine is smaller, particularly if the problem is not familiar before-hand.

Important versus unimportant tasks

The importance of the decision or judgement problems in an experiment is likely to influence both the way in which the problem is solved and the quality of the verbal protocols. In general, one may assume that more important tasks may generate more thorough information processing and more complete protocols. On the other hand, if the task is so important and demanding, it may be reasonable to assume that the subject becomes totally absorbed by the problem and the verbal protocols may again become less complete. Unfortunately, no conclusive results about the role played by the importance of a task have yet been reported.

Number of aspects in a task

The more aspects or cues in a decision problem or judgement task the more difficult it is on the average. Generally speaking, it seems difficult to obtain rich protocols for tasks with less than four attributes or cues as the cognitive process tends to become automatized quite rapidly. The less familiar a task the smaller the number of cues that can generally be used, but it seems as if four or more separate pieces of information are needed in order to secure reasonably rich protocols.

THE EXPERIMENTAL SETTING

Instructions to subjects

Written instructions which the subject reads first and then discusses with the experimenter (with the tape recorder on) seem to be the best way to tell the subject what to do. This ensures a high degree of conformity across subjects and controls their understanding of the instruction through the recording of the interaction between the experimenter and the subject. It also gives some information about the experimenter's behaviour which through very subtle cues may affect a subject's way of approaching a problem.

In think-aloud experiments the subject is told to think aloud all thoughts that come while solving the task. In retrospective verbal protocols the subject may also be required to report his/her thoughts or more restrictive instructions may be used. To exemplify, if a specific hypothesis is tested the subject can be instructed to give the order in which he/she processed different pieces of information by indicating this on a response sheet after each problem has been solved.

To make subjects familiar with the think-aloud technique it is recommended that they are given a training session on tasks similar to the experiment proper. It is difficult to give the optimal time for training as it varies from task to task, but it should not be too long (boring the subjects and leading to less dense reports) or too short (leaving the subjects without a habit of thinking aloud). For rather long decisions with complex and engaging material 20 to 30 minutes were used, or about one-third of the time required for the following experiment. This seems to be one extreme; when the subjects are making many repeated simple judgements or decisions, the training phase should not be long. Actually, the first trials may sometimes provide key information for understanding the development and characteristics of the cognitive processes. Such information may not appear at all once the subject's information processing has become routine. There is also a risk that if the training task is very similar to the experiment proper this may interfere with the subjects' reactions in the experiment. Therefore, it seems wise to record the training phase and also to keep track of unwanted effects of training.

Whenever the subject becomes silent in the training phase the experimenter intervenes with 'What are you thinking of now?' spoken in a neutral voice. Ericsson and Simon (1984) would argue for a probe of 'keep talking', which may be experienced as a less demanding probe causing less problems. The experimenter should be in the same room but positioned so that he/she does not have eye contact with the subject. This is to avoid non-verbal communication. A back-to-back position between the subject and experimenter has been found satisfactory as it does not give the subject a feeling of being watched. The experimenter may be busy doing some simple task which can be interrupted when the subject becomes silent.

Example of a think-aloud instruction

> As soon as you begin working on the problem, please start thinking aloud. The best way to do this is to be as spontaneous as possible. Tell me everything you are thinking as you are thinking it, even details or sidetracks that seem insignificant or embarrassing. If you think aloud spontaneously, you will soon forget that you are speaking at all. There is no need to explain to me why you are thinking what you are. You don't have to interpret or justify your approach to a problem. Just tell me what you are thinking at the moment. If you are silent for more than a few seconds, I will remind you by saying: Please tell me what you are thinking (Russo, Johnson, and Stephens, 1986, pp. 12, 13).

Microphone arrangement

It may sound utterly trivial that one should be reminded about the importance of the arrangement of the microphone if the protocols are tape recorded. However, we have made some unnecessary mistakes in the Stockholm group where, for instance, the microphone was too far away from the subject in one case and too close to the paper material used in the experiment in another case. This may give rise to some difficulties for the person who types the protocols. He/she will need more time and still perhaps produce incomplete protocols. To be safe, the microphone and tape recorder arrangements should not be easy to change by the subjects. The author has experienced how neglecting this problem caused an incomplete protocol in an experiment where a couple making a joint decision started arguing so intensely that they considered it best to turn off the tape recorder (cf. the following chapter).

Arranging for subject identification of alternatives

It is very important that the experimental situation is designed so that the think-aloud protocols always make it clear what alternative (and/or case) a subject considers at each point in time. To illustrate, if a subject who is making a choice between different houses talks about 'a wonderful garden' it is crucial to know with certainty which alternative that garden belongs to. The instruction therefore should emphasize that the subject always mentions what alternative he/she is attending to.

Careful instructions paired with experimental material that facilitates natural mentioning of alternatives are means to obtain protocols that are unambiguous as to what alternative is considered during different parts of the protocols. It is particularly important that the experimenter asks the subject, for example, 'What alternative are you considering now?', when the protocol becomes unclear at that point. In addition, the choice of information that the subjects are processing may facilitate the coding of the protocols. If, for instance, the alternatives in a decision task are all characterized by different and unique aspects this makes it possible to code the protocols unambiguously.

Typing the protocols and coding

Some researchers have coded the protocols directly from the tapes but it is still advisable to have the protocols typed. The length of a line should not be any longer than half the width of the paper used. Then the detailed coding can be written either between the typed lines and/or to the left or to the right of the text. The latter is better for shorter protocols where one statement can be typed on each line. Otherwise it is easier to write the codings on top of the typewritten text.

Experimenter characteristics

As made clear earlier, the interaction between the experimenter and the subject should be kept to a minimum when the subject is thinking aloud because it is well known that it is easy to communicate an experimenter's hypothesis about the behaviour that he/she expects the subject to reveal. However, the presence of the experimenter ensures that the subject knows that someone is listening to what he is saying even though the experimenter is silent.

The choice of experimenter is more important and more crucial than in many other types of experiments because of the risks of biasing the verbal protocols. The experimenter should be a person who can be silent in a pleasant and socially acceptable way so that the subject feels that he/she should produce the verbal protocol but without any feelings of unpleasant social pressure to do so. In this way it is the subject's behaviour that is studied and not reflections of the experimenter–subject interaction.

WHAT TYPE OF INFORMATION DO SUBJECTS REPORT?

Woodworth and Schlosberg (1954) describe the collection of retrospective protocols in the following way:

> Shortly after 1900 several investigators in different laboratories devised a form of experiment which was certainly straightforward and obvious enough. They asked *O* to solve some simple problem and then recount his conscious experience from the moment when the problem was given till the solution was reached. He was

instructed to *describe* his experience, not to explain it. His function was to provide the raw data which *E* would subsequently analyze and interpret ....

... On one main point the results obtained in different laboratories were in excellent agreement. All *O*s reported thinking of what we may call *objects* in a broad sense, including things, persons, events, and states of affairs. In short, their reports were like those you get if you ask a person to report what he sees in an actual scene or happening. Some objects thought about may be imaginary, and some may be rather abstract as when one thinks of 'the dog' as a kind of animal or of the relative importance of heredity and environment in making people different (Woodworth and Schlosberg, 1954, p. 815).

This description of retrospective verbal reports is quite to the point (cf. also Nisbett and Wilson, 1977; Ericsson and Simon, 1984). Most verbal protocols actually contain a lot about the information processed and very little or nothing about how it is processed. Therefore it is important to have a good theory or model which makes it possible to understand the data in a process-oriented language. Very rarely do verbal protocols themselves provide the theory for their understanding. Instead, the abundance of information tends to overwhelm the unsophisticated researcher, making it very difficult to find a structure for an understanding or an explanation of the process that produced so much data.

REPRESENTING THE JUDGEMENT OR DECISION TASK

Primitives

A representation system describes another system (in this case a psychological system) in symbolic form and its smallest units are called primitives. The primitives are related to their corresponding elements in the verbal protocols. Thus, the psychological system is fundamental, described by the representation system, and the verbal protocols provide information directly related to the representation system. Note that the primitives of the representation system should not necessarily be regarded as identical with the smallest units used in the coding scheme for the verbal protocols. A primitive may be an aspect, i.e. a particular level or value of an attribute describing a decision alternative (e.g. a certain amount of dollars is a value on the attribute of rent). It could also be an element in a set (as in mental arithmetics where the cardinal numbers and/or the units may be manipulated). While a representation system does not include any smaller units than its primitives, the smallest units in the coding scheme (to be elaborated below) may contain more than one primitive. The coding scheme units are chosen on practical grounds related to the quality of the protocols and the problem being investigated. For example, a coding scheme may use a sentence or a turn in a dialogue as their smallest unit and each of these smallest units may consist of more than one primitive in the theory used for analysing the protocol.

Relations

Representing cognitive processes requires a system with a set of relations between the primitives and more complex sets of units. Metric representations are most often used for representing cognitive processes in studies of judgement and decision making. For instance 'equal' and 'greater than' are important relations in such a representation system. These two relations may be defined only within an attribute (if that type of representation is chosen; below this way of representing decisions alternatives will be elaborated) or across attributes (as in regular analytical geometry). Note that the relations of the representation system may be much finer grained, in other words on a lower level, than those used in the coding scheme. For instance, an interval scale of attractiveness may be assumed in a representation system for choice between multiattribute alternatives, while it has been shown that it is difficult to code verbal protocols reliably with a higher precision than that represented by an ordinal scale of attractiveness (Svenson, 1974). Also, note how decision makers may take advantage of representing a decision task in a coarser metric in order to be able to find a dominant alternative (Montgomery, Chapter 2 in this volume).

The choice of representation system for decision problems may be more difficult than for problem-solving tasks because in the latter tasks there are usually well-defined primitives, rules, and goals to an extent that is not present in decision-making tasks (cf. Newell and Simon, 1972; Ericsson and Simon, 1984). In fact, when designing think-aloud experiments Ericsson and Oliver 'recommend that tasks should be selected that have correct answers or responses and that are also amenable to extensive *a priori* analysis' (Ericsson and Oliver, 1986, p.13). Generally speaking, however, this recommendation may be easier and more reasonable to fulfil in a problem solving task than in a decision-making task. This is because in a decision problem the goals and the rules for reaching them are determined by each individual him/herself. Furthermore, many decision problems are ill-defined, which adds to the difficulty in finding out what representation system is the best for representing the subjects' representation of the situation.

CODING THE PROTOCOLS

The system used for coding the protocols is founded on the representation system chosen by the researcher. In part, that system reflects what research problems are addressed and, in part, what prior knowledge exists in the area under investigation. The relations between the cognitive model, the coding scheme, the verbal protocols, and the coded protocol are illustrated in Figure 1.

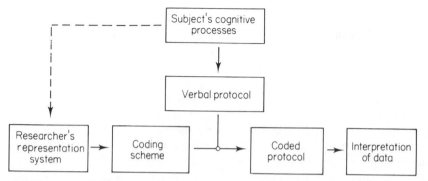

Fig. 1   Schematic representation of the process of collecting and interpreting verbal protocol data.

Dividing the protocol into units

In verbal protocols covering judgemental processes the smallest unit is usually the mention of a cue with or without a relation. In decision making a statement (e.g. a sentence with one main idea) or, if in doubt, any shorter unit can be used as the smallest unit. It is always advisable to have two independent coders split a few protocols into units before the coding starts to ensure that the same units are coded. The reliability of the division into units can be determined by correlating two independent judges. The correspondence between the judges' division into sentences should be high and a final division of the protocol agreed upon before proceeding to other parts of the coding. When dialogues between two persons are coded each turn or argument may be used as the smallest unit. If there are problems about determining the size of the smallest units it is recommended that a subdivision with smaller units is used.

Coding the units

The smallest units and/or relations between them are assigned to categories in the coding procedure. To exemplify, a statement (= smallest unit) may be classified as a positive evaluation of a particular aspect. Sometimes, the classification scheme as applied to the empirical data may not provide one and only one classification with certainty. By way of example, it may be hard to classify a passage in a written protocol as a simple information collection or an evaluative statement. In such cases it may be wise to introduce a priority order among the categories which, when in doubt, directs the coder to one and only one of the plausible categories. To exemplify, when a statement can reflect both information collection and evaluation the coding scheme may prescribe the classification of a statement as evaluative. In this way an increased reliability is gained at the price of a systematic bias in classification (that is controlled, however).

Relative and absolute evaluation

When investigating cognitive processes in judgement, reports like 'gee—this is big' (absolute evaluation) or 'this is bigger than that one' (relative evaluation) are examples of statements easy to code as they seem to imply significant attributions of values on a size attribute. In decision making, attractiveness evaluations or comparisons are corresponding relations which seem easy to code using categories derived from a multiattribute cognitive model.

Rules

A number of different rules or strategies (composed of one or several rules) are used by a decision maker or judge in arriving at the solution of a task. A number of such rules have been proposed for decision making, some of them having been summarized by Svenson (1979) along with many process studies of judgement and decision making. To illustrate, decision processes often seem to start with an initial screening involving application of a cognitive rule (which says that all alternatives that do not fulfil certain criteria should be eliminated from further search). At the same time or immediately thereafter a 'promising alternative' may be chosen and tested against the other remaining alternatives (cf. Montgomery and Svenson, 1983). This testing seems to be performed in more elaborate trade-off-type rules. In fact this general description approaches a general model for the cognitive processes leading to a decision (Montgomery, 1983).

Process model

One of the goals of process studies is to find a cognitive model that describes the thought processes leading to a judgement or a choice. Svenson (1985) coded think-aloud protocols from judgement of risk cumulated over time and found a general process model describing the steps or subgoals which governed the information processing leading to a judgement. The particular characteristics of this process differed from case to case depending on the particular information at hand, but the fairly simple general plan was the same for all cases.

An illustration of a model of judgement processes

In the Svenson (1985) study, the task subjects were asked to judge involved a set of hypothetical persons each of whom was exposed to different specified average risks of dying during different time periods of a year. The subjects were asked to judge the cumulated risk of dying during a year for each case. For example, a case might involve the high-risk exposure of 20.0 deaths per thousand persons a year during 3 weeks, a risk of 4.3 deaths per thousand a year during 33 weeks, and a risk of only 0.5 deaths per thousand a year during the remaining 16 weeks of the year. This is certainly not a familiar judgement task although some intuitive weighing of risks with exposure time is natural in everyday reasoning (e.g. 'but this risk is for only a short period of time'). For each case, the year was divided into three time periods varying in risk level.

Figure 2 gives the coded verbal protocol from one particular case (left column) with its coding based also on other cases judged by the subject. To the right in the figure a general process model is exposed which contains all the alternative models governing the information processing for all subjects. For this particular subject the parts of the right-hand flow diagram in which exposure times are relevant was applicable. Note that a process model has to be on the proper level of abstraction to be appropriate in the analysis of the data. Ideally, it should cover all subjects and cases and still be detailed enough to have something to say in a particular case. The illustrated protocol does not contain complete information about the process; some of it had to be inferred from other cases treated by the same subject.

It is quite important to note that this example does not need a cognitive representation system that differs much from the actual numbers given in each problem. This is typical of well-defined conceptual judgement tasks like the one just presented. However, if real and complex objects (like people) are judged it is by no means self-evident what cognitive representation will be used (e.g. what cues characterizing people do the judges use?). Then the experimenter has to find or construct such a model. Likewise, in more complex decision tasks (e.g. choices of homes, marriage partners, jobs) it is also necessary to describe the cognitive representation of the situation in an appropriate model. In the field of decision making, multiattribute models with different aspects characterizing the decision alternatives have been the prevailing general model choice. This will be illustrated below.

Verbal protocols from decision processes leading to the choice of a home

The researcher's model

Imagine a decision maker facing the decision of making the choice of a new home among a set of possible alternatives. In this case, not only are the aspects characterizing the homes relevant, as in a judgement task, but also the subjective value or attractiveness that the decision maker associates with each of the aspects is crucial for an understanding of the decision process. This means, in essence, that there are three different models for representing the situation: (a) one physical or objective, (b) one perceptual, conceptual, or subjective, and (c) one evaluative model. In the multiattribute model to be used here, a decision situation

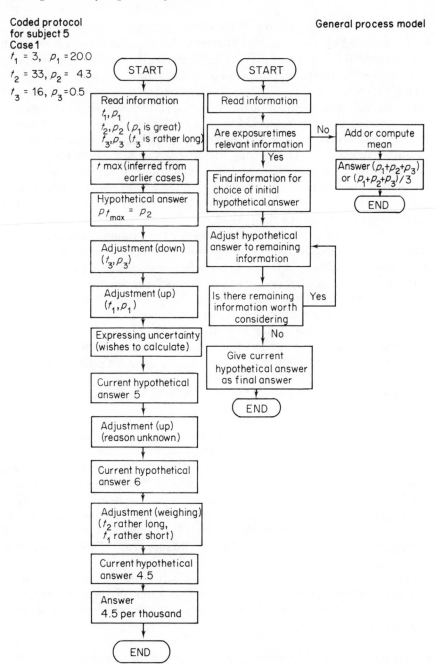

Fig. 2 An example of a verbal protocol, the coded protocol, and the process model representation for all subjects taking part in a judgement experiment. See text for further explanation. (From Svenson, 1985.)

is defined as consisting of two or more choice alternatives, each of which may be characterized by a set of *aspects* (the particular size, the rent of a home, etc.).

Furthermore, it is assumed that the decision maker's cognitive representation of these aspects corresponds to values on a set of dimensions or *attributes*. To exemplify, the particular size of a home perceived as an aspect of the decision maker represents a magnitude on the (subjective) attribute of size. As mentioned before, each aspect is also assumed to be experienced as more or less *attractive* by the decision maker. Thus, it is assumed than an aspect can be mapped on an attractiveness scale. There is one attractiveness scale for each attribute and the values on these scales need not be commensurable across attributes. To summarize, each home is characterized by a number of *objective* aspects (e.g. size in square metres, etc.). Each of these aspects has its *subjectively* perceived counterparts (e.g. perceived size—which may depend on plan of home, colours, etc.). Each of the subjectively defined aspects also has a value on an *attractiveness* scale (e.g. the bigger the home up to a certain optimal size the more attractive it is—when size increases beyond the optimal size attractiveness decreases again).

In a more exact description, a decision alternative is denoted $A_i(a_{11}, \ldots, a_{in})$, where a_{ij} stands for the attractiveness of, for example, a price (attribute j) associated with a house (alternative i). Note that only a rank order scale of (the subjective) attractiveness within each attribute is assumed so far. Thus, we do not assume *a priori* that trade-offs are or even can be made between two attributes, as many multiattribute models do (e.g. expected utility models).

The protocols

Table 1 lists the attributes used for the coding of think-aloud protocols in an early study (Svenson, 1974). When a subject used a more detailed analysis of one of the attributes (e.g. plan of house) new subattributes (e.g. a'_{i2} were created.

The smallest units in the protocols were statements. The most frequently used relation compared two aspects with each other in 'greater than', 'equal', and 'smaller than' relations on an attractiveness scale. To exemplify, the coding $a_{14} > a_{24}$ means that the subject has expressed a preference for house alternative 1 over alternative 2 on the attractiveness scale for distance from the city (defined perhaps through time, comfort, physical distance, etc.). This was called a comparative evaluation.

Table 2 illustrates the use of comparisons across alternatives as compared with absolute evaluations without any mention of another alternative (e.g. 'this is good'). It appears that comparative evaluations increase towards the very end of a decision process.

Coding protocols from dialogues: an hierarchical coding scheme

Sometimes it is not necessary to code the protocols in the detail just presented. In another study (cf. Svenson, Chapter 5 in this volume) couples who lived

Table 1 Representation of attractiveness of aspects used in the protocols. When further specification was given by a subject the aspects were differentiated and written specifications were added in the coded protocols (Svenson, 1974)

Code	Attribute number	Represents
a_{i1}	1	Plan of area (within the housing area)
a_{i2}	2	Plan of house: number of rooms, size, etc.
a_{i3}	3	Economic aspects: prize, loans, etc.
a_{i4}	4	Distance from the city, communications
a_{i5}	5	Part of town: suburb area, social status of area
a_{i6}	6	Recreation possibilities, closeness to water, etc.
a_{i7}	7	Standard of construction material and machines: wallpaper, washing machine, etc.
a_{i8}	8	Exterior appearance of house
a_{i9}	9	Service in area: schools, stops, etc.
a_{i10}	10	Ground-plot, size, type, etc.

together but did not have a house were instructed to make a choice between different houses on the market at the time. First, they made separate individual decisions based on information in authentic booklets without knowing that they were later expected to agree with their partner on a house.

Here the coding system was hierarchical and less detailed than in the earlier examples (Svenson, 1979). A coding unit was each 'turn' in the dialogues. Thus, sometimes several sentences constituted the smallest units coded although the representation system was the same as in the earlier description of individual choices. This creates problems because sometimes a unit could be classified into

Table 2 Distribution of absolute and evaluative statements over protocols (adapted from Svenson, 1974)

	Proportions					
	Complete protocols	First quarter	Second quarter	Third quarter	Fourth quarter	Last 15 statements
Absolute evaluations	0.71	0.64	0.72	0.77	0.71	0.57
Comparative evaluations	0.29	0.36	0.28	0.23	0.29	0.43

two different categories in the coding system. This was solved by always using the category that was higher in the heirarchy of the coding scheme.

CONCLUDING COMMENTS

It should be clear from this chapter that the author wishes to stress the importance of the psychological model that governs the collection and analyses of verbal protocols. Once a researcher has made the choice of a model (e.g. a multiattribute decision-making model), he has to sacrifice, to a certain extent, alternative models (e.g. scheme or script models) before he can start to analyse the protocols. This is more obvious in regular experimental designs in which one or a couple of hypotheses are tested, but it is just as true in any explorative think-aloud study. Thus, while think-aloud data on the surface may seem to be rather uncomplicated and permit access to a better understanding of psychological processes, reliability and validity requirements necessitate perhaps even more caution than in analyses of other types of data.

REFERENCES

Bainbridge, L. (1985). Inferring from verbal reports to cognitive processes. In M. Brenner, J. Brown, and D. Carter (Eds), *The Research Interview, Uses and Approaches,* Academic Press, London.
Ericsson, K. A., and Oliver, W. L. (1986). Methodology for laboratory research on thinking: task selection, collection of observations and data analysis. In R. Sternberg and E. Smith (Eds), *The Psychology of Human Thought,* Cambridge University Press, Cambridge.
Ericsson, K. A., and Simon, H. A. (1980). Verbal reports as data, *Psychological Review,* **87,** 215–51.
Ericsson, K. A., and Simon, H. A. (1984). *Protocol Analysis: Verbal Reports as Data.* MIT Press, London.
Montgomery, H. (1983). Decision rules and the search for a dominance structure: towards a process model of decision making. In P. C. Humphreys, O. Svenson, and A. Vari (Eds), *Analyzing and Aiding Decision Processes,* North-Holland and Hungarian Academic Press, Amsterdam/Budapest.
Montgomery, H., and Svenson, O. (1983). A think aloud study of dominance structuring in decision processes. In R. Tietz (Ed.), *Aspiration Levels in Bargaining and Economic Decision Making,* Springer, Berlin.
Newell, A., and Simon, H. A. (1972). *Human Problem Solving,* Prentice Hall, Englewood Cliffs, N.J.
Nisbett, R. E., and Wilson, T. D. (1977). Telling more than we can know: verbal reports on mental processes, *Psychological Review,* **84,** 231–59.
Payne, J. W., Braunstein, M. C., and Carroll, J. S. (1978). Exploring predecisional behaviour: an alternative approach to decision research, *Organizational Behavior and Human Performance,* **22,** 17–44.
Russo, J. E., Johnson, E. J., and Stephens, D. L. (1986). *The Validity of Verbal Reports,* Unpublished manuscript.

Shiffrin, R. M., and Schneider, W. (1977). Controlled and automatic human information processing: II. Perceptual learning, automatic attending, and a general theory, *Psychological Review*, **84**, 127–90.

Svenson, O. (1974). *A Note on Think Aloud Protocols Obtained During the Choice of a Home*, Report 421, Psychological Laboratories, University of Stockholm.

Svenson, O. (1979). Process descriptions of decision making, *Organizational Behavior and Human Performance*, **23**, 86–112.

Svenson, O. (1985). Cognitive strategies in a complex judgment task: analysis of verbal reports and judgments of cumulated risk over different exposure time, *Organizational Behavior and Human Decision Processes*, **36**, 1–15.

Watson, J. B. (1920). Is thinking merely the action of language mechanisms?, *British Journal of Psychology*, **11**, 87–104.

Woodworth, R. S., and Schlosberg, H. (1954). *Experimental Psychology*, Holt, New York.

ACKNOWLEDGEMENTS

This study was supported in part by the Bank of Sweden Tercentenary Foundation and in part by the US National Science Foundation under IST 8312482 to Perceptronics Inc. Any opinions, findings, and conclusions or recommendations expressed in this chapter are those of the author and do not necessarily reflect the views of the Bank of Sweden Tercentenary Foundation or the US National Science Foundation.

This chapter was written while the author was a Fulbright exchange visitor to Decision Research and Eugene Research Institute in Eugene, Oregon. I would like to thank all the people at the above institutions for making it possible to carry out this project. Lyn Blackshaw, Anders E. Ericsson, Kerstin Meyerhöffer, Henry Montgomery, Leisha Sanders, and Yvonne Waern made valuable comments on or assisted in typing earlier versions of this chapter.

5

Illustrating verbal protocol analysis: Individual decisions and dialogues preceding a joint decision

OLA SVENSON

The purpose of the present chapter is to present examples of verbal protocols for a discussion of some of the problems that are pertinent when coding such protocols. Basically, there are two ways of interpreting verbal protocols. First, a wholistic method may be used in which the meaning of the whole protocol is extracted by considering simultaneously all the parts of it in the interpretion. In various clinical situations this is often the case as well as in phenomenological analyses (Bullington and Karlsson, 1984). Such analyses may rely on certain central themes which the researcher tries to recognize in the protocol and which can increase an understanding of the protocol.

Second, the protocols may be analysed through a decomposition into parts which, when aggregated in different ways, can elucidate the cognitive processes that took place while the protocols were generated. In an early report by the present author (Svenson, 1974) both of these methods were attempted but in the present chapter only the second 'split and conquer' philosophy will be used.

The decision alternatives in the present study are represented as in previous process-tracing studies (Montgomery and Svenson, 1976; Svenson, 1979, Chapter 4 in this volume) and denoted $A_i(a_{i1}, a_{i2}, \ldots, a_{in})$ where a_{ij} stands for the attractiveness of an aspect on the attribute j for alternative i. The analysis focuses on the attractiveness of various aspects which may be illustrated by the attribute of size of a house. There is a *physical* size of a house (in square metres) and there is a *perceived* size of a house (the same size looks bigger if the walls are white than if they are dark) but here the focus is on the *attractiveness* of the perceived size of the house. To repeat, an alternative (e.g. a house) is

Process and Structure in Human Decision Making
Edited by H. Montgomery and O. Svenson. © 1989 John Wiley & Sons Ltd

characterized on a number of attributes (e.g. size, price, environment) and the specific attractiveness values on these attributes that characterize an alternative are called aspects.

In an earlier chapter (Chapter 4), details in the process of collecting the protocols were discussed. In this paper the transcription and analysis of verbal protocols will be treated in more detail with reference to concrete examples.

A subject participating in a think-aloud experiment verbalizes his/her thoughts and speaks them out loud to a tape recorder. The tape recordings are transcribed into a written document by a typist/coder. As will be shown below, some coding will be made already at this stage and some of the meaning of the protocol lost (e.g. meaning communicated through intonation). Because of this risk, in one early study the present author used data coded directly from the tapes by two independent coders (Svenson, 1974). However, this is a very time-consuming procedure and in most cases not worth the required time and costs. The typewritten protocol is coded in systematic analyses. This process will be exemplified below, starting with individual protocols. Following this, dialogues preceding a joint decision by two partners in a relationship will be presented.

INDIVIDUAL DECISION PROCESSES

Typing the tape recorded protocol

The following excerpt from a protocol was collected from a subject making a decision among five different one-family houses presented in authentic booklets for marketing the houses (Montgomery and Svenson, 1983):

> ... starting again and looking at Alby. It looks if you think of the area then I think it looks great. Lots of green around.
> Bollstanäs then. No ... now I'm looking at the cover (of the brochure). Well it was this one yes. It looks pretty dull if you look at ... when one looks at ... the map its location and such then it really does. Before I thought there were regular roads ....

The above transcription of the tape recorded protocol already involves some structuring of the information. This was done by asking the person typing to (a) use a period when she or he considered a sentence finished, (b) type a series of periods when there was silence for more than about 5 s (in this case), (c) start a new paragraph when the subject moved from one alternative to another one. These ways of initial structuring of the protocols are facilitated because the typist is able to listen to the original tape recording and this work is more difficult or impossible (in the case of (b)) to perform later on the basis of the written documents.

Dividing the typewritten protocol into statements

After having trained the two judges in dividing a protocol into statements they are asked to do this for all protocols. This can be done as in Table 1 with a slash after each statement. Here, the intonations in the tape recording have been used by the typist to locate periods in between different statements. In addition, pauses may also be used for dividing the protocols. Note that the protocol after statement 4 contains pauses and incomplete sentences. The division of the protocol in Table 1 poses little difficulty if these cues are used.

Coding the statements

The coding system used was comprised of ten attributes (attribute 1, plan of area (within housing area); attribute 2, plan of house, number of rooms, size, etc.) for the five alternatives. According to the notations introduced earlier a_{ij} denotes an aspect on attribute j for alternative i. More details of the coding system were presented earlier (Svenson, 1974, Chapter 4 in this volume) but here it is enough to know that attribute 1 signifies 'plan of area (within housing area)' and attribute 5 'part of town, suburb area, social status of area'. Info denotes information search or presentation without an evaluation. Capital letters denote whole alternatives as a whole and were used when no specific attribute was explicitly indicated in a statement.

The evaluative content of a statement was coded + if the attractiveness was positive and − if it was negative.

The codings suggested in Table 1 can be altered. For example, the explication of an evaluation (statement 3, 'Lots of green around') was not coded as such

Table 1 Example of a verbal protocol in which two alternatives (A_1 and A_2) are considered. Capital letters denote an alternative. The first index of the codes for a statement signify an alternative and the second an attribute. Positive and negative evaluations are denoted + and − respectively

---

Statement number, text, and coding

---

(1) Starting again and looking at Alby. A_1 (info)/
(2) It looks if you think of the area then I think it looks great. a_{11} +/
(3) Lots of green around. a_{11} +/
(4) Bollstanäs then. A_2(info)/
(5) No ... now I'm looking at the cover (of the brochure). A_2(info)/
(6) Well it was this one yes. A_2(info)./
(7) It looks pretty dull if you look at ... A_2 −/
(8) When one looks at ... the map its location and such a_{25} −/
(9) then it really does. a_{25} −/
(10) Before I thought there were regular roads. a_{21}(info)/

---

and only as another evaluative statement. A development of the coding scheme in Table 1 could devote a special category to such statements or include them in the evaluative coding immediately preceding them (statement 2, '... it looks great'). It is interesting to note how the coding of 'Lots of green around' depends on the context, viz. the immediately preceding statement. It is recommended in order to determine that the coders may not use more than, say, one or two immediately preceding statements of the context in their coding of a statement. This allows for some contextual coding without endangering the intercoder reliability and the logics of decomposition on which the present method of data is founded. The last sentence (10) indicates a negative evaluation if the whole protocol is taken into consideration. However, in the absence of any explicit evaluative statement the coding has to indicate information search or presentation.

Table 2 presents a segment of a protocol taken from the very end of another person's decision process. Here the division of statements is not as self-evident as in the former case. Statements 6 and 7 could be regarded as only one statement. However, when in doubt, the advice is to split into smaller units and therefore statements 6 and 7 were separated. The final stage in Table 2 shows comparisons between the final choice (A_3) and one of its competitors (A_4). Therefore, this is reflected in the codings of the relations which follow mathematical denotations. In fact, the protocol in Table 2 illustrates, very nicely, the end of a dominance-structuring process (see Montgomery, Chapter 2 this volume) in which the chosen alternative has become better than or about equal to its most serious competitor on all attributes worth considering.

Table 2 Example of a verbal protocol in which the two alternatives $(A_3$ and $A_4)$ are considered in the end of the decision process.

Statement number, text, and coding

.... (1) But what makes it possible to, that I can differentiate this home (A_3) from the house in Österåker (A_4), A_3, A_4 (info)/

(2) It is that A_3 has a clearly better disposition of the house, $a_{34} > a_{42}$/

(3) It is closer to the city. $a_{32} > a_{44}$/

(4) In other respects one can say that the areas are comparable with regard to municipal service and schools and centre. $a_{39} \approx a_{49}$/

(5) That's shops and such, that's about the same. $a_{39} \approx a_{49}$/

(6) I would choose A_3, $A_3 > A_4$/

(7) with a cost of 915 crowns per month and a pay down of 25 000. A_3(info)/

(8) That's the capital saved, that we have. (info)/

(9) (Now 45 minutes have passed/

(10) and the tape recorder hasn't stopped or has it?)

— End of protocol —

Integrating the information coded in a protocol

The coding system chosen for the analysis as well as the way of integrating the codings depend on the researcher's general purpose and his specific hypotheses.

If there are many different coding categories in the coding system then the intercoder reliability tends to go down and more data are needed to make differences in frequencies statistically significant. On the other hand, the capacity for detecting interesting cognitive processes may increase if a more elaborate coding scheme is used.

Verbal protocols can be used as support for hypotheses of what decision rules could have been used in the process (cf. Svenson, 1979). For example, it has often been reported that a decision involves an initial screening phase in which one attribute is examined across alternatives followed by a phase in which trade-offs are made between attributes through the application of more complex rules (Svenson, 1974, 1979). Such information can be secured in detailed analyses of individual protocols. A more elaborate coding scheme may be of great value in such analyses.

It is also possible to compute frequencies of simpler codings, as will be illustrated in the following example. Montgomery and Svenson (Chapter 7 in this volume) used verbal protocols from twelve subjects from whom the examples in Tables 1 and 2 were taken. Their purpose was to test a hypothesis that a decision process starts with the selection of a promising alternative which is then tested in a process involving attempts to restructure the decision situation so that this alternative dominates the others in the end. When one alternative dominates another this means that it is at least equally good as the latter on all attributes but better on at least one attribute. In such situations it is very easy to make a choice, but initially decision problems are not often structured in this way.

To test this hypothesis only a very simple coding system was needed. In fact, Table 1 illustrates most of the kinds of information that were needed. Through simple computations of frequencies and statistics on these counts it was possible to show that (a) the finally chosen alternative was given more attention (more statements) than its competitors and (b) that the choice was accompanied by a successively more positive evaluation (+ and − codings) of the chosen alternative and a correspondingly more negative evaluation of the non-chosen alternatives.

Furthermore, it was shown (c) that in the process of making a decision, positive aspects of the *chosen alternative* were mentioned about equally often in the first and second halves of a protocol. However, the *negative aspects of the chosen alternative were mentioned less often during the second half* of a protocol.

For the *non-chosen alternative* that was the most serious competitor to the chosen alternative the following was found. (d) The *positive aspects of the non-chosen alternative were mentioned much less frequently in the second half* of a protocol, but the negative aspects of the non-chosen alternative were mentioned as frequently in the first as in the second half of a protocol.

In conclusion, counts of frequencies of a very simple coding system indicated (with statistical significance) that in the process of making a decision the subjects played down the negative aspects of the chosen alternative and the positive aspects of the non-chosen alternative. This is a result predicted by the hypothesis of decision making as a process of dominance structuring (Montgomery, 1983; Montgomery and Svenson, Chapter 7 in this volume).

CODING DIALOGUES FROM COUPLES MAKING JOINT DECISIONS

Procedure

The purpose of this experiment was to explore the possibility of a meaningful decision theoretic analysis of tape recorded dialogues between two partners deciding on a common alternative. Each of six couples were asked to make a choice of a home among five different alternatives presented in the same booklets as in the previous examples given in this chapter. The total price and monthly costs for the homes were approximately the same across alternatives.

Before the subjects made their joint decisions they were asked to make individual choices of the home they found most attractive. They were also asked to think aloud; actually they were the subjects who generated the protocols from which the earlier examples were chosen. In the first experiment, however, they did not know that a second one would follow. But, there was another experiment following in which they were asked to make the choice of an alternative that both partners could agree on. Thus, after the individual decisions had been made the two partners in a couple were gathered in the same room with a tape recorder and asked to make a decision that both agreed on.

Only one of the six couples had made the same choice in the first stage so the process of agreeing on a common alternative included elements of conflict.

Coding the protocols

The typewritten dialogues were analysed in a code system where each unit was a statement defined as an uninterrupted string of words from either member of a couple. Thus, the length of a statement could range from one word to a few sentences. Each sentence was classified into one and only one of a number of categories by two independent coders. The coding categories were rank ordered hierarchically. When such an order is used it is possible to handle uncertainty when classifying a statement which may belong to two different categories. For example, a statement may contain two sentences each of which should be coded into different categories. If only one category can be used, the coding system must allow for one category dominating the other to determine one single code

Table 3 Categories of a system for evaluative coding of statements in dialogues between the partners of a couple. The system is hierarchical, implying that in case of uncertainty about which category a statement should be coded it is coded in the category higher in the hierarch (denoted by a smaller number)

Level in hierarchy	Denotation	Description of category
1	Crit	Discussion of, agreement on or presentation of criteria
2	Comp	Comparative mention of alternatives chosen by the members in a couple
	Comp(o)	Comparative mention of alternatives chosen by one of the partners and alternative not chosen by either of the partners (other)
3	A_m^+	Positive mention of alternative chosen by male
	A_m^-	Negative mention of alternative chosen by male
	A_f^+	Positive mention of alternative chosen by female
	A_f^-	Negative mention of alternative chosen by female
4	A_i^-	Negative mention of alternative not chosen by either of the partners
	A_i^+	Positive mention of alternative not chosen by either of the partners
5	Inf	Information about any fact
6	O	Other statements (e.g. questions, hmm, etc.)

for such a statement. The coding system in Table 3 was designed for this purpose. Priority is given for codes higher in the hierarchy in case of uncertainty about the coding category.

It is important to point out that a hierarchically organized coding scheme may also be quite helpful when coding verbal protocols from single subjects. Because of the rules of such a scheme a high reliability can be achieved even when the categories are subtle and difficult to use. Of course, a hierarchical coding scheme always means that pieces of information are lost, but this is done in a controlled way.

The coding system described in Table 3 was used for coding evaluative aspects of the dialogues describing the processes by which the different couples reached an agreement. Discussions of the criteria or values applicable in general for choosing a house (e.g. a discussion of the acceptable price in general) were classified into the category highest in the hierarchy, *Crit*. An explicit mention of the level of such a *criterion* was also coded into this category. When the focus of the statement was on the specific aspect characterizing an alternative (e.g. 'the price of this house ...') the statement was coded into *Comp* (comparison) or as an evaluative mention of an alternative (e.g. A_m^+).

Comparisons between alternatives could be performed either implicitly or explicitly with direct reference to an earlier statement. In both cases the code

of *Comp* was used. When the comparison was between the two alternatives
chosen by each of the partners in a couple respectively the code was *Comp*;
when another alternative was used in the comparison the code was *Comp* (*o*),
as shown in the table. *Comp* $(a_{ij} > a_{kj})$ can be used to identify alternatives and
attribute.

Any positive or negative mention of an alternative was coded in a category
belonging to level 3 in the hierarchy (A_m^+, A_m^-, etc). The index indicates that the
man (m), the woman (f), or neither one (i) had chosen the alternative. The plus
and minus signs represent positive and negative mention of an aspect belonging
to an alternative.

If non-evaluative information about an alternative was given, the statement
was coded into the category *Inf*. Other statements, questions, hmm, and
statements that could not be coded in any other category were coded O (other).

As mentioned earlier, most couples made different choices in the initial sessions
which is reflected in the protocols. Table 4 gives an example of the first part of
a protocol.

Table 4 clearly illustrates some difficulties in the coding of a verbal protocol.
First, statement 1 is a question about the partner's choice and this is not given
any specific code and is therefore lost in the coding system. Second, statement

Table 4 First part of protocol from a couple instructed to agree on the choice of a
common house

No.	Partner	Statement	Code
1	F	Why did you choose Smedby?	O
2	M	It would be nice to get cut of town sometimes, among other things.	Crit
3	F	What do you mean?	O
4	M	In a car, or 600 busses from Jarlaplan.	Inf
5	F	And then ... from Jarlaplan, well you go .... This assumes that one has a car.	$F:A_m^-$
6	M	But we already have a car.	Inf
7	F	Yes, but it's necessary to have a car to live out there, to be able to go to town.	$F:A_m^-$
8	M	Yes, but then we can afford it. A quarter of a million.	$M:A_m^+$
9	F	You have not thought about that we might need two cars if the kids go to school?	$F:A_m^-$
10	M	I am sure we can afford that too.	Inf
11	F	I don't think so.	Inf

Table 5 Last part of protocol from a couple instructed to agree on the choice of a common house

No.	Partner	Statement	Code
127	F	Mmm ... but look what a lot of green there is around Smedby.	$F:A_f^+$
128	M	Yes but there is also around the houses here. There is a couple, three hundred metres to the Alby lake.	$M:A_m^+$
129	F	Yes but not big ones like this.	Comp
130	M	Here is a future road.	$M:A_m^+$
131	F	Yes but it is far away. Lots of woods in between. I do not want to move to Alby.	$F:A_m^-$
132	M	I can live in Smedby. Are we then agreeing on that?	Decision
133	F	Yes	O
134	M	So we'll buy a house in Smedby.	
135	F	Mmm ... then we have ... we gain ten thousand in pay down.	$F:A_f^+$
136	M	Mmm ... on the other hand we loose 10 square metres.	$M:A_f^-$
137	F	Yes that's clear and win some windows.	$F:A_f^+$
138	M	OK then?	O
139	F	Yes	O

5 illustrates a statement that could be coded O or $F:A_m^-$. Only inference of the woman's attitude towards having to drive a car (clear from the context) makes it possible to code this statement in the higher category. This also applies for statements 7 and 9. A wholistic analysis of this part of the protocol shows an offensive woman and a defensive man. Third, the example illustrates that the units are so short that they very clearly contain only one main message, each of which makes the coding easier. This characteristic was typical of the protocols in this experiment.

Table 5 gives an example of the last part of another couple's protocol where the coding is rather straightforward.

Results

Of the six couples investigated the partners of only one had made the same initial choice. In all other protocols there were conflicts. One of these conflicts was so strong that no decision was reached and the tape recorder was turned off so that it did not register the later arguments between the partners. In the following only the five protocols from the couples with different initial choices will be analysed.

The protocols analysed here ranged in length from 139 to 394 statements and were coded by two independent coders. More than 90 per cent of all statements for each of the couples were coded in the same category by both coders. After the first independent codings the coders discussed their disagreements and decided which classification to use in the final joint coding.

The alternative preferred by the female was chosen by three of the five couples. As mentioned above, one couple could not agree on a common alternative and started quarelling and turned off the tape recorder after a long discussion. In the last couple the partners chose the alternative favoured by the male.

In general, the couples discussed only the two alternatives chosen by either one of the partners. Although other alternatives were sometimes mentioned during the two first thirds of the statements in a protocol the last third of a protocol never contained any comment or mention of any other alternative.

Frequencies of statements of different categories during different parts of the decision processes will be analysed first. Second, the ways of responding to some interesting types of statements will be highlighted. Third, conflicts (as manifested in three or more consecutive statements) will be discussed.

The frequencies of Inf and O were much greater across all protocols than the frequencies of any other single type of statement. As these categories were not as informative as the others for understanding the discussions, the categories of Inf and O will not be focused on in the following. It is clear that they would have to be split into subcategories to be of real interest in the analyses of the dialogues.

Arguments during different stages of the decision process

Each protocol was divided into six equal parts and the percentages of statements of different types calculated for each couple and part of protocol. The mean percentages over the five couples were then computed. The four categories of level 3 (Table 3) of the coding system were plotted in Figure 1.

The categories plotted in Figure 1 all describe statements in favour of one partner's alternative or statements with negative mention of the other partner's alternative. Statements in these categories were frequent during the discussions, as shown by the high percentages indicated in the figure. The first letter in the key for a curve denotes the source of a statement—male (M) or female (F). The plots in Figure 1 show means over the proportions of different statements in five protocols; i.e. each subject was given the same weight when the mean proportions were computed.

Interpreting Figure 1 shows that the woman starts with a great proportion of negative statements about the man's alternative (18 per cent), but very few

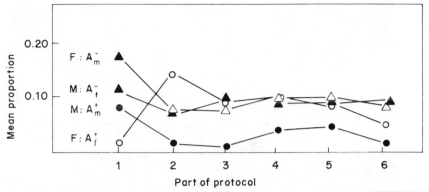

Fig. 1   Mean proportion for five couples of the male's (M) and female's (F) positive or negative mention of male (A_m) and female (A_f) alternatives.

positive statements about her own alternative. However, during the second part of the protocol she has reversed the relation so that she now speaks more favourably about her own alternative than negatively about her partner's. Note that the data are regarded as purely descriptive and that no far-reaching conclusions can be drawn due to the small number of couples investigated.

As the woman's alternative was the one the couples agreed on in three of four cases this tendency could also be present when the corresponding plot is drawn for winner (W) and loser (L) respectively. Figure 2 shows the same and stronger tendency that the winner starts talking negatively about the loser's alternative and only later starts to talk positively about his/her preferred alternative. Again, the sample is too small for any conclusions regarding general tendencies but the figure shows what type of information can be obtained from think-aloud protocols.

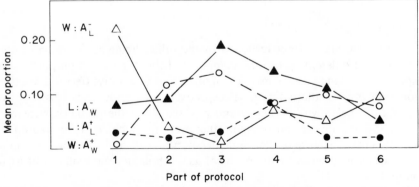

Fig. 2   Mean proportion for four couples of the winner's (W) and loser's (L) positive or negative mention of winner's (A_W) or loser's (A_L) alternatives.

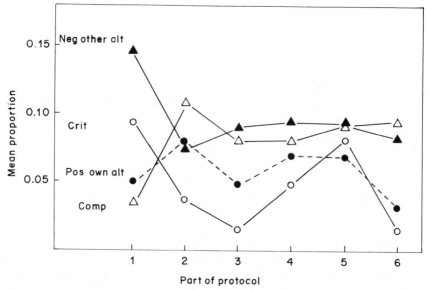

Fig. 3 Mean proportions of categories over parts of protocol.

Figure 3 shows proportions of criterion statements that are negative about the partner's alternative and positive about one's own, and comparative statements. As before, most of the significant action seems to take place during the first sixth of a protocol. A more detailed analysis (not related here) shows that the first 30 statements are crucial. It is between the first and second sixth that the initial high proportion of negative evaluations of the other partner's alternative drops. This result may be used as a hypothesis to be tested in further research.

Interaction between the partners

To study how one partner responds to the other, frequencies of consecutive statements of different types were computed. Table 6 gives the proportions of responses following positive mention of one's own alternative (A_1) and negative about the other's alternative (A_2) respectively. (The frequencies of negative mention of one's own alternative and positive about the partner's were very small and insignificant and therefore they were not included here.) Note that the table gives a picture of the whole decision process and therefore the initial phase which is atypical of the protocol as a whole does not stand out as in Figure 3.

The winner–loser distinction does not expose any clear differences not present in the male–female grouping, which will therefore be used as this analysis can

Table 6 Proportions of responses in trial $(n+1)$ to positive statements about one's preferred alternative in trial n and to negative statements about the other's preferred alternative. The proportions were based on all statements from five (female–male) couples

Response in trial $n+1$ by	Statement in trial n					
	Positive about own alternative (A_1)			Negative about other's alternative (A_2)		
	Male Female	Female Male	Total	Male Female	Female Male	Total
Inf	0.22	0.41	0.35	0.22	0.34	0.29
Other	0.15	0.27	0.24	0.25	0.16	0.20
A_1^-	0.48	0.08	0.19	0.02	0.06	0.06
A_2^+	0.08	—	0.02	0.15	0.18	0.17
A_1^+	0.04	0.11	0.09	—	0.02	0.01
A_2^-	—	—	0.00	0.10	0.02	0.05
Crit	—	0.03	0.02	0.10	0.10	0.10
Comp	0.04	0.08	0.08	0.10	0.11	0.11
Total no. of statements	27	66	93	40	62	104

be based on more data (five couples instead of four because of the couple never agreeing on any alternative).

Most of the reponses to a positive statement about one's own alternative or a negative about the partner's choice concern discussion of or seeking information or statements concerning other things than clear evaluations of the alternatives preferred by either partner. In only about 10 per cent of the cases the statements analysed here were followed by comparisons of the preferred alternatives. As shown in Figure 3, this proportion is lower in the initial phase of the discussion. More discussion of the criteria for evaluation seems to follow the negative mention of the partner's alternative (0.10) than a positive about one's own alternative.

The most striking difference between men and women concerns the response to a positive statement about one's own alternative. Here, the female responds by talking negatively about the man's alternative in 48 per cent of the cases, while the male only responds negatively to 8 per cent of these statements. The differences between the percentages for the two classifications depend to a large extent on the couple where the man's alternative was chosen and the couple not reaching an agreement. However, the difference remains also after exclusion of the data from the couple not reaching an agreement (48 per cent decreases to 38 per cent while the 8 per cent for the male remains the same).

In all, Table 6 shows that categories Inf and O (cf. Table 3) were the most frequent in the protocols. Therefore, it is natural that the most common sequence of two consecutive statements involved one of these categories. By far the most common sequence Inf (trial n) / Inf (trial $n + 1$) occurred in as many as 23 per cent of the cases (close to the chance expectation of 20 per cent). The second most common sequence was O (n) / Inf $(n + 1)$, which often denoted a question and a response. Another frequent combination was an evaluative expression followed by information A_m^+, A_m^-, A_f^+, or A_f^- (n) / Inf $(n + 1)$ which occurred in 9 per cent of the cases. However, almost all other contingencies were smaller than that number. A more detailed analysis showed that negative statements about the other's alternative were given more frequently in comparisons than in absolute terms later in the protocols. This illustrates the potential of coded think-aloud data to elucidate psychological processes.

Conflicts and conflict resolution

The verbal data may also be used to describe explicit conflicts between the partners. In order to do so, sequences of statements indicating conflict in a chain of three or more statements were identified for more detailed analysis. Two consecutive statements were classified to indicate a conflict in such a chain if they concerned the same alternative but were coded with opposite evaluations, i.e. (M : A_m^+, F : A_m^- — the man mentioning his own alternative positively followed by the woman saying something negative about that alternative), (M : A_f^-, F : A_f^+), (F : A_f^+, M : A_f^-), or (F : A_m^-, M : A_m^+). Comparisons indicating how good one's own alternative was (in relation to some other alternative) or how bad the other's was (coded Comp) were also accepted as a link in a conflict chain of statements.

Not surprisingly, the couple that could not reach an agreement had more conflicts (eight) than the other couples (three to five conflicts each). Of the eight conflicts encountered by that couple two were solved by the partners agreeing and three by changing the topic or asking about facts. The remaining three conflicts seemed not to be solved at all or were solved in very unclear ways.

The four couples agreeing on common choices had fifteen conflicts in total. Eight of these conflicts were solved by one of the partners agreeing with the other (by, for example, changing the criterion for acceptance). Of the remaining seven conflicts three were solved by changing topics and four conflicts were solved in unclear ways.

This experiment has shown again that verbal protocols contain important information about cognitive processes. The stagewise character of the human decision-making process was illustrated in the processes reflected in the protocols. It is interesting to note that much of the changes in the pattern of communication between the partners of a couple seems to take place very early during the discussions. This parallels the findings by Montgomery and Svenson

(Chapter 7 in this volume) for individual protocols, also indicating that the final choice may be predicted from early parts of the protocols. Therefore it is tempting to offer the hypothesis that, to the members of a couple, the choice often may be clear very quickly on some psychological level and that the rest of the dialogues reflect psychological processes in which the subjects try to legitimate the choice already made. Many negative arguments about the other's alternative in the very beginning of the dialogue seems to be the strategy of the winning partner in the couples investigated here. It would be interesting to explore the generality of this finding in future research.

CONCLUDING COMMENTS

The present chapter has exemplified how verbal protocols from think-aloud experiments and dialogues can be coded and analysed. A decision theoretic framework was used when defining the coding categories in both cases. Although the coding systems stressed simplicity it was illustrated that even very simple coding systems can produce interesting facts about complex psychological processes. Even though the results were presented for illustrative purposes the analyses also illustrate how think-aloud data can generate research hypotheses which can be tested in subsequent studies.

REFERENCES

Bullington, J., and Karlsson, G. (1984). Introduction to phenomenological research, *Scandinavian Journal of Psychology*, **25**, 51–63.

Montgomery, H. (1983). Decision rules and the search for a dominance structure: towards a process model of decision making. In P. C. Humphreys, O. Svenson, and A. Vari (Eds), *Analyzing and Aiding Decision Processes*, North-Holland and Hungarian Academic Press, Amsterdam/Budapest.

Montgomery, H., and Svenson, O. (1976). On decision rules and information processing strategies for choice among multiattribute alternatives, *Scandinavian Journal of Psychology*, **17**, 283–291.

Svenson, O. (1974). *A Note on Think Aloud Protocols Obtained During the Choice of a Home*, Report 421, Psychological Laboratories, University of Stockholm.

Svenson, O. (1979). Process descriptions of decision making, *Organizational Behavior and Human Performance*, **23**, 86–112.

ACKNOWLEDGEMENTS

This research was supported by grants from the Swedish Council for Research in the Humanities and Social Sciences and the Bank of Sweden Tercentenary

Foundation. Many people took part in the work reported here and among them I would like to thank Kerstin Meyerhöffer who did most of the very important and competent typing of the protocols, Gunnar Karlsson, Göran Hagert, and Liselotte Müller who coded the protocols from which parts were sampled in this chapter. Henry Montgomery's many comments have also been very valuable for the work reported here.

6

Three methods for analysing decision making using written documents

Irmtraud N. Gallhofer

and

Willem E. Saris

Since the last decade, the study of decision making in psychology and political science has focused increasingly on the constraints and determinants of the individual decision process (Allison, 1971; George, 1980; Jervis, 1976; Kozielecki, 1981; Simon, 1979; Von Winterfeldt and Edwards, 1986; Wright, 1984), although it is apparent, particularly in politics, that besides the individual context, the small group and organizational context play a part.

It is generally recognized nowadays that human decision makers, when confronted with uncertainty and value complexity — which is mostly the case in non-routine political decision making — deviate from the rational or analytic choice paradigm. In order to cope with the complex environment decision makers constrain or simplify the situation in one way or another.

By conceiving decision making as a cognitive process, the theoretical framework of cognitive psychology is established. In this chapter we shall introduce three empirical methods for analysing decision making frequently used in the study of political decisions, although they can also be applied to all kinds of human decision making in non-routine situations. Each of these methods describes specific aspects of the decision-making process. The methods are the following:

(a) *The cognitive mapping (CM) method,* originally developed by Shapiro and Bonham (1973) and by Axelrod and his associates (1976),

Process and Structure in Human Decision Making
Edited by H. Montgomery and O. Svenson. © 1989 John Wiley & Sons Ltd

(b) *The empirical decision analysis (EDA) method,* developed by Gallhofer and Saris (1978, 1979, 1986b) and
(c) *The multiple paths to choice (MPC) method,* originally developed by Gross-Stein and Tanter (1980) and further elaborated by Maoz (1981).

Besides their theoretical background, these methods have in common that they have been applied empirically, resulting in significant research findings.

How far these methods overlap or not will be one of the topics of this chapter. It could be possible that each deals with a different part of the decision-making process. Therefore, we shall elaborate schematically the different stages characterizing cognitive decision making and indicate the position of each of the methods in this scheme. Furthermore, the differences in data generation and sources will be discussed and some quality criteria for text analysis data will be introduced. Thereafter, each method will be presented separately and applied to one and the same text in order to get a clearer insight into the differences and similarities of the methods.

DIFFERENT STAGES OF THE COGNITIVE DECISION-MAKING PROCESS

In the literature (e.g. Vlek and Wagenaar, 1979; Jabes, 1982; Kozielecki, 1981) the decision-making process is hypothetically divided into several phases or stages. Table 1 summarizes the relationship between the various phases of the decision-making process and the three empirical methods introduced in this chapter.

First there is a *diagnostic phase* where a concrete problem is recognized. The decision maker wants either to preserve the status quo or to change it. At this stage he/she will try to interpret the specific situation. The cognitive mapping

Table 1 Relationship between the various phases of the decision-making process and the three empirical methods of analysis

Methods	Phases					
	Diagnosis	Structuring	Evaluation	Revision	Choice	Action
Cognitive mapping (CM)	Yes	No	No	No	No	No
Empirical decision analysis (EDA)	No	Yes	Yes	No	Yes	No
Multiple paths to choice (MPC)	No	Yes	Yes	Yes	Yes	Yes

method mainly investigates the beliefs and values that influence this interpretation of the situation.

After diagnosing the situation, a decision maker searches for possible alternative courses of action, identifies the consequences of such courses of action, and establishes whether or not uncertainty is involved in the occurrence of possible consequences. This step is called *structuring*. Then he evaluates the consequences and the probabilities; this is called the *evaluation* stage. Finally, there remain two possibilities: either he searches for new information on the probabilities of specific consequences or for new consequences in order to revise the decision problem (*revision* step), or he makes his *choice* immediately. Both empirical decision analysis and multiple paths to choice investigate the structuring, evaluation, and choice stages and determine the decision rule used. The EDA method, however, does not investigate the revision phase; this is because it takes a single document produced by a decision maker as the unit of analysis.

Table 1 shows *action* as the final step, i.e. the implementation of the decision. It is clear that in order to arrive at action, individual decision makers will engage in some collective process. The MPC method also investigates this step. However, we shall not deal with this last phase in this chapter.

CODING UNITS AND CONCEPTS

All three methods use written documents for analysis. First, concepts have to be extracted from the documents.

In the CM method the concepts consist of a decision maker's beliefs about a specific topic. The EDA and the MPC method make use of concepts derived from decision theory as it has been developed by statisticians and experimental psychologists (e.g. Von Neumann and Morgenstern, 1947; Edwards, 1961; Fishburn, 1964; Kenney and Raiffa, 1976). In addition, the MPC method also makes use of a set of concepts relating to process models.

Table 2 gives an overview of the coding units and concepts necessary for the different methods. The term *recording unit* in Table 2 refers to the specific part of text which is characterized by being assigned to a concept (Holsti, 1969). Table 2 shows that all the methods use 'themes', i.e. assertions about some subject, *not only keywords in context*. With respect to the *context unit*, i.e. the largest body of text that may be searched to characterize a recording unit (Holsti, 1969), the methods differ slightly. For the decision theoretic concepts, smaller units, such as complete sentences, are searched, while beliefs and concepts referring to process models are spread over larger units, such as paragraphs.

Since the three methods infer that the concepts relate directly to the internal structure of a decision maker, there is a second coding step which consists of mapping the cognitive structure of decision makers, based on the concepts

Table 2 Coding units and concepts for the three approaches

Approaches	Concepts	Recording unit	Context unit	Graphical representation of the cognitive structure
CM	Specific beliefs	Theme	Paragraph	Cognitive map
EDA	Decision theoretic concepts	Theme/ single word	Complete sentence	Decision tree
MPC	Decision theoretic concepts	Theme	Complete sentence	Decision tree

already extracted from the relevant documents. This is done graphically in the form of decision trees (EDA,MPC) and in path diagrams ('cognitive maps') in the CM method.

Illustrations of the codings will be given in the sections that relate to each method separately.

DATA SOURCES

Table 3 indicates the data sources for the three methods. The primary sources for the CM method are open-ended interviews. The EDA method relies on

Table 3 Data sources for the three methods

Data sources	CM	EDA	MPC
Primary documents referring to historical decisions, e.g. minutes of governmental meetings, reports from advisers	Yes	Yes[a]	Yes
Public documents referring to contemporary decisions, e.g. parliamentary debates, official statements	No	Yes	Yes[a]
Open-ended interviews with decision makers and/or advisers	Yes[a]	No	Yes[a]

[a] Indicates the preferred material.

governmental meetings, reports from advisors, and coded telegrams, i.e. all material that is classified for a certain period. In contrast with the EDA method, the MPC method, since it concentrates on contemporary decisions, makes use of interviews and public documents, such as parliamentary debates and official documents. In summary, one can say that the diversity of the source material is a function of the decision-making aspects under investigation. One can see that there is a considerable overlap of data used by the different methods. This raises the interesting question as to what results the different methods obtain from the same text. Are they deriving the same conclusions? If not, is this due to the concepts used or to the parts of the text chosen for analysis?

SOME QUALITY CRITERIA FOR TEXT ANALYSIS METHODS

From the above it is clear that this chapter deals with three methods for text analysis intending to derive a decision maker's opinion of the decision process based on documents produced by him/her. Since it is clear that the derived opinion is not necessarily identical to the true opinion of the author, it seems appropriate to discuss briefly various factors that might influence our text analytic derivations. Figure 1 indicates the relationship between the true opinion of the author of a document and his/her derived opinion.

Fig. 1   Relationship between the true opinion of the author of a document and his derived opinion.

Figure 1 shows that text analysts are mostly engaged in deriving characteristics from documents, which are not directly observed. We assume that the stronger the relationship between the true opinion of the author and the document he/she produced, the more manifest his/her true opinion will be in the text. This means that he/she will express his/her opinion in an unambiguous way, using synonymous expressions when repeating it.

Another important issue relates to the factors which might influence the production of the text. Since decision makers address their documents to different audiences, the text might be influenced by their perception of the opinion(s) of the audience(s). This is due to the fact that our authors are mostly dealing with controversial issues. In order to convince the audience or to justify a point of view they will try to influence the opinion(s) of the audience(s).

Besides the perception of the opinion of the audiences, the text produced by the author might also be influenced by the linguistic variation of the formulation. This constitutes a big difference from survey research where a set of stimuli (questions with categories) are presented to the subject who chooses from a fixed set of answers. When producing a text the author is free to express him/herself as he/she wishes. The usage of style may vary because of the great variety of linguistic structures available in natural language and/or on purpose because of the usage of different argumentation techniques. To be less abstract, some variations in linguistic formulation which may occur in the same text, produced by the same author and relating to the same topic will be given as an example:

'The authorities have reached an agreement with the squatters' or
'the authorities have spared the city of a new spate of riots' or
'the authorities have bowed before the law of the jungle'.

This example shows three possible variations of evaluating the act of the authorities. The first version is neutral while the other two sentences contain metaphors representing differing views.

Figure 2 summarizes the major factors which in our opinion influence the production of a text.

Another factor which influences the interpretation of the opinion expressed in a text is the coding method. In order to analyse the text the researcher has to establish *coding rules*. By coding rules we mean a set of specifications given to the human coder in order to perform his/her task. First concepts, which have to be extracted from the document, must be defined. Then proper coding units have to be specified: the smallest segment of text that is classified as a concept (*recording unit*) and the largest body of text which is searched for recording units (*context unit*).

The choice of these units is a crucial decision the researcher makes, since they must be meaningful with respect to the concepts. If the concepts have to be

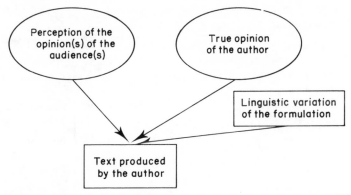

Fig. 2   Factors that influence the production of a text. Characteristics indicated with circular forms refer to unobserved characteristics.

represented in cognitive structures, then rules have to be established for the construction of these structures.

Based on these coding rules, coders individually produce interpretations of the opinion expressed by the author in the document. The interpretations of several coders seldom agree perfectly. This is due to errors of interpretation: coders can interpret the coding rules differently and they might be careless. Thus the clearer the coding rules and the more careful the coders are (the last might be achieved by a selection after an intensive training), the more coders will agree. Remaining differences between coders can be clarified by discussion and a joint judgement of the opinion can be produced. From the above it is clear that a coding method must be replicable in order to be a reliable instrument.

The efforts which have been undertaken to assess the stability and reproducibility of data analysed by the three methods introduced in this chapter are reported for each method separately in Gallhofer, Saris and Melman (1986a, 1986b). However, reliability is only a prerequisite for the validity of the instrument (the degree to which we measure what we want to measure by our derived opinion, i.e. the true opinion of the author of the text).

Validation studies are very difficult since frequently there is no external information available in order to corroborate the results obtained by text analysis and one therefore must rely on partial or indirect corroboration. Figure 3 summarizes a possible validation design and shows a relation between the true opinion of the author and the true consequences of his/her opinion which could be conceived as, for example, acts or conclusions from opinions or arguments. For both, the opinion and the consequences, written material exists that can be subjected to text analysis.

The texts about consequences can consist, for example, of written reports relating to the acts or event data. Based on the derived opinion a prediction of

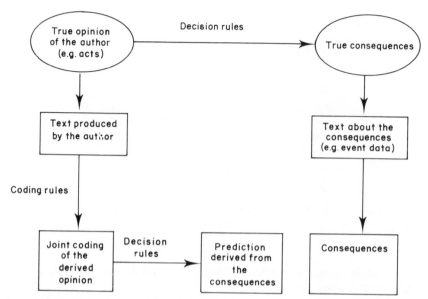

Fig. 3   Validation design of a text analysis instrument. Characteristics indicated with circular forms refer to unobserved characteristics.

the consequences, i.e. acts, can be made. If the derived consequences coincide with the prediction of the consequences then one can say that the instrument measures what it intends to measure.

Having dealt with those factors which we consider important to bear in mind when using text analysis instruments, we now introduce the three methods.

COGNITIVE MAPPING (CM) METHOD

As mentioned above, this method was developed by Shapiro and Bonham (1973) and Axelrod (1976). It relates to the diagnostic phase of decision making and investigates the beliefs and values playing a role in the explanation of events. The cognitive structure of an individual, i.e. his/her cognitive map, is conceived of as a causal diagram of beliefs. In order to construct a cognitive map, the following text analytic steps must be performed:

(a) Within each paragraph (context unit) of the document, themes of causal assertions (recording unit) of the following type are detected:

$$\text{Cause concept} \xrightarrow[\text{causal link}]{+/-} \text{effect concept}$$

Sentences like 'high defence expenses increase the chances of war' or 'security is in the best interests of our nation' would be represented as follows:

High defence expense $\xrightarrow{\quad +/- \quad}$ chances of war

The more security $\xrightarrow{\quad + \quad}$ the better for the interests
of our nation

The second example shows clearly that sentences have to be transformed in causal language if they do not literally express an increase or a decrease in something. A positive causal link is obtained if the cause and effect concepts have the same direction, i.e. if both increase or decrease. In the case where the one increases while the other decreases, the causal link is negative. A sentence like 'if we insist on a clear answer, Germany's confidence in us will be shaken' would be transformed as follows:

The more we insist $\xrightarrow{\quad - \quad}$ the less German confidence

(b) Cause and effect concepts are further classified into four different kinds of concepts:

Affective concepts (*A concepts*), which are immediate policy objectives of the decision maker. These concepts thus relate to one's own side.

Cognitive concepts (*C concepts*), which consist of beliefs about the behaviour or intentions of the opponents.

Policy concepts (*P concepts*), which are the available alternatives that the decision maker perceives.

Value concepts (*V concepts*), which consist of very abstract values like the national interest, security, etc.

(c) Based on the causal assertions which were detected, a cognitive map is then constructed where the V concepts are placed on the right-hand side of the map, the P concepts on the left-hand side, with C and A concepts somewhere in the centre.

We proceed with constructing a cognitive map based on a text (quoted below) which relates to minutes of the Dutch Council of Ministers in October 1914 and contains the speech of the Minister of Foreign Affairs. The Cabinet had to decide in this meeting whether or not they should stay neutral during World War I. The Germans had begun an offensive against Belgian Antwerp in order to gain access to the sea. As the Netherlands controlled the estuary of the Western Scheldt and the access to Antwerp, this military operation put the Dutch government in a precarious situation. Should they stay neutral or choose the British or the German side? This was the decision issue at stake in this debate.

The Minister of Foreign Affairs agrees with the Chairman and declines firmly to ask the question neither in the way the Ministers of Navy and War proposed nor in the amended version of the Minister of Agriculture.

Our own interests have not been threatened yet; we can only guess, but do not know, how the war will end. This is therefore not the right moment to take sides, although our interests are closer to the British, especially with respect to our colonies.

If we ask the question, it will look like a call to stop or a taking sides. It is inconceivable that Germany will answer categorically at this stage of the war that it will not keep Antwerp or that it will only occupy it temporarily. Although it is unlikely that Germany will wish to incorporate Belgium, it will either answer evasively, or politely give us to understand that Germany's intentions are no concern of ours.

Shall we lay this statement on the table or shall we insist on a clear answer?

The latter could cause trouble, perhaps even war, and certainly would shake German confidence in our neutrality, which is of paramount importance.

To change our official position of neutrality now would not be in our interests, especially since we declared it so loudly and since Germany explicitly said that it would respect our position.

The Minister of War's plan to grant the guarantors of Belgium's neutrality [France, Britain, eds.] access to our neutral territory in order to force back the German army is even less justifiable. Although it is unlikely that the British would even consider entering the Western Scheldt to relieve Antwerp, any British warship that tried would be sent to the bottom by the German artillery. Actually it is unclear what we would gain at the final peace settlement by pressing the Germans now. If we have to enter the war and Germany wins the war, we have to pay the piper. If the British are victorious then we cannot expect much reward, at most an equivalent piece of land from Germany in exchange for Dutch Flanders and the Scheldt, which will be given as compensation to Belgium.

If the war ends with no clear winner, then we are left with a partially destroyed country and a shaken confidence on the part of our Eastern neighbour on whom we depend so much economically.

The occupation of Antwerp is in no case worth any of these things.

That we would get into trouble with the British [i.e.that they take over the Dutch colony Indonesia, authors,] if we do not speak at all is not to be expected. (Translation from the Dutch original, in *Bescheiden betreffende de Buitenlandse Politiek van Nederland*, RGP IV, 1895–1919)

Figure 4 shows the cognitive map of the Minister of Foreign Affairs. In order to discover patterns in the belief system of the decision maker one can investigate, for example, which concepts are most important to the decision maker. The most important concepts are defined as those that are most central in the belief system, which means that a lot of arrows go in (so called indegrees) and out (outdegrees) of this specific concept.

In order to facilitate the computation we represent the indegrees and outdegrees of our map in a table, which is called a valency matrix (Axelrod, 1976, p. 350). Table 4 shows the indegrees and outdegrees of the several concepts. The computation of the centrality scores of the concepts can be done by computing the indegrees and outdegrees for each concept separately.

The indegrees (Id) of concept i can be computated by summing up the

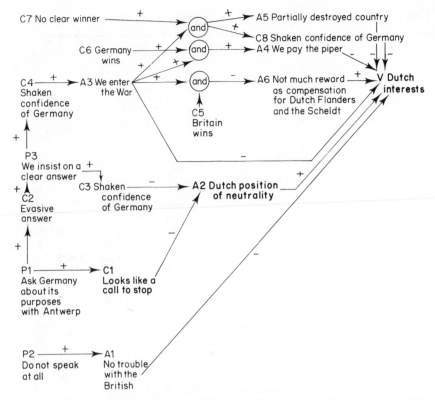

Fig. 4 Cognitive map of the Minister of Foreign Affairs. Parts of the map indicated in bold characters refer to concepts not used in the other two approaches.

absolute values of the elements of column j:

$$\mathrm{Id}(j) = \sum_{i=1}^{n} v_{ij}$$

The outdegrees (Od) of concept i are obtained by summing the absolute values of the elements of row i:

$$\mathrm{Od}(i) = \sum_{j=1}^{n} v_{ji}$$

In order to obtain the centrality score of concept i the total degree (Td) of the concept has to be computed. It consists of the sum of the indegrees and outdegrees of concept i:

$$\mathrm{Td}(i) = \mathrm{Id}(i) + \mathrm{Od}(i)$$

Process and structure in human decision making

Table 4 Valency matrix of the cognitive map of the Dutch Minister of Foreign Affairs

	P1	P2	P3	C1	C2	C3	C4	C5	C6	C7	C8	A1	A2	A3	A4	A5	A6	V	Absolute sum of out-degrees
P1				1	1														2
P2														1					1
P3						1	1												2
C1															−1				1
C2			1																1
C3															−1				1
C4													1						1
C5																		−1	1
C6																1			1
C7											1						1		2
C8																		−1	1
A1																		−1	1
A2																		1	1
A3											1	1	1			−1	−1		5
A4																		−1	1
A5																		−1	1
A6																		1	1
V																			0
Absolute sum of in-degrees	0	0	1	1	1	1	1	0	0	0	2	1	2	1	2	2	2	7	24

These computations show that the concept of 'Dutch interests' and 'entering the war' have the highest centrality scores, i.e. they were most important to the decision maker:

$$\text{Td (Dutch interests)} = 7(\text{Id}) + 0(\text{Od}) = 7$$

$$\text{Td (we enter the war)} = 1(\text{Id}) + 5(\text{Od}) = 6$$

Such computations are especially interesting if there are maps for different decision makers relating to the same situation. One can then see how decision makers differ in the interpretation of the event and one can try to explain why they differ by means of external characteristics like party affiliation, position in the government, etc.

Another way to analyse cognitive maps is to compute the total effect (i.e. the sum of the direct and indirect paths) of each policy alternative on the value concept. In this way one can detect a policy alternative which can be chosen, namely the one with a positive impact. The computation of the total effect for the two policy alternatives in our example is as follows.

First the indirect effects of P1 and P2 on V (notice that there are no direct effects of P1 or P2 on V in this map) are computed. In order to obtain the sign of these effects the direct effects, consisting of $+$ or $-$, leading via specific paths to V are multiplied. This is indicated by $*$:

$$P1*C1*A2*V = + * - * + = -$$

$$P1*C2*P3*C3*A2*V = + * + * + * - * + = -$$

$$P1*C2*P3*C4*A3*A6*V = + * + * + * + * + * - * + = -$$

$$P1*C2*P3*C4*A3*A4*V = + * + * + * + * + * - = -$$

$$P1*C2*P3*C4*A3*A5*V = + * + * + * + * + * + * - = -$$

$$P1*C2*P3*C4*A3*C8*V = + * + * + * + * + * + * - = -$$

$$P2*A1*V = + * - = -$$

Then we take for each policy alternative the sum of its effects on V. Since the total effect is negative for both policy alternatives according to the CM method, the decision maker would have to search for another policy alternative.

In this section we have presented cognitive mapping only briefly. For a more detailed presentation of this method, we refer to Bonham and Shapiro (1986).

THE EMPIRICAL DECISION ANALYSIS (EDA) METHOD

This method was developed by Gallhofer and Saris (1986b) in order to determine the decision makers' choice, based on argumentation in governmental meetings and reports of top officials, etc. The theoretical framework of EDA is similar to MPC insofar as both methods are based on decision theory.

In order to analyse a document of a decision maker using EDA, the following text analytic steps have to be performed:

(a) Coders have to extract *the decision theoretic concepts* which are:
available actions for one's own party (A),
possible actions of the opponent(s) (AO),
possible outcomes for one's own party (O),
subjective probabilities of the outcomes and the actions of the opponents (P),
subjective values or utilities of the outcomes (U).
(b) From these concepts a decision tree is constructed which gives an overview of the argumentation in a chronological sequence.

For a more detailed exposition of the text analysis see Gallhofer and Saris Chapter 17 in this volume and Gallhofer, Saris and Melman (1986b, appendix 3). Figure 5 displays the decision tree derived by the EDA method from the text of the Dutch Minister of Foreign Affairs quoted above.

Figure 5 shows that two actions were considered. The possible outcomes with their subjective values and new developments are indicated in chronological

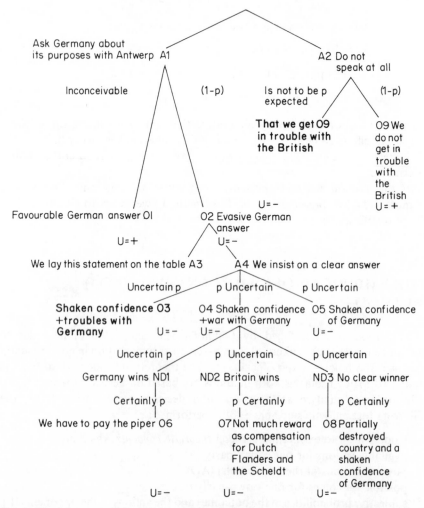

Fig. 5 Decision tree of the Minister of Foreign Affairs according to the EDA method. ND stands for 'new development' which indicates an event caused by fate. The parts of the decision tree indicated with bold characters refer to parts omitted in the other approaches.

sequence. In order to determine the choice rule based on the decision tree, which only indicates the structuring and the evaluation, decision rules specifying how people choose are necessary. The first step in determining the decision rule is to reduce the decision tree into a table. Table 5 presents this reduction.

The table shows that all the intermediate outcomes of the decision tree leading to a final branch are summarized together. In this way one obtains outcomes for S1 and S2. Sometimes these outcomes can be elaborated into systematic dimensions across strategies. In this case it can be seen that the dimensions are not systematically used by the decision maker according to the EDA method. For example, the relations with the British are only mentioned in two outcomes. The summary of the probability of the occurrence of outcomes is made by taking the 'products' of the verbal probability statements leading to a specific final outcome. Taking, for example, the product of the probabilities of A1 leading to O7 (Figure 5) one obtains '(1-inconceivable)∗uncertain∗uncertain∗certainly', which is at most 'uncertain' since the product of the probabilities cannot be greater than the smallest probability and 'uncertain', however, does not indicate a size.

In order to determine the decision rule one must establish the appropriate class of decision rules which could be applied, based on the information of utilities and probabilities summarized in Table 5.

In Gallhofer and Saris (Chapter 17 in this volume) we give a detailed classification of decision rules according to the type of information they require with respect to probability and statements. Four classes of decision rules are mentioned. Class I, which contains the subjective expected utility (SEU) model, requires utility and probability statements that can be quantified. This means that the verbal statements should at least indicate a rank ordering. Class II consists of utility statements that are not quantifiable since they only indicate whether something is positive or negative, while the probability statements indicate a rank-ordering. Class III, containing various multiattribute utility models, requires utility statements which can be rank ordered and probability statements which only indicate whether something is possible or not. Class IV refers to decision rules which require utilities and probabilities without rank orders.

Since Table 5 shows—with the exception of two probability statements (which are zero)—utilities and probabilities without rank orders, models of class IV are appropriate. In class IV two rules are mentioned: the reversed Simon rule, which consists of excluding all the strategies leading with certainty to negative outcomes as long as there is another strategy which might lead to a positive outcome, and Simon's rule, which states that one has to select the (first) strategy that only leads to satisfactory outcomes. If we apply the reversed Simon rule to the data we see that it fits. Since the chosen strategy (S2) only leads to satisfactory outcomes Simon's rule also applies to the data. We therefore conclude that the reversed Simon and Simon's rule can explain the choice of the decision maker.

Table 5 Summary of the decision tree of the Minister of Foreign Affairs

Strategies	Outcomes							
	Positive answer	Evasive answer + shaken confidence + troubles	Evasive answer + shaken confidence + war + we have to pay the piper	Evasive answer + shaken confidence + war + exchange of territory	Evasive answer + shaken confidence + war + destroyed country	Shaken confidence	Trouble with the British	No trouble with the British
S1: Ask Germany	$p = 0$ $U = +$	$p = \text{possible}$ $U = -$	$p = \text{possible}$ $U = -$	$p = \text{possible}$ $U = -$	$p = \text{possible}$ $U = -$	$p = \text{possible}$ $U = -$		
S2: Do nothing (chosen)							$p = 0$ $U = -$	$p = \text{certain}$ $U = +$

THE MULTIPLE PATHS TO CHOICE (MPC) METHOD

This method was introduced by Gross-Stein and Tanter (1980) and further developed by Maoz (1981). It mainly deals with contemporary political decisions and therefore uses various documents from one decision maker, relating to the same decision situation, in order to reconstruct the decision tree and to reveal the decision rule used. The documents consist of public material such as parliamentary debates, official statements, etc., since primary documents such as minutes of the Council of Ministers are not accessible for recent issues.

In order to study decisions according to the MPC method the following text analytic steps have to be performed:

(a) Each document is analysed separately by the coders on the basis of a questionnaire (for further details on this questionnaire, see Maoz, 1986). By means of the questionnaire the coders extract the following decision theoretic concepts:
policy alternatives,
possible events, i.e. actions of the opponents, intermediary outcomes,
value dimensions of the possible events,
subjective probabilities of the possible events.
(b) The coders quantify the probability and value dimensions (for further details, see Maoz, 1986, appendix 4).
(c) If there is more than one text available relating to the same decision situation, steps (a) and (b) are repeated.
(d) Based on the concepts found, the coders construct a decision tree.

Figure 6 represents a decision tree according to the MPC method based on the text of the Minister of Foreign Affairs quoted above. This tree shows three available alternatives, followed by event branches with probability statements, and on the final branches the value dimensions of the events are indicated. Value dimensions with an asterisk refer to inferred values, i.e. values that were not mentioned literally in the text but were inferred by the coders based on their knowledge of the event. In this way a very complex decision tree is generated with multiple value dimensions, which are systematically used for each alternative.

However, the decision tree is not complete with respect to alternative 3. As the figure shows, no value dimensions are present at the ending branches of this alternative. The coders probably could not infer them from this text. This implies that no multiattribute decision calculus can yet be computed in order to derive the choice. According to the MPC method one would have to search for additional documentary material to complete the information about alternative 3 in order to perform the calculus for the choice.

From the above it will be clear that the MPC method shows a tendency to produce multiattribute choice rules, since it allows many inferences in order to

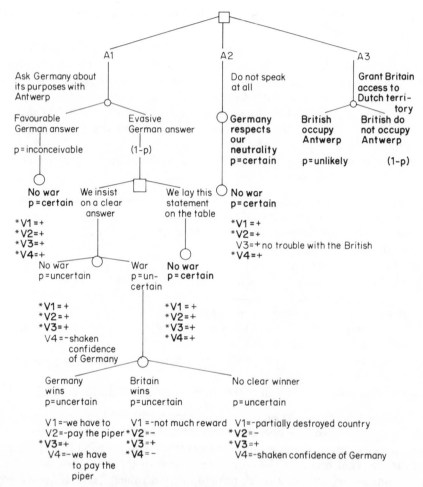

Fig. 6   Decision tree according to the MPC method. The symbols indicate the following: □ an alternative fork; ○ an event fork; *V means a value dimension inferred by the analyst, i.e. not mentioned literally in the text. The values relate to the following dimensions: V1 = territorial losses/gains; V2 = neutrality; V3 = relations with Britain, V4 = relations with Germany.

obtain the same value dimensions for each strategy. This is in contrast with the empirical decision analysis method, presented above.

After having briefly described the three approaches, a final overview of the similarities and dissimilarities is in order. This will be done first by a comparison of the concepts used. Table 6 summarizes the concepts of the three methods. Subsequently, we shall concentrate on the similarities and dissimilarities of the results of analyses of the same text.

Table 6 Similarities and dissimilarities in the use of concepts in the three methods

CM	EDA	MPC
Policy alternatives (P concepts)	Available actions of one's own party (A)	Policy alternatives of one's own party (A)

Beliefs about
   the behaviour of
   other actors
   (C concepts)
	Possible actions
	of the opponents
	(AO)
		Intermediate events

—	Possible outcomes (O)	Intermediate events

Causal links	Subjective
	   probabilities
	   (P)
		Subjective
		   probabilities
		   (P)

Value concepts (V concepts)	Subjective values/utilities (U)	Value dimensions (V)

Beliefs about
   immediate policy
   objectives
   (A concepts)
	—	—

SIMILARITIES AND DIFFERENCES IN CONCEPTS USED

Table 6 shows that all methods make use of the concept of *policy alternatives*. In the MPC and the EDA methods this concept has a predominant place since it constitutes the first step of a decision tree. In the CM method, however, before analysing the subsequent paths which relate to policy alternatives, the antecedent paths are explored.

The perceived *possible actions of the opponent(s)* are primarily studied in the EDA method. The MPC method does not make use of this concept separately. It falls within the category of intermediate events. The *beliefs of a decision maker about the behaviour of other actors* (C concepts) in the CM method are partially similar to the possible actions of the opponents when they relate to actions. However, they may also relate to intentions. *Possible outcomes* for the decision maker are represented in the EDA and MPC methods, although there is a difference in definition. The EDA instrument considers all the consequences for the decision maker resulting from his/her own actions and from the actions of the opponents as outcomes, both intermediate and final oucomes. In the MPC method, on the other hand, outcomes are considered as *intermediate events* in the decision tree. In terms of the EDA method they include possible actions of the opponent(s) and/or consequences that are not final.

Subjective probabilities are used identically in the EDA and MPC procedures. The *causal linkages* between concepts in the CM method are conceptually fundamentally different from probabilities. Uncertainties are ignored in this method. However, the causal linkages fulfil the same function in the cognitive structure with respect to connecting concepts with each other.

Value concepts are used in all procedures; however, the concepts differ slightly. The *value dimensions* of the MPC relate to the final consequences in the decision tree which are considered to be of multiple attributes. In the EDA method 'subjective values' are assigned to all kinds of outcomes (intermediate and final ones) in a decision tree. These values may be simple or multidimensional, depending on the formulation of the decision maker. When studying the text analysis instrument of the EDA method, the reader will notice that outcome statements often partially overlap with value statements. Nevertheless, we decided to distinguish these two concepts in order to provide clear coding instructions. The 'value' concepts of CM are more abstract since they relate to more general concepts like national interests, security, etc.

From the above it is clear that the MPC and EDA approaches are most similar. Dissimilarities between these approaches consist mainly in the way they aggregate the data, and the concept definitions used in practice. The differences in concept definitions have been indicated above. Therefore we concentrate on the *aggregation* phase in this section. In the EDA method the level of analysis consists of the argumentation of a decision maker in *one* document, while the MPC method, because of its use of more fragmentary material, aggregates across *all* documents concerning one decision maker relating to a specific decision. This constitutes a fundamental difference and may also have a considerable impact on the description of the data in terms of decision rules. More precisely, it could show a tendency—almost absent in the findings revealed by the EDA method—of multiattribute subjective utility models being used.

The CM method studies the beliefs of individual decision makers. It relates to a diagnostic phase in which a concrete problem is appearing. It is clear that the concepts differ from the other two approaches which relate to the structuring, evaluation, and choice phases.

From this discussion of the similarities of the concepts we see that there are considerable differences between the approaches. That makes it all the more interesting to see what the consequences are of the applications of these approaches to the same text, which will be the topic of the next section.

APPLICATION OF THE CM, EDA AND MPC METHODS TO THE SAME TEXT

In this section we want to compare the results obtained from applying the CM, EDA, and MPC methods to the text of the Minister of Foreign Affairs. Figures

4, 5, and 6 summarized the cognitive map, respectively the decision trees, according to the EDA and MPC methods, derived from this text. The analyses were done by the developers of these methods.

When considering the cognitive map derived from this text (Figure 4) one sees that the Dutch interests are the most central concept in the belief system of the Minister. The second concept of major concern to the decision maker (also in terms of centrality) is the concept of entering the war. The map also visualizes the two available policy alternatives, namely to ask the question about Germany's intentions with Antwerp or to do nothing. If one computes the total effect for each policy alternative on 'the Dutch interests' one obtains a negative effect for both alternatives. This means that the Minister considered the situation precarious, according to the cognitive mapping method, whatever he did.

Figure 5 summarizes the argumentation of the Minister in a decision tree based on the EDA method. The same alternatives as in Figure 4 are considered, however in a more literal way. One can find sentences from the text. Since in the EDA method subjective probabilities are also used, one can draw the conclusion from the decision tree that the alternative of not speaking at all leads with certainty to a positive result while when asking the question the satisfactory result is 'inconceivable' and a variety of uncertain, negative outcomes could occur.

The decision tree in Figure 6 relates to the MPC method. The first two alternatives are identical with the ones the previous procedures mentioned. The third alternative relates to granting the British access to Dutch territory. Since it was insufficiently elaborated by the Minister, it was omitted from the cognitive map and the EDA tree, while in the MPC method additional documents, even those from other decision makers, would be searched for additional information in order to complete the argumentation. Earlier we have already seen that the MPC method allows for a great deal of logical inferences, especially with respect to value dimensions. Since the four value dimensions, i.e. territorial losses/gains, neutrality, relations with Germany, relations with Britain, were not systematically used by the decision maker for each alternative, the researcher inferred their values by reasoning. According to MPC the 'do nothing' option would lead with certainty to positive values. However, when quantifying the value dimensions and the probabilities (for a possible procedure see Gross-Stein and Tanter, 1980, pp. 347–52), it might eventually turn out according to the SEU model that the alternative of asking the question would have a higher expected utility than the alternative the decision maker chose.

DIFFERENT RESULTS

From the above it is clear that, despite some overlaps, the results obtained by the three methods are nevertheless different.

When one is studying the derived cognitive map and the two versions of decision trees represented in Figures 4,5, and 6 in terms of use of parts of text and concept use one obtains a classification of five distinct categories.

First, there is a category containing *different concepts and different parts of text*. This is, for example, the case with the abstract value concept of Dutch interests and the beliefs about the immediate policy objectives like the Dutch position of neutrality, which are only used in the CM method. This is quite evident, because one can expect that concepts with different meanings relate to different parts of the text.

The second category refers to *different concepts which relate to the same part of the text*. This means that the same parts of the text have a different interpretation. It is mainly the case with outcomes and actions of the opponents of the EDA method that are interpreted as intermediate events, respectively value dimensions in the MPC method and some C and A concepts of CM. For example, 'an evasive answer' is classified as an outcome in EDA, in MPC as an intermediate event, and in CM as a belief about the behaviour of other actors.

The third category relates to *extralinguistic logical inferences*. By this category we understand, for example, inferences based on probability statements in the EDA method, indicating that alternative outcomes are also possible. These are then classified as the negation of the concept mentioned in the text (for further explanations see Gallhofer, Saris, and Melman, 1986a.) Many value dimensions and many intermediate events of MPC are also based on extralinguistic inferences. In the CM method these inferences frequently occur with direct links to the value concept.

The fourth category considers *parts of the text which could, in principle, be classified by all the approaches, but which were left out by one or more methods*. The reasons for the omission might be either that this part was considered unimportant or that the omission shows carelessness in coding. When studying Figures 4, 5 and 6 one sees, for example, that the policy alternative 'to grant Britain access to Dutch territory' was omitted in the EDA and CM method whereas MPC made use of it and another time CM omitted such a concept while it was used in EDA and MPC.

The fifth category refers to the *same concepts and the same parts of text*. This category contains available actions (EDA) or policy alternatives (MPC, CM) that are identical.

DIFFERENCES IN LANGUAGE AND STRUCTURE DETERMINE THE RESULTS

When one is comparing the cognitive map with the decision trees one salient difference is the use of language, which also relates to differences in structures. However, both types of structures make use of consecutive sequences of arguments. The language of the cognitive map is *causal*. For example, the sentence 'that we would get into trouble with the British if we do not speak at all is not to be expected' is transformed into a cause and effect variable with a causal link in terms of whether the cause variable increases or decreases the effect variable. The transformation of the above sentence can be as follows: the less we speak (cause) the less we get into trouble with the British (effect); causal link: using 'the less' twice indicates that there is a decrease in both variables in the same direction and therefore the link is +. If one variable decreased while the other increased the link would be −. This is, for instance, the case with the link of A1 (Figure 4), 'the less trouble we get with the British' and V (Figure 4), 'the more the Dutch interests are guaranteed'. Thus, most of the sentences in the text have to be transformed into this causal language and thereafter they are related directly or indirectly to the value variable 'Dutch interests'. The value variable functions as an explained variable. Based on the total effect of the links, one can diagnose which paths in the map have a positive impact on the value variable.

The language of decision trees, on the other hand, is *conditional and probabilistic*.

The reformulation of the above sentence is straightforward: if we do not speak at all (A) it is not to be expected (P) that we would get into trouble with the British (O). Both in the EDA and in the MPC method one selects these successive conditional and probabilistic sequences which are evaluated in terms of separate outcomes and not by a global value as in the CM method. Since conditional statements are difficult to formulate in the usual causal diagrams the conditions under which the war could end (literally indicated in the text) were handled in Figure 4 by using an auxiliary construction with 'and'. Taking these differences into account a translation of the causal scheme to a decision tree formulation is quite understandable.

Although the language for both decision approaches is the same, there were considerable differences between the EDA and MPC versions of the decision tree. These differences relate to the more *frequent use of extralinguistic logical inferences in the MPC method* whereas in the EDA method these inferences are restricted to negations of outcomes based on probability statements. In the MPC method these inferences relate to all kinds of concepts and especially to value dimensions. For all ending branches of the tree, the value dimensions mentioned one way or another in the document are evaluated by the coders. The parts of the structures labelled in bold characters in Figure 6 make this clear to the reader.

CONCLUSIONS

The discussion in the last section shows that the three approaches lead to three different interpretations of the 'opinion' of the decision maker. This means that the interpretation is method specific. Even the two approaches, EDA and MPC, which apparently use the same theoretical framework, lead, in this case, to different results. Nevertheless, it is most likely that the author of the document would have preferred one opinion above the others.

This is a situation that arises very frequently in any form of social science research. It is only by external validation that it is possible to determine which method is more valid than any other and therefore further research is needed to elucidate this problem.

We have seen that an important difference between EDA and MPC is the way intermediate events and values are used. In the second method one is more inclined to specify outcomes as dimensions of a final outcome which is then evaluated, whereas the first method indicates these events as intermediate outcomes and does not infer value statements unless there is an indication in the text. Detailed interpretation research would be required to determine which method is correct in relation to a particular research problem.

The CM method introduces a somewhat different conceptual scheme. In this case it would also be useful to study whether people agree with both the causal and the probabilistic interpretations.

It thus remains to be shown in the future which of the approaches brings us closer to the true structure of ideas of decision makers in specific situations. In order to give some guidelines for potential users of the three methods we suggest that the CM method can be applied best to situations where decision problems are signaled and diagnosed. In this way, the beliefs that will play a role in the future decision are assessed. By studying cognitive maps of several decision makers involved in the diagnosis of the situation, comparisons of beliefs across decision makers can be made and, for example, trends with respect to the future choices can be predicted. An alternative to the CM method would be the scenario method developed by Biel and Montgomery (Chapter 14 in this volume).

The EDA method is appropriate for the study of the structuring, evaluation, and choice rules of individual decision makers. Single documents should be used where decision makers explain their choice in detail. MPC claims to study the same as EDA, but using fragmentary textual material, it aggregates across documents. However, by aggregating across documents and inferring systematic value dimensions the MPC method produces, in our opinion, MAUT SEU rules. We suggest that MPC should be used in this way only for the study of group decisions, which cannot be tackled otherwise.

REFERENCES

Allison, G. T. (1971). *Essence of Decision*, Little Brown, Boston.
Axelrod, R. (Ed.) (1976). *Structure of Decision*, Princeton Univeristy Press, Princeton, N.J.
Bonham, G. M., and Shapiro, M. J. (1982). The cognitive process method and policy analysis. In G. Hopple (Ed.), *Biopolitics, Political Psychology and International Politics*, Frances Pinter London: pp. 210–35.

Bonham, G. M. and Shapiro, M. J. (1986). The cognitive mapping method. In I. N. Gallhofer, W. Saris, and M. Melman (Eds), *Different Text Analyses Procedures for the Study of Decision Making*, Sociometric Research Foundation, Amsterdam, pp. 29–52, 125–40.
Edwards, W. (1961). Behavioural decision theory, *Annual Review of Psychology*, **12**, 473–98.
Fishburn, P. C. (1964). *Decision and Value Theory*, Wiley, New York.
Gallhofer, I. N. (1978). Coders' reliability in the study of decision making concepts, replications across time and across topics. In *Methoden en Data Nieuwsbrief*, Vol. 1, Sociaal Wetenschappelijke Sectie van de Vereniging voor Statistiek, Amsterdam, pp. 58–74.
Gallhofer, I. N., and Saris, W. E. (1979). An analysis of the argumentation of decision makers using decision trees, *Quality and Quantity*, **16**, 411–30.
Gallhofer, I. N., Saris, W. E., and Melman, M. (Eds) (1986a). *Different Text Analyses Procedures for the Study of Political Decision Making*, Sociometric Research Foundation, Amsterdam.
Gallhofer, I. N., Saris W. E., and Melman M. (1986b). The empirical decision analysis approach. In I. N. Gallhofer, W. E. Saris, and M. Melman (Eds), *Different Text Analyses Procedures for the Study of Political Decision Making*, Sociometric Research Foundation, Amsterdam, pp. 53–68, 141–52.
George, A. L. (1980). *Presidential Decisionmaking in Foreign Policy: The Effective Use of Information and Advice*, Westview Press, Boulder, Colo.
Gross-Stein, J., and Tanter, R. (1980). *Rational Decision Making. Israeli's Security Choices*, 1967, Ohio State University Press, Columbus.
Holsti, O. R. (1969). *Content Analysis for the Social Sciences and Humanities*, Addison Wesley, Reading, Mass.
Jabes, J. (1982). Individual Decision Making. In A. McGrew and M. J. Wilson (Eds), *Decision Making Approaches and Analysis*, Manchester University Press, Manchester, pp. 53–9.
Jervis, R. (1976). *Perception and Misperception in International Politics*, Princeton University Press, Princeton, N.J.
Kozielecki, J. P. (1981). *Psychological Decision Theory*, Reidel, Dordrecht
Maoz, Z. (1981). The decision to raid Entebbe: decision analysis applied to crisis behaviour, *Journal of Conflict Resolution*, **25**, 677–707.
Maoz, Z. (1986). The multiple paths to choice method, In I.N. Gallhofer, W.E. Saris, and M. Melman (Eds), *Different Text Analyses Procedures in the Study of Political Decision Making*, Sociometric Research Foundation, Amsterdam, pp. 69–96, 153–72.
Shapiro, M. J., and Bonham, G. M. (1973). Cognitive process and foreign policy decision-making, *International Studies Quarterly*, **17**, 147–74.
Simon, H. A. (1979). Information processing models of cognition, *Annual Review of Psychology*, **30**, 120–141.
Vlek, Ch., and Wagenaar, W. A. (1979). Judgement and decision under uncertainty. In Michon *et al.* (Eds), *Handbook of Psychonomics*, Vol.2, North-Holland, Amsterdam, pp. 253–345.
Von Neumann, J. and Morgenstern, O. (1947). *Theory of Games and Economic Behavior*, Princeton University Press, Princeton, N.J.
Von Winterfeldt, D., and Edwards, W. (1986). *Decision Analysis and Behavioral Research*, Cambridge University Press, Cambridge, Mass.
Wright, G. (1984). *Behavioural Decision Theory, An Introduction*, Penguin Books, Harmondsworth, Middlesex.

Part III
Experimental studies

Introduction

Henry Montgomery

and

Ola Svenson

In the following seven chapters the structure and process of decision making are studied in the psychological laboratory. All chapters report experiments in which decision making is examined as a process over time. Two main categories of process-tracing methods are used, viz. think-aloud protocols and information-board techniques. The latter type of method denotes techniques for making subjects externalize their search of information about choice alternatives. This is done by requiring subjects to interact with some kind of data storage (information board). Information-board techniques were used in three of the studies reported here (Dahlstrand and Montgomery, Sundstroem, and Tyszka). As we used the term, information boards could be manifested in many ways. In the present studies they corresponded to a concrete physical lay-out (Sundstroem), to a video screen connected to a computer (Dahlstrand and Montgomery), and to information provided orally by the experimenter (Tyszka). One study (Svenson and Edland) illustrates a more indirect route to obtaining information about decision processes, namely by manipulating the time available to subjects for making a decision and investigating how such a manipulation affects the choices.

In this introductory chapter we will first briefly discuss the reliability and validity of the two types of process-tracing methods mentioned above in the light of the six pertinent studies. Thereafter, we will use the data presented here to look for a common picture of how people structure and process information in a decision-making task.

The reliability of a process-tracing method may be assessed in at least two ways, namely across different judges using the same method (*interjudge reliability*) or across different methods used to tap the same information-processing activities (*intermethod reliability*).

Process and Structure in Human Decision Making
Edited by H. Montgomery and O. Svenson. © 1989 John Wiley & Sons Ltd

The interjudge reliability gives information about how much different judges using a given system of judgemental categories agree when coding a given data collection. This type of reliability obviously is relevant when qualitative data such as think-aloud reports are at hand. In two of the think-aloud studies presented here interjudge reliabilities are presented (Maule and Montgomery and Svenson). In one of these studies (Montgomery and Svenson) the reliability was very high (95 percent agreement). One reason for the high reliability is probably that the coding system used required very limited interpretative efforts as the number of categories were quite few and easy to use (e.g. to determine whether a positive, negative, or a neutral value expression was used). Moreover, the protocols were subdivided into fairly small units each of which was coded separately. As noted by Svenson (Chapter 4 in this volume) small coding units are recommendable. Using small coding units implies that it will be easier for the coder to pay attention to all relevant information within each unit and in this way a high interjudge reliability may be attained. In Maule's think-aloud study the entire protocol served as a coding unit. In line with this fact, the interjudge reliability was lower (54 percent agreement). The fact that most disagreements were identified as errors of omission, which were easily resolved, indicates that the interjudge reliability indeed could have been made higher by using smaller coding units. However, according to Maule judges found it easier to make their codings when the relevant words were embedded in rather large units. Obviously, coding units should not be so small that it is necessary to pay too much attention to information in surrounding units in order to make valid codings (see Ericsson and Simon, 1984, p. 276). Hence although the reliabilty of a coding system may increase with smaller coding units the validity may decrease inasmuch as coders will fail to take relevant information into account. In any case, the two studies discussed above show that it is possible to reach a high interjudge reliability in codings of verbal protocols.

As mentioned above, another type of reliability is computed *across methods*. In other words, it may be asked whether different process-tracing methods yield the same results when applied to behaviour related to a given task. The present set of studies offers two possibilities to assess intermethod reliability. Dahlstrand and Montgomery followed up Montgomery and Svenson's think-aloud study by using a computerized information-board technique to elicit behaviour in a choice problem structurally similar to the problem used by Montgomery and Svenson. In general, the results were very similar across the two methods. With both methods it was found that subjects tended to spread out their attention to and evaluation of different alternatives in the same way over time. Tyszka's studies also resulted in convergent results for data produced by an information-board technique and think-aloud instructions respectively. It is worthy of note that the information-board technique used by Tyszka differed largely from the one used by Dahlstrand and Montgomery, relying largely on communication between subject and experimenter as opposed to communication between subject and computer in the Dahlstrand and Montgomery study. The results now reported suggest that the choice of process-tracing method need not depend on the type of information produced. Rather the choice may be dictated by practical considerations such as how easy it is to implement the method (easier with the think-aloud method) or how easy it is to code the data produced (easier with information-board techniques).

We will now turn to discussing the *validity* of the process-tracing methods used in the present studies. Primarily, we will focus on whether these methods yielded results that are meaningful from a theoretical point of view and fit into the structure of knowledge already existing in the field. Two perspectives could be adopted to address this issue. First, it may be asked whether the methods used *confirm* predictions made from a particular theory. Second, it may be asked whether the methods lead to a *development* of theoretical and empirical knowledge in the field.

Let us first discuss the extent to which existing theories were confirmed in the present process-tracing studies. In three of the studies dominance-search theory, i.e. the idea that decision making implies a search for a cognitive representation in which one alternative dominates (Montgomery, Chapter 2 in this volume), was in the foreground (Dahlstrand and Montgomery, Montgomery and Svenson, and Tyszka). A number pf predictions were made from the theory and the results were generally in line with these predictions. The predictions concerned details on how alternatives are treated at different stages of the decision-making process. It is difficult to imagine how knowledge about these issues could have been obtained without using some kind of process-tracing method. Ranyard's think-aloud protocols exemplify how subjects' thought processes may be described by the so-called non-linear additive difference rule suggested by Tversky (1969). His data also confirm Tversky's (1972) suggestion that decision makers simplify a decision problem by sorting alternatives according to their similarity. It may be concluded that the usage of think-aloud data in this case further corroborated ideas that earlier have been confirmed in analyses of final choices and judgements. Maule's study started out from Kahneman and Tversky's (1979, 1984) prospect theory and predictions were made regarding the relationship between subject's choices and their framing of the decision problem. Again, the predictions were confirmed although the data also suggested ways of framing a decision problem that were outside the scope of prospect theory (e.g. in terms of moral principles).

The latter finding points to the second perspective on the validity of process-tracing methods mentioned above, namely the extent to which they contribute to the *development* of existing theories and knowledge structures of decision making. More specifically, two of the present studies produced results that were unexpected but certainly interesting from a theoretical point of view. Maule's investigation suggests that moral issues may be an important ingredient in a descriptive theory of decision making. Sundstroem found that when subjects lack external memory aids, information-search behaviour in a decision task is affected by the number of attributes rather than by the number of alternatives. This finding suggests that one way of developing a process theory of decision making is to consider how the decision maker's memory limitations determine how he/she adapts to the structure of given information.

Although process-tracing methods have proved quite successful in decision-making research, both verbal protocols and information-board techniques are limited in at least one important respect. Presumably, they are not very useful for studying quick, more or less automatic processes. Think-aloud reports mainly mirror deliberate, conscious mental processes and are especially suited for tapping verbal information processes (Ericsson and Simon, 1980, 1984). By definition, information-board techniques do not give information about processes that cannot be externalized in terms of some kind of interaction between the decision maker and his/her environment. It is difficult to imagine how quick, automatic, and unconscious mental processes could be externalized in this way without disrupting the process. Usage of eye-movement data, however, may be one way of tracing automatic information processes, although this method is technically complicated. Another less complicated, but perhaps cruder, way is exemplified in Svenson and Edland's study. This study was concerned with decision making under time pressure in a relatively simple choice task. Obviously, such a task invites quick information processing. In order to obtain information about subjects' information processing the choice alternatives were constructed by means of pilot studies in such a way that final choices (under time pressure versus under no time pressure) would provide the information asked for. The Svenson and Edland investigation exemplifies a research problem where process-tracing methods have to be replaced by other well-thought-through experimental arrangements to make it possible to draw interesting conclusions about decision-making processes from subjects' final choices. In this way, research on decision-making processes may swing back and forth like a pendulum between process-tracing studies and experimental designs focusing on only one or a few stages of the process.

We will now leave the methodological issues and instead briefly discuss what the present studies have told us about man as a decision maker. When it is possible, we will also relate the findings presented here to the theoretical papers of this volume. More specifically, we think there are three issues which are of special interest in the present studies, namely (a) the importance of framing and restructuring in decision making, (b) the different stages of a decision-making process, and (c) the importance of context for decision-making processes.

Ever since Kahneman and Tversky's (1979) seminal paper it has been repeatedly demonstrated that final choices are dependent on how a decision problem is framed or structured. In this connection, it is important to distinguish between the *objective* framing of a problem, e.g. how the experimenter has framed a decision problem to subjects, and the decision maker's own personal or *subjective* framing of a given problem. Kahneman and Tversky's studies were mainly concerned with objective framings inasmuch as they examined how different objective framings affect subject's choices (e.g. Kahneman and Tversky, 1979, 1984; cf. also Fischhoff, 1983). A number of the present studies deal with the subjective framings of a given problem. Maule demonstrates how problems used by Kahneman and Tversky (1984) are framed in different ways by different subjects. It was also found that these personal framings determine subjects' choices. Ranyard discusses a number of heuristics that decision makers use to simplify the representation of a problem, such as rounding of numerical values and similarity grouping. It is interesting to note that the heuristics discussed by Ranyard may be added to the examples of 'subheuristics' in decision making discussed by Huber in his theoretical paper in this volume (Chapter 1). Ranyard also presents data showing that subjects sometimes restructure the goal of a decision task. For example, in a selling price task involving gambles it was found that even when subjects were urged to maximize they often restructured this goal and instead set a price aiming at securing or avoiding the opportunity to play. (For a discussion of how goals in decision making may be described, see Huber, Chapter 1 in this volume). Svenson and Edland's data suggest that under time pressure decision makers will simplify their representation of a problem by focusing on negative aspects of the most important attribute. Sundstroem manipulated the objective framing of a decision-making problem by making alternatives or attributes more or less salient. By and large, these manipulations produced rather weak effects on subjects' information-search behaviour. Sundstroem's data suggest that subjects' information-search behaviour in a decision task does not always follow directions suggested by the framing of the problem. Obviously, subjects' behaviour results from an interaction between their own goals and features of the decision situation (cf. Ranyard's discussion of this issue), and the impact of these factors may vary across tasks and subject populations.

Decision maker's framing or structuring of a choice problem is emphasized in dominance-search theory (Montgomery, Chapter 2 in this volume). The key assumption of this theory is that decision makers search for a cognitive representation in which one alternative dominates the others. Such a representation is called a dominance structure. It is assumed that the search for a dominance structure implies that a decision process typically could be subdivided into four stages. These stages are pre-editing (screening out unimportant attributes and alternatives with too negative aspects), finding a promising alternative (i.e. finding a candidate for the final choice), dominance testing (of the promising alternative), and dominance structuring (attempts to 'repair' dominance violations). Similar descriptions of decision-making stages but with less emphasis on search for dominance are given in Huber's and Karlsson's theoretical papers in this volume (Chapter 1 and 3 respectively). We now touch upon the second issue referred to above, viz. the stages of a decision-making process. Evidence for all four stages assumed in dominance-search theory is presented in the Montgomery and Svenson and in the Dahlstrand and Montgomery studies. Tyszka's review of previous research presents evidence for what he calls negative and positive preselection of alternatives. This distinction corresponds closely to screening of alternatives and finding a promising alternative in dominance-search theory. Hence, the three aforementioned studies largely support dominance-search theory. However, so far there is only limited knowledge about how decision makers actually process information in each stage. For example, in the dominance-structuring stage it is possible to conceive of a number of operations that the decision maker may use in order to eliminate or neutralize a dominance violation (see Montgomery, 1983, Chapter 2 in this volume), but at the present moment there seems to be only limited knowledge about when and how often each of these operations is used. Little is also known about when and how often people require a more or less perfect (or more or less fully developed) dominance structure in order to make a decision (see Montgomery, Chapter 2 in this volume).

A recurring finding in cognitive psychology is the importance of factors limiting subjects' possibilities of processing information in an efficient way. Seemingly small variations of such context factors may produce large effects on subjects' information processing (e.g. Bransford and Johnson, 1972; Zukier and Pepitrone, 1984). Some of the present studies illustrate three powerful context factors, which all have to do with limits to or constraints on subjects' possibilities of efficient information processing. Sundstroem's study shows the importance of *memory requirements* for decision makers' search behaviour. (See also the think-aloud study described in Huber's theoretical paper, Chapter 1 in this volume.) Svenson and Edland's study resulted in dramatic effects of *time pressure* on subjects' final choices. Tyszka's study revealed that *lack of familiarity* with choice alternatives may affect how alternatives are evaluated (more positive evaluations and more comparisons between alternatives for non-familiar alternatives; see also Huber's think-aloud study, Chapter 1 in volume). All three studies suggest that constraints give rise to interesting qualitative changes in subjects' information processing; i.e. introducing constraints into a choice situation does not necessarily just make subjects' information processing less efficient (quantitative change) but rather it may imply that subjects use different tactics or strategies when processing the information (qualitative change) in order to make the best of the given situation. For example, if a decision maker has limited knowledge about an alternative he/she may make the best of the situation by comparing this alternative to another given alternative rather than searching in vain for knowledge that may be used for an independent evaluation of the alternative. To express it simply, people in general adapt to constraints and this is also true for decision situations.

As a final word, the present studies may be seen as a move towards a *psychology* of decision making. They have resulted in some additional understanding of

internal processes and structures in decision making compatible with already
known facts about the human mental apparatus.

REFERENCES

Bransford, J. D., and Johnson, M. R. (1972). Contextual prerequisites for understanding:
some investigations of comprehension and recall, *Journal of Verbal Learning and
Behavior*, **11**, 717-26.
Ericsson, K. A., and Simon, H. A. (1980). *Verbal Reports as Data, Psychological Review*,
87, 215-51.
Ericsson, K. A., and Simon, H. A. (1984). *Protocol Analysis: Verbal Reports as Data*, MIT
Press, London.
Fischhoff, B. (1983). Predicting frames, *Journal of Experimental Psychology: Human
Learning and Memory*, **9**, 103-16.
Kahneman, D., and Tversky, A. (1979). Prospect theory: an analysis of decisions under
risk, *Econometrica*, **47**, 263-91.
Kahneman, D., and Tversky, A. (1984). Choices, values, and frames, *American Psycholo-
gist*, **39**, 341-50.
Montgomery, H. (1983). Decision rules and the search for a dominance structure: towards
a process model of decision making. In P. C. Humphreys, O. Svenson, and A. Vari
(Eds), *Analyzing and Aiding Decision Processes*, North-Holland and Hungarian
Academic Press, Amsterdam/Budapest, pp. 343-69.
Tversky, A. (1969). Intransitivity of preferences, *Psychological Review*, **76**, 311–48.
Tversky, A. (1972). Elimination by aspects: a theory of choice, *Psychological Review*, **79**,
281-99.
Zukier, H., and Pepitrone, A. (1984). Social roles and strategies in prediction: some
determinants of the use of base rate information, *Journal of Personality and Social
Psychology*, **47**, 349–60.

7

A think-aloud study of dominance structuring in decision processes

and

OLA SVENSON

Decision making involves a series of perpetual, cognitive, and evaluative processes. In everyday routine decisions, these processes may be fairly quick and automatic and, as a consequence, difficult to examine for the researcher. On the other hand, when new and complex decision situations occur, there will be a demand for slower, more deliberate, and conscious information-processing activities. Such processes are profitably studied by means of concurrent verbal reports from the subject or, put differently, by using a think-aloud technique (Ericsson and Simon, 1980). The think-aloud technique and other process-tracing methods (e.g. eye-movement records) have been used in a number of studies of decision making in new and complex situations (Payne, 1976; Payne and Braunstein, 1978; Svenson, 1974, 1983; cf. also Montgomery and Svenson, 1976; Svenson, 1979; Montgomery, 1983). One purpose of these studies has been to describe the decision maker's structuring of the situation and another to examine how different decision rules are used within a particular structure for arriving at a final choice among the alternatives. A review of findings bearing on these issues was presented by Svenson (1979).

In the present investigation the decision alternatives are described as in previous process-tracing studies (e.g. Svenson, 1974). A decision alternative is denoted A_i $(a_{i1}, a_{i2}, \ldots, a_{in})$, where a_{ij} stands for the attractiveness of an aspect on the attribute j for alternative i (e.g. the attractiveness of a salary (attribute j) associated with a job offer (alternative i)). Note that only a rank-order scale

Process and Structure in Human Decision Making
Edited by H. Montgomery and O. Svenson 1989 Published by John Wiley & Sons Ltd

of (the subjective) attractiveness within each attribute is assumed so far. Thus, we do not assume *a priori* that trade-offs are or even can be made between two attributes as most models in the economy do (e.g. expected utility models).

Recently, Montgomery (1983) proposed that a decision process consists of a series of structuring and restructuring activities whereby the representation of the decision situation is successively changed. The goal of these activities is to arrive at a representation in which one alternative can be *justified* for oneself and others as being the best choice (cf. Slovic, 1975; Tversky, 1972,; Ranyard, 1982). Montgomery (1983) assumed that the ideal representation for justifying a decision is a structure in which the rule of dominance is applicable. A decision alternative dominates other alternatives if it has at least one advantage on one attribute compared to all the other alternatives and is not worse than any other alternative on any attribute. To illustrate, A_1 dominates A_2 iff for $j = 1$, n, $a_{1j} \geq a_{2j}$ and for at least one $j = k$, $a_{1k} > a_{2k}$. The dominance rule is regarded as an axiom in most decision theories (e.g. Edwards, 1954). As is easily realized, this rule leads to short arguments and is associated with a clear cognitive structure. Hence, it is easy to justify a decision when the dominance rule is applicable.

Unfortunately, the dominance rule is often not applicable in its pure sense. Still, it may be possible to create a representation of a decision situation which in some sense allows the dominance rule to be used. The decision maker may create what Montgomery (1983) called a *dominance structure*. This is a representation in which (a) one alternative, A_i, is better than the other alternatives on at least one attribute and (b) where all disadvantages of A_i, if any, have been eliminated, neutralized, or counterbalanced in one way or another. In Montgomery's (1983) paper, it was assumed that a decision process may be seen as a search for a dominance structure. When this goal has been attained, the decision maker knows that he/she can justify his/her decision.

The view of decision making as a search for dominance may be related to the idea that decision processes can be seen as a hypothesis-testing activity (cf. Janis and Mann, 1977). Montgomery (1983) assumed that the decision maker, at an early stage, hypothetically chooses one alternative as a candidate for the final choice. However, this hypothetically preferred alternative has to fit in a desired dominance structure. If violations of dominance in favour of this alternative are found, the decision maker continues to a dominance-structuring phase of the decision process in order to handle these violations. In this phase, the decision situation is tentatively restructured in an effort to make the promising alternative dominant. For instance, if the promising alternative is better in all respects except that it is a little more expensive, the decision maker may consider the costs of all alternatives to be within his/her limits of expenditure and look upon them as approximately equal on the attribute of costs. This would make it possible to justify the choice very easily. If the decision maker fails to neutralize a dominance violation, he/she may attempt to change the representation of the decision more drastically and/or to find a new promising alternative to test in a second round.

The purpose of the present think-aloud study of decision making was to present new information about the information search and evaluative processes used for arriving at a decision. In particular, the data were interpreted in relation to the idea that decision making includes a hypothesis-testing process involving dominance structuring. To achieve this end, two main aspects of the decision process were studied, viz. subjects' attention to and evaluation of different choice alternatives during different parts of the process. These measures were also computed for particular attributes in more detailed analyses. Generally, it was predicted that the finally chosen alternative would receive more attention and be more positively evaluated than other alternatives long *before* it is definitely chosen. These predictions follow from the idea that the choice of a decision alternative is preceded by a hypothesis that this alternative is the best one. It was also predicted that the pattern of attractiveness of the aspects across alternatives should be closer to a dominance structure at later stages of the decision process than in the earlier stages. For instance, if a non-chosen alternative was more attractive on one attribute than the chosen one in the beginning of the decision process, this difference 'in the wrong direction' was predicted to be smaller towards the end of the decision process.

METHOD

Decision alternatives

Five different one-family houses were presented in great detail in authentic booklets for marketing the houses. The information about the five alternatives was issued from the same bank-affiliated agency and given in a standard type of format. At the time of the experiment, the houses were under construction and for sale. The price and monthly expenses were almost constant across the alternatives. All houses were located in the Stockholm region.

Subjects

The twelve subjects were recruited through the Department of Psychology at the University of Stockholm. In fact they were six couples each of whom had one of the partners studying at the Department. All subjects were living in apartment houses and had future possibilities to buy one of the houses which constituted the choice alternatives. The subjects had never before taken part in a similar experiment.

Procedure

The subjects were instructed that they should imagine themselves in a situation where they could buy one of the homes described in the brochure. The choice should be made according to the subjects' own opinions and personal situation with a few changes. The changes were that the subjects had the down-payment required in a bank deposit and that their salary would be sufficient to be able to pay the annual costs for all the choice alternatives. In addition, the subjects were instructed that they (irrespective of their present situation) had a family consisting of two adults and two children less than 10 years old.

All decisions were made in individual sessions where the subjects were instructed to think aloud in the same way as reported earlier by Svenson (1974). A tape recorder registered all that was said during the experiment. In the first and training stage of the experiment, the subjects were given only two choice alternatives not included in the set of five alternatives later used in the experiment proper. These training alternatives were very similar to the later alternatives. In this way, the subjects learned how to think aloud and became acquainted with the task. During the training stage, the experimenter was seated in an adjoining room (to avoid visual contact) with the door open so that he/she could hear what the subject said. Whenever the subject remained silent the experimenter asked in a neutral voice 'What are you thinking of now?' This training required 20 to 30 minutes. In the first part of the training session the experimenter asked the subjects to think aloud more often than later, which indicates the usefulness of a training stage before collecting the verbal protocols.

In the second stage, the main experiment was conducted with the subject alone with a tape recorder. The process of making a choice among the alternatives required 30 to 45 minutes.

Coding the verbal protocols

Each protocol was typed from the tape recordings during the sessions. The protocols were then split up into statements. The criterion for identification of a statement was that it should refer to one idea. Many statements corresponded to what would normally be regarded a sentence. When in doubt, a statement was always made shorter rather than longer. A statement could be very short as exemplified by the mentioning of an alternative with an added evaluation, e.g. 'Alby—good'.

Two coders decomposed the protocols into statements independently of each other. The interjudge reliability was very high (more than 95 per cent identical statements). The deviations were discussed by the coders and were then eliminated, which gave one final sequence of statements for each protocol.

Each statement was then coded as evaluatively neutral, positive, or negative and also with regard to which of the following attributes (1 to 11) it concerned (cf. Svenson, 1974): (1) plan of area (within housing area); (2) plan of house (number of rooms, size, etc.); (3) economic aspects; (4) distance from city, communications, etc.; (5) part of town (surburban area, social status of area, etc.); (6) recreational possibilities (closeness to water, etc.); (7) standard of construction material and machines (wallpaper, washing machine, etc.); (8) exterior features of house; (9) service in area (schools, shops, etc.); (10) ground plot (size, etc.); (11) date when house would be completed. A last category referred to global statements of an alternative as a whole such as 'this is a good alternative'. In all cases where attributes were analysed separately, the global statements were excluded.

The *attention* paid to an alternative was defined as the number of statements referring to that alternative during a given part of a protocol. The *evaluation* of an alternative was measured by the index (the number of positive statements − number of negative statements)/total number of statements. This index ranged from − 1.0 for only negative statements to + 1.0 for only positive statements.

RESULTS

Attention and evaluation of alternatives

Each protocol was divided into four parts, each containing the same number of statements within necessary rounding errors. Attention and evaluation studied within each of these fourths to illustrate the development of the decision process. The finally chosen alternative was identified for each subject, as the study of that alternative was regarded as particularly interesting. For instance, it would be interesting to find out when in the decision process this alternative was differentiated from its competitors. The other choice alternatives were identified by ranking them with respect to the amount of attention paid during the whole decision process. In particular, the most attended non-chosen alternative was considered worth studying as this alternative may be regarded as the most successful competitor to the chosen alternative.

Overall attention

Inspection of individual data revealed that half of the subjects (six) paid little or no attention (three or less statements) to the finally chosen alternative during the first fourth of the protocols. Therefore, the data were analysed separately for subjects who atteneded to the finally chosen alternative during the first part of a protocol and those who did not.

Figure 1 shows arithmetic means of attention for each of these two groups plotted against part of the protocol. The top panels give data for attention and the bottom panels for evaluations. The data summarized in Figure 1 were

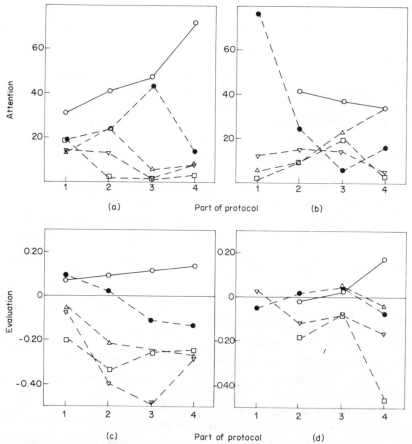

Fig. 1   (a, b) Attention to and (b, c) evaluation of decision alternatives as a function of part of the protocol. Part of the protocol corresponds to fourths of the protocol (in terms of number of statements). (a) and (c) show data for subjects attending to the finally chosen alternative in the first fourth of the protocol and (b) and (d) show data for subjects paying little or no attention to the finally chosen alternative in the first fourth of the protocol (three or less statements). (○ chosen alternative; ● most attended non-chosen alternative; △ second most attended non-chosen alternative; ▽ third most attended non-chosen alternative; □ least attended non-chosen alternative.) Attention was operationalized as the number of statements for a given alternative and part of the protocol; for the definition of evaluation, see text.

analysed by a three-way analysis of variance with repeated measures of the two last factors mentioned below. The factors were defined as follows: (1) group of subjects (chosen alternative attended to (more than three statements) versus not attended to during the first fourth of the protocol), (2) time (first, second, fourth, etc., of the protocol)—the first fourth was, for obvious reasons, excluded when the data consisted of evaluative indices of which one of the groups had no data, and (3) alternative (all five alternatives or finally chosen alternative versus other alternatives, see below). All evaluative measures based on less than three statements were excluded from the analysis to ensure a sufficient degree of reliability of the data. This led to a few cases of missing data for individual subjects. In these cases the missing value was replaced by the evaluative index computed for the preceding fourth of the protocol for the appropriate alternative and subject. Hence, it was assumed that no (or little) attention paid to an alternative implied no change in the evaluation of that alternative.

The analysis of variance conducted for attention included all five alternatives. One significant main effect was obtained, viz. for the alternative, $F (4,40) = 32.27$, $p > 0.01$. As can be seen in Figure 1, this effect reflects the fact that as soon as the finally chosen alternative was attended to by the subjects it also drew, on the average, most attention.

Three interactions were significant, viz. group × alternative, time × alternative, and group × time × alternative. We will first comment on the time × alternative interaction, $F (12, 120) = 2.99$, $p < 0.01$. This interaction mainly concerned the attention paid to the finally chosen alternative and the most attended non-chosen alternative respectively, in the first and the last fourth of the process. In the first fourth of the process the most attended non-chosen alternative received most attention on the average (in all 564 statements for this alternative versus 196 statements for the finally chosen alternative) whereas in the last fourth, the situation was completely reversed (165 statements for the most attended non-chosen alternative versus 627 statements for the chosen alternative). However, these tendencies were not uniform across the two groups (Figure 1a and b), which is reflected in the group × time × alternative interaction, $F (3, 39) = 4.64$, $p < 0.01$. More exactly, the dominating role of the most attended non-chosen alternative in the first fourth of the process was restricted to the group of subjects who did not attend to the finally chosen alternative during that part of the process (Figure 1b). In the other group the attention was more evenly spread out across all five alternatives at the beginning of the process (Figure 1a). During the latter part of the process there was in this group a tendency to increasing differentiation between the amount of attention given the chosen alternative and the other ones. There was no such tendency in the group who did not attend to the finally chosen alternative in the beginning of the process. In all, more attention was paid to the finally chosen alternative by subjects attending to this alternative at the start of the process than by the other subjects, which is reflected in the group × alternative interaction, $F (4, 40) = 5.48$, $p < 0.01$.

It should be noted that the analysis of variance on the attention data are partly confounded by the fact that attention was used for dividing the subjects into groups. The grouping criterion used implies, by definition, that in the *first* fourth of the process the *chosen* alternative will receive more attention in the one group than in the other one. To control for this confounding effect, two additional analyses of variance were conducted in which we excluded either the first fourth of the process or the chosen alternative from the analysis. Of particular interest are the interactions involving the group factor. The following of these interactions were significant, namely group $\times$ alternative, F (4, 40) = 3.02, $p < 0.05$, when the first fourth of the process was excluded, and group $\times$ time $\times$ alternative, F (8, 80) = 2.38, $p < 0.05$, when the first fourth of the process was excluded, and F (9, 90) = 5.47, $p < 0.01$, when the chosen alternative was excluded. Thus, these results support the interpretations of the results from the complete analysis of variance.

Overall evaluation

The analysis of variance conducted for evaluations of the alternatives was a three-way analysis as before (group of subjects $\times$ time $\times$ alternative). The alternative factor was defined in two ways: (a) the chosen alternative versus the most attended non-chosen alternative and (b) the chosen alternative versus the arithmetic means of the evaluations of all non-chosen alternatives. Due to too many cases of missing data it was not feasible to include all the five alternatives as levels on the third factor in case (b).

Not surprisingly, the chosen alternative tended to be more positively evaluated than the other ones (see Figure 1c and d), which is reflected in significant alternative effects, $F(1, 10) = 9.23$, $p < 0.05$ (chosen alternative versus most attended non-chosen alternative) and F (1.10) = 60.96, $p < 0.01$ (chosen alternative versus means of the four remaining alternatives). No other main effect was significant.

Two types of interaction were significant, viz. time $\times$ alternative (both analyses) and group $\times$ alternative (chosen alternative versus means of the remaining four alternatives).

The time $\times$ alternative interaction, F (2, 20) = 14.39, $p < 0.01$ (chosen alternative versus most attended non-chosen alternative), and F (2, 20) = 9.73, $p < 0.01$ (chosen alternative versus means of the four remaining alternatives), implies, as can be seen in Figure 1, that subjects tended to differentiate more between the chosen alternative and the other ones at the end of the process than in the earlier parts. This differentiation tended as a rule to be stronger when the chosen alternative was attended to from the very beginning of the decision process (Figure 1d) as compared to when this was not the case (Figure 1c), which is reflected in the significant group $\times$ alternative interaction, F (1, 10) = 9.27, $p < 0.05$. Figure 1 shows that this interaction also implies that the chosen alternative became more positively evaluated sooner than *all* its competitors for subjects who had attended to the finally chosen alternative in the beginning of the process.

Attention and evaluation combined

A striking result noted above is that in the first fourth of the process, the most attended non-chosen alternative almost completely dominated those subjects' attention who initially did not attend to the finally chosen alternative. (This was true for five of the six subjects in this group.) There was no such tendency with regard to the chosen alternative for subjects who attended to that alternative in the beginning of the process. It may be asked whether these differences in *attention* reflect *evaluative* differences in different parts of the first fourth of the protocol. In particular, it may be interesting to compare subjects' initial impressions of the two alternatives with impressions later in the first fourth of the protocol. To do so, the first fourth of the protocol was broken down into fifths (in terms of number of statements). Evaluation indices were then computed for the two alternatives for the first fifth in which they appeared and for the remaining part of the first fourth of the protocol. (As before, cases with three or less statements were excluded.) For subjects primarily attending to the non-chosen alternative, the initial impression of this alternative tended to be more favourable than it was later, $M = 0.11$ and -0.09 respectively, $t (4) = 7.10$, $p > 0.01$. For subjects attending to the chosen alternative there was an opposite but non-significant trend with regard to the non-chosen alternative, $M = -0.03$ and 0.09 respectively, $t (4) = 1.85$. (Here one subject was excluded who only attended to the chosen alternative during one of the fifths.) It can be tentatively concluded that the reason for the large amount of attention paid to the most attended non-chosen alternative by five of the subjects was that these subjects did not want to leave aside an alternative which first was positively evaluated but then found to be less attractive.

Predicting final choice from attention and evaluation

Table 1 gives distributions of attention and evaluation for the chosen alternative as compared to the other alternatives for each fourth of the protocols. Cumulated data across fourths of protocols are also given in the table. An $\times$ in the table indicates that the chosen alternative was given most attention in the corresponding fourth (or cumulated fourths) of the process. When little or no attention was paid to the chosen alternative (three or less statements) this was marked by — in the table. When another alternative than the chosen one received most attention or was most highly evaluated, this was indicated by $\bigcirc$.

Considering the attention paid to the chosen alternative *within* each fourth of the process it can be seen that after half the decision process, six of the twelve subjects paid most attention to the chosen alternative during the preceding fourth of the process. It is interesting to note that only three subjects (2, 5, and 11) paid most attention to the chosen alternative during both of the two last fourths of the decision process. However, seven of the twelve subjects paid most attention to the chosen alternative during the last fourth of the process.

Table 1 Distributions of attention (number of statements in a fourth of a verbal protocol) and of the evaluation index (number of positive statements – number of negative statements)/(total number of statements) for finally chosen alternative and the remaining alternatives. When the finally chosen alternative was given most attention or evaluated higher than the others, this is shown by an × in the table. When the most attention was given to another alternative, this is denoted by ○ in the table. A line indicates that little or no attention was paid to the chosen alternative (three or less statements)

	Percentile	1	2	3	4	5	6	7	8	9	10	11	12	number of subjects giving chosen alternative most attention/highest evaluation
Attention within fourth of protocol	0.25	×	│	×	│	×	○	○	│	│	×	○	│	3
	0.50	○	○	×	○	│	×	×	×	×	│	×	○	6
	0.75	○	×	×	○	×	○	○	│	○	×	×	×	6
	1.00	×	×	○	×	×	×	×	│	○	×	○	○	7
Cumulative attention	0.25	×	○	×	○	×	×	×	○	○	×	×	○	3
	0.50	×	×	×	○	×	×	×	○	×	×	○	○	6
	0.75	×	×	×	○	×	×	×	○	×	×	×	○	8
	1.00	×	×	×	○	○	×	×	│	×	×	×	│	9
Evaluation within fourth of protocol	0.25	×	│	│	│	│	○	○	│	│	│	×	│	2
	0.50	×	○	×	○	×	×	×	×	×	○	×	×	7
	0.75	×	×	×	○	×	×	×	│	○	×	×	○	8
	1.00	×	×	×	○	○	○	○	×	│	○	○	○	10
Cumulative evaluation	0.25	×	│	│	│	×	×	×	│	×	○	×	│	2
	0.50	×	×	○	○	○	×	○	×	○	×	×	×	7
	0.75	×	×	○	○	×	×	×	×	○	○	×	×	8
	1.00	×	×	○	○	×	×	×	×	○	○	×	×	8
Total number of statements		322	268	196	723	378	319	515	454	386	601	359	396	

The *cumulative* attention is a somewhat better predictor of the final choice. After half the process, this measure predicts the choice for six subjects, as is also the case for the *within* attention. However, after the third and last fourth of the process, the final choice is predicted for eight and nine subjects respectively, as compared to correct predictions for six and seven subjects respectively for the *within* attention.

Turning to the evaluations, it can be noted that evaluations *within* a fourth of the protocol and the *cumulative* evaluations predict the same number of choices in the first, second, and third fourths of the protocol. The number of correct predictions for these parts of the protocol is about the same as for cumulative attention. Moreover, the correct predictions provided by the attention and evaluation measures largely concern the same subjects. For example, seven of the eight correct predictions for cumulative attention and within evaluation after the third fourth of the protocol concern the same subjects. The overall best prediction of the final choice is provided by the evaluations during the last fourth of the protocol which predict ten of the twelve choices.

Finally, it can be noted that the length of the process (in terms of number of statements) appears to be unrelated to whether subjects attended or did not attend to the finally chosen alternative in the beginning of the process. It might have been expected that the former group of subjects would have made a quicker decision since they started earlier to differentiate between the finally chosen alternative and the other ones (see Figure 1).

Test of the dominance-structuring hypothesis

The results presented below concern the hypothesis that the pattern of attractiveness of aspects across alternatives is closer to a dominance structure at later stages of the decision process than in the earlier stages. In general, the risk of violating dominance is greater the *less* attractive the *chosen* alternative is on a particular attribute and the *more* attractive a *non-chosen* alternative is on a particular attribute. Hence, to approach a dominance structure, the decision maker will primarily change negative evaluations of the chosen alternative (into less negative evaluations) and positive evaluations of non-chosen alternatives (into less positive evaluations) on specific attributes. It was predicted that these changes, if any, would be stronger than changes of positive evaluations of the chosen alternative and of negative evaluations of non-chosen alternatives, since the latter evaluations have a greater probability of being compatible with a dominance structure. The plots in Figure 2 are a test of this prediction.

The data in Figure 2 are means of evaluation indices for the chosen alternative and most attended non-chosen alternative respectively. The evaluation indices were computed for each half of a protocol or negative aspects respectively in the first half of the protocol. Hence, Figure 2 shows how subjects' evaluations changed from the first half of the protocol to the second half. To ensure sufficient

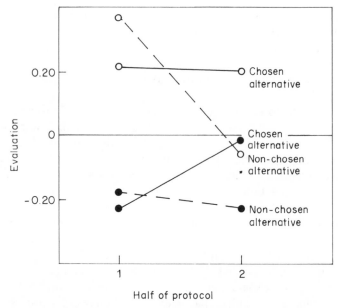

Fig. 2   Evaluation (see text) of chosen alternative (straight lines) and most attended non-chosen alternative (dashed lines) in the first and second half of the protocol on either attributes with positive evaluation (O) or with negative evaluation (●) in the first half of the protocol.

reliability and to make comparisons across halves of the protocol meaningful, the computations were only based on those cases where there was a total of at least four statements within the same set of attributes in both halves of the protocol. Thus each line in Figure 2 is based on a subset of the twelve subjects with the number of included subjects varying from eleven (chosen alternative with primarily positive aspects in the first half of the protocol) to five (non-chosen alternative with primarily positive aspects in the first half of the protocol).

The results in Figure 2 are entirely in line with the predicted pattern. There are no significant changes from the first to the second half of the protocol when the evaluations are in the 'correct direction' in the first half of the protocol: $t(10) = 0.17$ (chosen alternative), $t (5) = 0.74$ (non-chosen alternative). On the other hand, there are marked and statistically significant changes in the predicted direction when the evaluations are in the 'wrong direction' in the first half of the protocol: $t (6) = 2.53$, $p < 0.05$ (chosen alternative), $t (4) = 2.95$, $p < 0.05$ (non-chosen alternative).

A more straightforward but less quantitative test of the dominance-structuring hypothesis can be done with the data presented in Table 2. These data are based on a classification of the evaluative relations between the chosen and most attended non-chosen alternatives across all subjects and attributes. The data

Table 2 Number of cases for different relations between evaluative indices for chosen and most attended non-chosen alternative (each attribute and each subject) during the first and second halves of the decision process. A_c stands for chosen alternative and A_a for the most attended non-chosen alternative. $A_c > A_a$ indicates that A_c was more positively evaluated than A_a measured by the evaluation index (see text), $A_c = A_a$ that the alternatives were equally evaluated, and so on. A_c^+ indicates that A_c was positively evaluated and — that A_a was not attended at all. A_c^0 indicates that alternative A_c was neutral according to the evaluation index

| First half of protocol | Second half of protocol | | | | | | | | | | Totals in groups | Totals in groups of category |
	1	2	3	4	5	6	7	8	9	10		
Chosen alternative more positive												
1. $A_c > A_a$	16	2	1	3	—	—	2	1	4	4	33	
2. A_c^+, —	3	1	1	1	—	—	—	1	—	—	7	42
3. —, A_a^-	1	—	—	1	—	—	—	—	—	—	2	
Non-chosen alternative more positive												
4. $A_c < A_a$	8	3	—	3	—	1	2	1	6	5	29	
5. —, A_a^+	—	—	—	—	—	—	—	—	—	1	1	32
6. A_c^-, —	—	—	—	—	—	—	—	—	—	2	2	
Alternatives equal or no information												
7. $A_c = A_a$	5	1	—	2	—	—	—	—	2	2	10	
8. —, A_a^0	—	2	—	—	—	—	—	—	4	3	9	58
9. A_c^0, —	2	1	1	—	—	1	3	—	1	1	9	
10. —, —	4	3	—	—	—	1	1	1	2	18	30	
Totals in category	39	12	3	10	0	3	8	4	17	36	132	
Totals in group of categories (1–3, 4–6, and 7–10)		54			13				65			

show how these relations changed from the first half of the protocol to the second half. The first three categories in the table indicate evaluative relations (according to the earlier presented index) in favour of the chosen alternative for a subject on an attribute. Categories 4 to 6 indicate that the most attended non-chosen alternative was more positively evaluated than the chosen alternative, while categories 7 to 10 do not indicate differences in attractiveness between the alternatives on the attribute and subject under consideration.

The totals in the groups of categories give some interesting information. First, the chosen alternative tended to be positively evaluated only a little more often in relation to the non-chosen alternative during the second half of the decision process (54 compared with 42). Second, the most striking result is the drastic change for evaluative relations favouring the non-chosen alternative. Evaluations of attributes where comparisons are unfavourable for the chosen alternative decrease from 32 to 13 from the first to the second half of the protocols. Third, the number of non-diagnostic cases is about the same during the first and second halves of the decision process.

Out of the 42 cases with the chosen alternative evaluated *more* positively during the first half, the evaluations changed in the opposite direction during the second half in 5 cases (12 per cent) and the difference was ignored in 12 cases (29 per cent). In 32 cases the chosen alternative was evaluated *less* positively during the first half but here the proportion of change was higher, 11 cases (34 per cent). Thus, when a comparison on an attribute was in favour of the non-chosen alternative, there was a tendency to re-evaluate that particular comparison. This re-evaluation led to a switched rank order on the attribute in 34 per cent of the cases. In all, violations of the dominance in favour of the chosen alternative during the first half of a decision process were re-evaluated or ignored during the second half of the decision process in 87 per cent of the cases.

DISCUSSION

The present study is based on the assumption that decision making can be seen as a search for a dominance structure. This search is assumed to involve hypothesis-testing activities, i.e. the hypothetical choice of an alternative and subsequent tests of whether this alternative is the best. In the present study, we investigated whether there is support for the dominance-structuring assumption in the pattern of attractiveness of aspects across alternatives in different parts of the process. We will first, however, discuss those results that are primarily related to the hypothesis-testing assumption.

In the later parts of the verbal protocols, there was a tendency towards increasing differentiation between the chosen alternative and the other ones, particularly for evaluation data. This tendency suggests that the final choice of an alternative was preceded by some kind of hypothetical choice of that alternative. (Note that the think-aloud protocol ended as soon as the subject declared his/her final decision.) Individual data suggested that for at least half of the subjects, the hypothetical choice of the finally chosen alternative could have been made already in the first half of the process.

It is interesting to note that the length of processes was independent of whether subjects attended or did not attend to the chosen alternative at the beginning of the process. However, one difference between subjects attending to or not attending to the chosen alternative at the start is that the former subjects tended to spread out their attention over several alternatives in the first fourth of the process whereas the latter subjects almost exclusively attended to one alternative (the most attended non-chosen alternative). A comparison of these results with evaluation data suggested that the dominating role of the non-chosen alternative for some subjects in the beginning of the process was due to the fact that this alternative first was positively evaluated but then was soon found to be less attractive. This suggestion may be expressed in terms of the idea that decision processes involve hypothesis-testing activities; i.e. the large amount of attention paid to the non-chosen alternative by five of the subjects may reflect a failure to confirm an initial hypothesis that this alternative was a promising one. It is possible that these subjects did not want to leave aside the non-chosen alternative since they hoped (in vain) to find information that could restore the initially favourable impression. This hypotheses is in line with earlier findings that people find it difficult to give up a policy that initially is favourable but later becomes less favourable (Staw, 1976).

The results which primarily are related to the dominance-structuring assumption were uniformly in accordance with that assumption. Hence, the pattern of evaluations of aspects across alternatives was closer to a dominance structure in the later parts of the process than in the earlier parts. It should be borne in mind, however, that our analysis of subjects' dominance structuring was fairly crude with an emphasis on overall quantitative measures rather than on fine-grained analysis of the contents of the verbal protocols. An analysis of the latter type would also be of interest since dominance structuring could be of many types and on different qualitative levels (see Montgomery, 1983). Still it is interesting that such highly qualitative data as the think-aloud protocols used in this study also give meaningful quantitative results.

REFERENCES

Edwards, W. (1954). The theory of decision making, *Psychological Bulletin*, **51**, 380–417.
Ericsson, K. A., and Simon, H. A. (1980). Verbal reports as data, *Psychological Review*, **87**, 215–51.
Janis, I. L., and Mann, L. (1977). *Decision Making*, The Free Press, New York.

Montgomery, H. (1983). Decision rules and the search for a dominance structure: towards a process model of decision making. In P. C. Humphreys, O. Svenson, and A. Vari (Eds), *Analyzing and Aiding Decision Processes*. North-Holland and Hungarian Academic Press, Amsterdam/Budapest, pp. 343–69.

Montgomery, H., and Svenson, O. (1976). On decision rules and information processing strategies for choices among multiattribute alternatives, *Scandinavian Journal of Psychology*, **17**, 283–91.

Payne, J. W. (1976). Task complexity and contingent processing in decision making: an information search and protocol analysis, *Organizational Behaviour and Human Performance*, **16**, 366–87.

Payne, J. W., and Braunstein, M. L. (1978). Risky choice: an examination of information acquisition behaviour, Memory and Cognition, **6**, 554–61.

Ranyard, R. H. (1982). Binary choice patterns and reasons given for simple risky choice, *Acta Psychologica*, **52**, 125–35.

Slovic, P. (1975). Choices between equally valued alternatives, *Journal of Experimental Psychology: Human Perception and Performance*, **1**, 280–7.

Staw, B. M. (1976). Knee-deep in the Big Muddy: a study of escalating commitments to a chosen course of action, *Organizational Behaviour and Human Performance*, **16**, 27–44.

Svenson, O. (1974). *A Note on Think Aloud Protocols Obtained during the Choice of a Home*, Report 421, Psychological Laboratories, University of Stockholm.

Svenson, O. (1979). Process descriptions of decision making, *Organizational Behaviour and Human Performance*, **23**, 86–112.

Svenson, O. (1983). On the exploration of verbal protocols from decision processes. In P.C. Humphreys, O. Svenson, and A. Vari (Eds), *Analyzing and Aiding Decision Processes*, North-Holland and Hungarian Academic Press, Amsterdam/Budapest, pp. 371–82.

Tversky, A. (1972). Elimination by aspects. A theory of choice, *Psychological Review*, **79**, 281–99.

ACKNOWLEDGEMENTS

This chaper is reprinted from R. Tietz (Ed.) (1983), *Aspiration Levels in Bargaining and Economic Decision Making*, Springer-Verlag, Berlin, pp. 366–83.

The chapter was supported by the Swedish Council for Research in the Humanities and Social Sciences and by the Tercentenary Fund of the Bank of Sweden.

We wish to thank Ulf Dahlstrand, Ulla-Stina Johansson, Gunnar Karlsson, and Kerstin Meyerhoffer for their help with transcribing and analysing the protocols.

8

Information search and evaluative processes in decision making: A computer-based process-tracing study

ULF DAHLSTRAND

and

HENRY MONTGOMERY

A number of process-tracing techniques have been used in studies of the cognitive and evaluation processes preceding a decision (for a review, see Svenson, 1979). Analysis of think-aloud data is perhaps the most commonly used method. This technique yields a detailed description of the decision process, but it produces such a wealth of unsystematic data that it may be hard to find and interpret interesting trends and structures.

Another technique is to record what information the decision maker attends to during the decision process. For example, in a study by Payne and Braunstein (1978), the subjects were asked to press appropriate keys on a computer keyboard to get a desired piece of information on a video screen. However, the same information-search pattern may imply several different decision strategies or so-called decision rules. Therefore, it is difficult to draw inferences about the decision process from the information-acquisition behavior alone (e.g. Svenson, 1979; cf. also Klayman, 1983).

The present study of decision making used the same technique as Payne and Brunstein (1978). In addition, the subjects were required to evaluate the attractiveness of each piece of information requested. The subjects were also required, at regular intervals during the experimental session, to rate how eligible each alternative was.

Process and Structure in Human Decision Making
Edited by H. Montgomery and O. Svenson 1989 Published by John Wiley & Sons Ltd

The purpose of the study was twofold, viz. (a) to develop an easily manageable technique for process-tracing studies of decision making and (b) to use this technique to test the validity of a process model of decision making proposed by Montgomery (1983). This model describes the decision process as going through four phases in order to find a representation of the decision situation in which one alternative can be seen as dominant over the others. The four phases, pre-editing, finding a promising alternative, dominance testing, and dominance structuring, are assumed to be associated with different decision rules.

The pre-editing phase includes screening of alternatives. To accomplish this, the conjunctive decision rule may be applied. This rule implies that alternatives which are non-acceptable on any attribute are discarded in the following decision process. In the next phase, the decision maker makes a hypothetical choice of an alternative that seems to be promising. A promising alternative may be found by looking for an alternative that is very attractive on any attribute (the disjunctive rule). The main concern in the dominance-testing phase is to see if the rule of dominance is applicable. This is the case when the promising alternative is represented as having at least one advantage compared to the other alternatives, and no disadvantages. Disadvantages, if any, are eliminated or neutralized in the dominance-structuring phase by such operations as de-emphasizing the importance of attributes on which the promising alternative is unattractive, enhancing positive aspects associated with the promising alternative, and compensating a disadvantage by an advantage, which may be seen as using an additive rule.

The results of the think-aloud study by Montgomery and Svenson (1983) supported the idea that decision processes involve attempts to construct a dominance structure, which justifies the choice of a tentatively chosen alternative. More specifically, it was found that subjects tended to enhance their attention to and evaluation of the finally chosen alternative long before the actual choice. In the present study, we were interested in confirming these results. We also explored the idea that different decision rules have different functions such as screening, finding a promising alternative, and guiding the final choice.

METHOD

Subjects

Twenty-six persons between 20 and 40 years of age, mostly students of psychology, were paid for their participation in the experiment.

Choice alternative

The alternatives were five realistic medium-sized flats at different locations in Göteborg. Each flat was described, sometimes in great detail, on eight attributes, viz. rent, location, size, standard, plan of the flat, type of house, surroundings, public transports. Information about one aspect at a time could be presented on a video screen connected to an H-89 microcomputer. An aspect refers to a characteristic of an alternative on an attribute (e.g. the rent of a particular flat).

Procedure

The subjects (Ss) were asked, in individual sessions, to choose one of the flats with respect to the Ss' own circumstances. The street names of the flats and the attributes describing the flats were presented on the video screen in two columns. The flats and the attributes were also introduced by letters (A to E) and numbers (1 to 8) respectively. The S was introduced to pick out optional information about the flats by pressing the 'letter' key corresponding to a flat and the 'number' key corresponding to an attribute, and then a 'finish' key. The specified information was displayed on the video screen as well as a graphical scale. The end points of the scale were defined as 'bad' and 'good' respectively. By adjusting a marker on the scale, the S was required to rate the attractiveness of the requested aspects. If the S forgot to adjust the marker, nothing happened when he/she pressed the 'finish' key. Otherwise, the original menu of the street names and the attributes was displayed again. Then, the S was free to pick out a new piece of information. After each tenth aspect presentation, the S was asked to rate how eligible each alternative was, on a similar scale as the one mentioned above. The end points of this scale were defined as 'a small chance' (to be the finally chosen alternative) and 'a large chance' respectively.

There were no restrictions on the amount of information that could be requested. The S could decide at any time in the session.

In summary, the following data were recorded by the computer for each S: (a) the sequence of aspects attended to by the S, (b) ratings of the attractiveness of each presented aspect, and (c) ratings of eligibility of each alternative after each tenth aspect presentation. The latency of each aspect presentation was also recorded. The sessions lasted about 30 minutes.

RESULTS

Definitions

The attention paid to an alternative was defined as the number of trials on which the S requested information about that alternative. The evaluation of an alternative was defined as the arithmetic mean of the attractiveness ratings of that alternative on specific attributes.

The choice alternatives were identified in the same way as in the previous think-aloud study (Montgomery and Svenson, 1983). First, the finally chosen alternative was identified for each S. It was considered interesting to find out when and how this alternative differentiated from its competitors. Second, the other choice alternatives were identified by ranking them with respect to how much the S attended to each of them during the whole decision process. Of these alternatives, the most attended to non-chosen alternative was considered to be particularly interesting to study as this alternative may be regarded as the main competitor to the chosen alternatives.

Overview of individual decision processes

Figure 1 summarizes the records of each decision process. It can be seen that the length of the process varied from 10 to 54 trials (aspect presentations) with most Ss requiring around 20 trials to reach a decision. The latencies of the trials were quite stable after the third trial and lasted typically between 10 and 20 seconds. Already after ten trials a total of fourteen Ss (54 per cent) rated the finally chosen alternative as more eligible than the others. This is indicated in Figure 1 by a vertical line crossing the bar on the corresponding trial. In the last phase of the decision process, nineteen Ss either paid most attention to the finally chosen alternative or had the highest mean evaluation of it, or both.

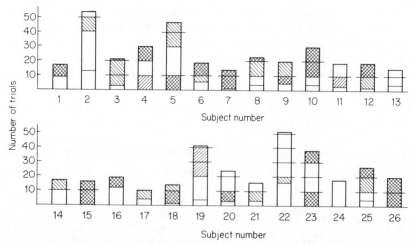

Fig. 1   Data on individual subjects. The height of each bar corresponds to the length of the decision process (number of trials) for a particular subject. Patterned areas denote most attention paid to the chosen alternative (//////), or highest mean evaluation of chosen alternative (\\\\\), or both most attention to and highest mean evaluation of chosen alternative (╫╫╫╫), within the corresponding phase of the decision process (trials 1–10, 11–20, etc.). The lowest horizontal line in each bar corresponds to the first trial on which the chosen alternative was attended to. The horizontal lines crossing the bars indicate that the subject on the corresponding trial was rated to be chosen as the alternative more likely than the others to become the finally chosen alternative.

Attention and evaluation

To study how the attention to and evaluation of different alternatives changed over time each record of Ss' decision processes was divided into three parts, denoted as the initial, middle, and final part. The initial and final part comprised five trials each, provided that both the chosen and the most attended non-chosen alternative was attended to on any of the initial or final five trials. If this was not the case, these parts of the records corresponded to the minimum number of consecutive trials, counted from the start or the end of the records, containing trials on which the S attended to both the chosen alternatives and the most attended non-chosen alternative. The middle part of the record was simply that part which remained when the initial and final parts had been delimited. This way of dividing the records ensured that the initial and final stages of the decision processes were approximately comparable within and across Ss despite the considerable variability in the length of the processes (see Figure 1).

The attention and evaluation data were analysed by a time × alternative analysis of variance with repeated measures on both factors. Time refers to part of the record (initial, middle, and final part). The alternative factor refers to the choice alternatives, identified as described above, and included either all five alternatives or only the chosen alternative and the most attended non-chosen alternative. One S (No. 17, see Figure 1) was excluded from the analysis since his decision process was too short to be divided into an initial, middle, and final stage, according to the definitions given above.

When there were missing data on Ss' evaluation of a given alternative in a given part of the record, the evaluation of that alternative was assumed to be the same as in the preceding part, if any. The attention paid to an alternative in a given part of the record was calculated as the proportion of trials on which Ss requested information about the alternative. The end points of the evaluation scales were defined as 0 and 1 respectively. Arithmetic means of attention and evaluation are plotted against part of the protocol in Figure 2.

For attention there was a significant main effect of the alternative factor when this factor only comprised the chosen and the most attended non-chosen alternative, $F(11, 24) = 5.09$, $p < 0.05$. (The effect of the alternative factor with all five alternatives included is confounded by the fact that attention was used for identifying the non-chosen alternatives). Figure 2a shows that the chosen alternative during the entire decision process tended to draw more attention than any other alternative. However, the attention paid to the most attended non-chosen alternative was almost the same as for the chosen alternative in the middle part of the process. The alternative × time interaction was significant when all five alternatives were included, $F(8, 192) = 3.33$, $p < 0.01$. It can be seen in Figure 2 that this interaction reflects a tendency to increasing differentiation between the chosen alternative and the other alternatives in the final part of the process.

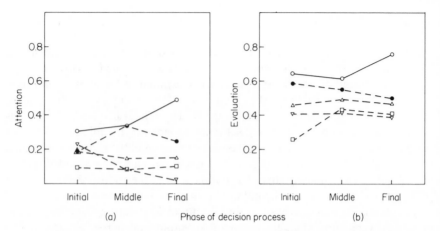

Fig. 2   (a) Mean attention to and (b) evaluation of choice alternatives in different stages of the decision process (see text). ○ Chosen alternative; ● most attended non-chosen alternative; △ second most attended non-chosen alternative; ▽ third most attended non-chosen alternative; □ = least attended non-chosen alternative. Attention was operationalized as the proportion of trials on which a given alternative was attended to.

The analysis of variance conducted for evaluation only included the chosen alternative and the most attended non-chosen alternative since there were too many missing values for the other alternatives. There was a strong effect of the alternative factor, $F(1, 24) = 49.45$, $p < 0.001$. As shown in Figure 2b, the chosen alternative tended to be definitely more positively evaluated than its main competitor in all parts of the process. However, the gap between the two alternatives tended to increase as the process proceeded. This result is corresponded by a significant alternative × time interaction, $F(2, 48) = 6.76$, $p < 0.01$.

Decision rules

The process model discussed above implies that a decision process is seen as involving a number of local decisions, all of which may be conducted according to different decision rules. Apart from the final decision, there are at least two types of local decisions, viz. (a) screening (i.e. discarding unacceptable alternatives) and (b) finding a promising alternative. Below, we examine how well different decision rules predict such local decisions as well as the final decision. The following four decision rules are considered.

The maximin rule

Choose that alternative whose least attractive aspect is more attractive than the least attractive aspects of other alternatives. This rule is closely related to the conjunctive rule, which prescribes that a chosen alternative should exceed certain minimum values on all attributes.

The maximax rule

Choose the alternative whose most attractive aspect is more attractive than the most attractive aspects of other alternatives. This rule is closely related to the disjunctive rule, which prescribes the choice of an alternative that exceeds a certain (relatively high) criterion value on at least one attribute.

The lexicographic rule

Choose that alternative which is more attractive than other alternatives on the most important attribute. The most important attribute was defined as that attribute which the S attended to first.

The additive rule

Choose that alternative for which the mean of attractiveness values is greater than for other alternatives.

Table 1 shows how often these rules predict (a) the alternative with the *unique* highest eligibility rating in different parts of the process and (b) the finally chosen

Table 1 Frequency of successful predictions of alternative with highest eligibility rating after 10, 20 trials, etc.) for non-chosen and chosen alternatives and of final choice according to different decision rules (MIN = maximum rule, MAX = maximax rule, LEX = lexicographic rule, ADD = additive rule)

Prediction	Decision rule				No rule applicable	Number of cases
	MIN	MAX	LEX	ADD		
Alternative with highest eligibility rating but not later chosen	2	5	6	3	5	12
Alternative with highest eligibility rating and later chosen	14	19	12	16	3	28
Final choice	12	18	11	20	2	26
Total	28	42	29	39	10	66

alternative. The alternative with the highest eligibility rating was assumed to reflect the finding of a promising alternative. In some cases, this alternative did not turn out to be the finally chosen alternative. These cases are treated separately (see the first row in Table 1). It can be seen that in general there were fewer successful predictions in these cases than when the alternative with the highest eligibility rating turned out to be chosen (second row in Table 1). The overall most efficient rule is the maximax rule, closely followed by the additive rule, but with the other rules well behind. The maximax rule was particularly efficient for predicting preliminary choices (first and second rows in Table 1) whereas the additive rule was slightly more efficient for predicting final choices (third row in Table 1).

Table 2 illustrates how well different decision rules predict not only the chosen alternative but also how Ss ranked the remaining alternatives in terms of the attention paid to them. The ranks were predicted by first, as before, using a decision rule for predicting the chosen alternative (i.e. an alternative with rank 1). Then this alternative was eliminated and the rule was used for predicting an alternative among the remaining four alternatives, and so on. For all alternatives with a given rank (say all chosen alternatives, i.e. alternatives with given rank = 1), the means of of the predicted ranks were computed. These means are shown in Table 2. It seems reasonable that alternatives with low ranks may correspond to alternatives which had not passed a screening test and because of this considered not worth while to attend to in the following process. This hypothesis is compatible with the tendency shown in Figure 2 that the least attended alternatives receive more attention in the beginning of the decision process than in the later phases in the process. The better a decision rule discriminates among the lower ranks, say ranks 3 to 5, the more efficient it may be for screening decisions. Table 2 shows that the lexicographic and maximin

Table 2   Mean of predicted ranks of alternatives according to different decision rules for given ranks of alternatives (rank 1 = chosen alternative, rank 2 = most attended to non-chosen alternative, rank 3 = second most attended to non-chosen alternative, rank 4 = third most attended to non-chosen alternative, rank 5 = fourth most attended to non-chosen alternative)

Decision rule	Given rank				
	1	2	3	4	5
MIN	2.13	2.87	2.65	3.37	3.80
MAX	1.54	2.38	3.08	3.98	3.98
LEX	2.52	2.23	2.69	3.60	4.06
ADD	1.33	2.75	3.27	3.71	3.78

rules are most efficient for these discriminations. The additive and maximax rules are best at discriminating among the higher ranks; i.e. these rules are best at differentiating the chosen alternative from its main competitors.

The results shown in Tables 1 and 2 may be summarized as follows. Final choices and selection of a promising alternative tend to be based on the most attractive aspects (maximax rule) with caution taken to other aspects (additive rule). By contrast, rejection of alternatives tends to be based on the most unattractive aspects, i.e. on the most unattractive aspects on the most important attribute (lexicographic rule) or on the most unattractive aspects within an alternative (maximin rule).

DISCUSSION

The present data suggest that a person facing a choice among several multiattribute alternatives may proceed as follows. First, he/she discards those alternatives that are unfavourable on the most important attribute or are extremely unfavourable on any other attribute. Then the decision maker evaluates the remaining alternatives on new attributes and identifies that alternative whose most attractive aspect is more attractive than the most attractive aspect of the other alternatives. This alternative becomes a promising alternative. Next, the decision maker checks whether the promising alternative is acceptable on further attributes. These checks will be more or less biased in favour of the promising alternatives; i.e. the promising alternative will draw more attention and be more positively evaluated than other alternatives. If the promising alternative is found acceptable, it is chosen. If it is not, a new promising alternative may be selected, but how this is done is difficult to find out from the present data.

The decision process described above is largely in line with the dominance-structuring model proposed by Montgomery (1983). The tendency to base the selection of a promising alternative on attractive aspects and the rejection of other alternatives on unattractive aspects obviously facilitates the construction of a dominance structure favouring the promising alternative. Moreover, neglecting the non-chosen alternatives and bolstering the chosen alternative in the latter part of the decision process imply that there will be few dominance violations for the chosen alternative. This way of approaching dominance may seem rather primitive. In an earlier discussion of the dominance-structuring model (Montgomery, 1983), it was assumed that the normal way of approaching a dominance structure is to eliminate dominance violations that actually have occurred. By contrast, the subjects in the present study seem to have facilitated their choices by simply preventing dominance violations to occur. How typical this is for real-life decisions remains to be investigated. However, it seems safe to conclude that the present results generally support the dominance-structuring model, including the idea that different decision rules may serve various local functions in the search for a dominance structure. Finally, it can be concluded that it is possible to get interesting results by the computer-based process-tracing technique used in the present study.

The evaluation in the final part of the decision process mostly concerned new attributes to which Ss had not attended earlier in the process. Across all Ss, 44 out of the 71 evaluations of the chosen alternatives in the final part of the records concerned new attributes. The corresponding frequencies for the most attended non-chosen alternative were 25 'new' evaluations out of a total of 37 evaluations. For the repeated evaluations, there was no significant difference between the 'first' and the 'repeated' evaluations. This implies that the differentiation between the chosen and non-chosen alternatives in the final part of the decision process was mostly due to 'new' evaluations, since these evaluations were more common than the 'repeated' evaluations.

It may be asked whether the tendency to more favourable evaluations of the chosen alternative, as the decision process proceeded, is the only cause of the choice of that alternative or if it is also an effect of a preliminary choice of the chosen alternative before the final choice is made. To differentiate between these possibilities, the eligibility ratings were used as data on preliminary choice in the process. For each S the alternative with the highest eligibility rating after ten trials was identified irrespective of whether this alternative was chosen later or not. The evaluation of that alternative in the remaining part of the record was compared with the evaluations of the other alternatives in the same part of the record. From this comparison we excluded all cases where the S repeated an evaluation made on the first ten trials of an alternative on a given attribute. Sixteen Ss had sufficient data for this comparison. It was found that the alternative with the highest eligibility rating on the average was significantly more positively evaluated than the other alternatives on the trials used for the comparison, $t(15) = 2.35$, $p < 0.05$, mean difference being 0.18 on the 0–1 scale. This result is compatible with the idea that Ss in the later part of the decision process tended to facilitate a final choice of a tentatively chosen alternative. Hence, the tendency to increasing differentiation between the chosen and the non-chosen alternatives towards the end of the decision process may be an effect of a preliminary choice of the finally chosen alternative. (It may be noted that the final choices were spread fairly evenly across all five alternatives. This implies that the results discussed above could not be due to specific characteristics of a particular alternative.)

REFERENCES

Klayman, J. (1983). Analysis of predecisional information search patterns. In P. C. Humphreys, O. Svenson, and A. Vàri (Eds), *Analysing and Aiding Decision Processes*, North-Holland and Akadémiai Kiadó, Amsterdam/Budapest.

Montgomery, H. (1983). Decision rules and the search for a dominance structure: towards a process model of decision making. In P. C. Humphreys, O. Svenson, and A. Vàri (Eds), *Analysing and Aiding Decision Processes*, North-Holland and Akadémiai Kiadó, Amsterdam/Budapest.

Montgomery, H., and Svenson, O. (1983). A think aloud study of dominance structuring in decision processes. In R. Tietz (Ed..). *Aspiration Levels in Bargaining and Economic Decision Making*, Springer-Verlag, Berlin.

Payne, J. W., and Braunstein, M. L. (1978). Risky choice: an examination of information acquisition behavior, *Memory and Cognition*, **6**, 554–61.

Svenson, O. (1979). Process descriptions of decision making, *Organizational Behavior and Human Performance*, **23**, 86–112.

ACKNOWLEDGEMENTS

This chapter is reprinted from *Acta Psychologica* (1984), **56**, 113–23.

The chapter was supported by a grant from the Swedish Council for Research in the Humanities and Social Sciences.

9

Positive and negative decision frames: A verbal protocol analysis of the Asian disease problem of Tversky and Kahneman

A. JOHN MAULE

Recent research has identified the importance of the 'decision frame' in determining choice behaviour (Kahneman and Tversky, 1979, 1984; Tversky and Kahneman, 1981). The term decision frame has been used to describe the internal representation that an individual has for a particular decision problem and 'refers to the decision maker's conception of the acts, outcomes and contingencies associated with a particular choice' (Tversky and Kahneman, 1981). It has been argued that an individual's decision frame may differ in crucial ways from a formal representation of the problem, thereby leading to inconsistencies in choice behaviour. To illustrate, consider an example used by Tversky and Kahneman (1981). Subjects were presented with the following problem:

> Imagine that the US is preparing for the outbreak of an unusual Asian disease, which is expected to kill 600 people. Two alternative programs to combat the disease have been proposed. Assume that the exact scientific estimates of the consequences of the programs are as follows:
>
> 1(A)   If Program A is adopted, 200 people will be saved.
> 1(B)   If Program B is adopted, there is one-third probability that 600 people will be saved and two-thirds probability that no people will be saved.
>
> Which of the two programs do you favour?

Another group of subjects was given exactly the same cover story but the two

Process and Structure in Human Decision Making
Edited by H. Montgomery and O. Svenson. © 1989 John Wiley & Sons Ltd

programmes were presented in a different way:

2(A)   If Program C is adopted, 400 will die.
2(B)   If Program D is adopted, there is a one-third probability that nobody will
die and a two-thirds probability that 600 people will die.

Whilst the two versions of the problem are formally identical, Tversky and Kahneman report that out of a group of 152 subjects, 72 percent chose the riskless option, 1A, in the first version, which highlights lives saved. In contrast, a second group of 155 subjects was given the second version which highlights lives lost and 78 percent chose the risky option 2B. Since the two versions are formally identical this represents inconsistent behaviour, violating notions of rational choice. Tversky and Kahneman suggest that the two versions induce subjects to adopt different decision frames and explain why this should occur in terms of a new theory of individual choice called *prospect theory*. In prospect theory the decision-making process is divided into two phases: an editing phase responsible for developing a decision frame and an evaluation phase during which the framed courses of action are evaluated as a basis for choice. In the editing phase a number of information-processing operations are assumed to be applied to the problem as presented so as to develop a decision frame. These operations can alter the incoming information in crucial ways. Although Kahneman and Tversky (1979) identify several such operations, one of these, the coding operation, is of central importance in explaining the inconsistencies of choice in the Asian disease problem. The coding operation is assumed to occur when people evaluate the worth of outcomes associated with different courses of action (or what Kahneman and Tversky call 'different prospects'). Evaluation is assumed to occur in terms of changes from a current reference point, rather than each prospect evaluated in terms of its final state of wealth. The preceding experience or immediate context is assumed to define a neutral point which acts like an anchor. Subjects are assumed to assess value in terms of changes from this neutral point and this is in contrast to traditional utility theories, which describe outcome in terms of total wealth. Thus any prospect has the potential to lead to a gain, loss, or to maintain the status quo, and this is crucial in the activity of framing. In addition, the amount of the gain or loss is important, and Kahneman and Tversky present a hypothetical value function that relates the amount of gain or loss to the subjective value for an individual. This function is illustrated in Figure 1.

While a full description of this function is not included here, there are some important features revelant to the present discussion. In the domain of gains the curve is concave such that the difference between £50 and £100 is of greater subjective value than the difference between £950 and £1000. This explains why, given a choice between a riskless prospect of £800 for

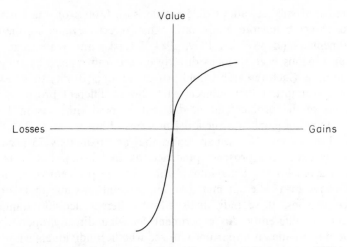

Fig. 1 A hypothetical value function. (After Tversky and Kahneman, 1981.)

sure and a risky prospect of £1000 with probability 0.8 and £0 with probability 0.2, individuals prefer the riskless prospect. The two prospects are formally equivalent in terms of expected monetary pay-off, but the concave shape of the value function leads to a risk-averse preference. Risk aversion in the domain of gains is a robust finding across many different choice situations (Tversky and Kahneman, 1981).

In contrast to this, in the domain of losses the situation is reversed. Consider the reverse gamble involving choice between a riskless prospect of a sure loss of £800 and a risky prospect of a loss of £1000 with probability 0.8 and a loss of £0 with probability 0.2. As argued above, the subjective value of the certain prospect is higher, but since this is a loss rather than a gain, the prospect is more aversive, so subjects are risk seeking and choose the risky prospect. Tversky and Kahneman (1981) reported many examples of subjects exhibiting risk-seeking behaviour in the domain of losses. Thus, for the Asian disease problem presented earlier, the reference point for the first version is that everybody dies, with each prospect associated with possible gains from this. The second version assumes a reference point where nobody dies and the two prospects maintain this or are associated with losses. Thus subjects are expected to be risk averse in the first version and risk seeking in the second, a prediction supported by the data.

Prospect theory considers other elements of choice situations like subjective probability. However, the present paper focuses exclusively on the extent to which the theory provides a satisfactory account of the Asian disease problem and so these other elements will not be considered. Although prospect theory does provide an explanation for what might otherwise appear inconsistent behaviour, there are some problems with this account. First, previous research has inferred that subjects adopt different decision frames on the basis of an analysis of choice behaviour alone, rather than directly evaluating the frames used (Kahneman and Tversky, 1979, 1984; Tversky and Kahneman, 1981). There is an obvious need to focus directly on the frames used by subjects in choice situations. Such research would provide an opportunity to assess more directly the assumption that subjects who choose different prospects in the two versions of the problem adopt different frames, with version 1 of the problem in terms of gains and version 2 in terms of losses.

Second, Tversky and Kahneman report that approximately 75 per cent of their subjects chose the prospect predicted by the theory, but there is no explanation given for the behaviour of the other 25 per cent or what leads them to behave in a different manner. One can only assume that, for some unspecified reasons, these individuals adopt different decision frames and thereby choose differently. An experiment focusing directly upon decision frames should provide an opportunity to see whether individuals who behave inconsistently with respect to prospect theory use different frames. Finally, Tversky and Kahneman present data from experiments using a between-subjects design, though a stronger test of the theory is possible using a within-subjects design. The former design considers only choice behaviour for one version of the problem per subject, yet the theory predicts how subjects should choose across both versions. These authors do mention that within-subjects experiments have provided support for the theory, but do not present any supporting data. It is important to determine how many subjects show a reversal of preference when given both versions of the problem and the present experiment uses a within-subjects analysis of the Asian disease problem to assess this.

Though there is a clear need for a direct evaluation of the decision frames used by subjects, such research raises certain methodological problems, given that this requires identifying the internal representation that an individual has for a particular problem. These issues have been discussed by researchers investigating human problem-solving behaviour (e.g. Newell and Simon, 1972), where the use of verbal protocols has been advocated. Subjects are required to think aloud as they solve a problem and this provides the basis for identifying the internal representations associated with problem-solving activity. Though there has been much disagreement concerning the reliability and validity of this methodology, Ericcson and Simon (1984) argue that the concurrent verbal protocol, in certain situations, may provide an appropriate method. The present experiment required subjects to provide concurrent think-aloud protocols while they performed the Asian disease problem. The two versions of the problem were presented on separate occasions and the protocols were analysed to assess the decision frame in each case. It was predicted that:

(a) Those subjects who behave consistently with prospect theory, choosing different prospects in the two versions of the problem, should reveal different decision frames in each case, with gains highlighted in version 1 and losses highlighted in version 2.

(b) Those subjects who behave inconsistently with respect to prospect theory should reveal different decision frames from those whose choices are consistent with the theory.

In addition, the experiment will include a comparison of choice behaviour founded on between and within-subject analyses.

METHOD

Subjects

Twelve subjects were recruited from the student population at Huddersfield Polytechnic. None of them had any previous experience of decision theory or decision research.

Materials

Three decision problems were adapted from, and in the case of the filler problems simplified as compared with, those used by Tversky and Kahneman (1981). Each version of the problem was typed on a separate sheet of paper. Though the two versions of each problem were equivalent, one was constructed in terms of the domain of gains (DG), the other the domain of losses (DL). One of the problems was the Asian disease problem outlined above and this was the major focus for analysis. However, two further problems were presented so as to make it less likely that subjects would recognize the problems in the second session and remember the response given in that session. The other two problems were as follows:

Problem two

Imagine that you face the following pair of concurrent decisions. First examine both alternatives and then indicate the one you prefer:
Version 1 (in the domain of gains)
A) A sure gain of £250.
B) A 25% chance to gain £1000 with a 75% to gain nothing.

Version 2 (in the domain of losses)
A) A sure loss of £750
B) A 75% to lose £1000 with a 25% to lose nothing.

Problem three

Which of the following options do you prefer?
Version 1 (in the domain of gains)
A) A sure win of £36
B) An 80% chance to win £45 with a 20% chance to win nothing.

Version 2 (in the domain of losses)
A) A sure loss of £36
B) An 80% chance to lose £45 with a 20% chance to lose nothing.

Procedure

Subjects attended two sessions and were presented with a different version of each problem at each session. The sessions were at least two weeks apart, thereby minimizing memory for choice on the earlier version of the problem. Versions of the problem were counterbalanced across sessions and the order of problems within a session was randomly determined.

In both sessions subjects were asked to provide think-aloud protocols as they were solving all of the problems. Instructions required subjects to read the problem aloud and then to say aloud all that came into their minds, whilst solving the problem, regardless of whether it appeared of relevance. They were told that a prolonged period of silence would lead to a prompt from the experimenter. Instructions outlined the need to identify the preferred course of action and that there were no right or wrong answers; rather, it was a matter of judgement. Although protocols were taken for all three problems, analysis was undertaken only for the Asian disease problem.

RESULTS

The first part of this section considers subject's choice behaviour, while the second describes the analysis of the protocols generated when solving the Asian disease problem.

Choices between the risky and riskless options

Table 1 presents details of the number of subjects choosing the riskless and the risky alternatives for each version of the three problems. In each case a relatively high percentage of subjects preferred the riskless option for version 1 (assumed to be framed in terms of gains), while a relatively high percentage preferred the risky option for version 2 (assumed to be framed in terms of losses.) These findings are consistent with those reported by Kahneman and Tversky (1981).

A within-subject analysis was undertaken to determine how many subjects showed the reversal of preference in choice behaviour across the two versions

Table 1   The number of subjects choosing the riskless and risky alternatives for the two versions of each of the three problems

	Problem 1		Problem 2		Problem 3	
	Version 1	Version 2	Version 1	Version 2	Version 1	Version 2
Riskless alternative	10	5	12	1	9	4
Risky alternative	2	7	0	11	3	8

of the same problem. For problem one, six subjects showed this reversal, eleven subjects for problem two and seven subjects for problem three. However, subjects who showed a reversal of preference for one problem did not always show this pattern with the other problems. Two subjects failed to show a reversal for any of the problems, three subjects showed one reversal, five showed two reversals, and two subjects showed a reversal of preference for all three problems. It is perhaps interesting to note that across the three problems there were only three instances of reversals in the opposite direction (i.e. choosing the risky alternative when the problem was framed in terms of gains and choosing the riskless alternative when framed in terms of losses). Thus reversals were much more likely to be in the direction predicted by prospect theory.

The within-subjects analysis does provide support for prospect theory with between 50 and 93 per cent of subjects showing the reversal in preference across the two versions of the three problems. However, this does raise the problem of explaining the basis of choice for the remaining subjects and identifying the reasons for these differences. The analysis of the verbal protocols was undertaken to investigate these issues.

Analysis of the verbal protocols

The verbal protocols generated during the Asian disease problem were transcribed from audio-tape to typescript and then, following the procedure outlined by Svenson (Chapter 4 in this volume), broken down into units. Svenson suggests that protocols should be divided into short elementary units of meaningful text so that the frequency of each type of unit can be established. However, the present analysis was simpler than those considered by Svenson since it involved identifying the presence of certain key words and synonyms of these words. A pilot study indicated that judges found this easier when the words were embedded in relatively larger units, and so larger units were used for the present analysis. All protocols were retyped with double spacing and one unit typed per line. Examples of protocols formatted in this way are presented in Appendix 1.

The number of words contained in each protocol was used as a measure of protocol length and this provided a basis for comparing the protocols across the two versions of the task. The mean number of words per protocol for version 1 of the problem was 76 and version 2 was 93. This difference just failed to reach statistical significance using a related T-test ($T = 1.808$, 11d.f.).

The next phase of the analysis involved identifying the frames used by the subjects. Despite the fact that Tversky and Kahneman (1981) provided a definition of the decision frame, it is not at all clear how this should be operationalized to allow details of a frame to be identified from a verbal protocol. In the present experiment two schemes were developed. The first of these involved counting the frequency with which subjects referred to saving and losing lives. Tversky and Kahneman argued that subjects frame the two versions of the problem in terms of gains (i.e. saving lives) and losses (i.e. losing lives), so words relating to the saving and losing of life should reflect the adoption of these different frames. It was predicted that the frequency of usage of these words should be different across the two versions of the problem. Two judges were given instructions to read the 24 protocols, underlining each word or group of words which referred to saving or losing life, putting an S or L in the margin next to the underlined word(s). Judges were given the 24 protocols in two different random orders and having completed the analysis independently, discussed and resolved any differences. Judges disagreed in 11 of the 24 protocols, in nine cases disagreement was over one statement, and in two cases over two statements. The discrepancies were readily resolved since in most cases they were identified as errors of omission by one or other of the judges. In addition to the words 'saving' and 'losing', judges also identified other words as relevant, including 'survived', 'kill', 'loss', and 'die'.

The mean number of occasions that subjects referred to saving or losing life for each version of the problem is illustrated in Table 2. A Wilcoxon test was used to compare the frequency of saving and losing statements for each version of the problem separately. For version 1 there was a significant difference ($T = 7$, $p < 0.01$), showing that subjects generated more saving than losing statements. The reverse was true for version 2 of the problem, with subjects generating more losing than saving statements ($T = 12$, $p < 0.05$). Insofar as these statements in the protocol reflect the decision frame, the findings support the notion that subjects adopted different frames when completing the two versions of the problem. There were some interesting individual differences, with some subjects using only saving or losing words within a particular protocol while others used both classes of words. Discussion of these differences is deferred till a second data analysis scheme is outlined in the next section.

Table 2 The average number of words or group of words concerned with saving and losing life included in the verbal protocols for the two versions of the Asian disease problem

	Saving	Losing
Version 1	3.6	1.2
Version 2	1.75	3.7

A second, *post hoc*, scheme for data analysis was undertaken following an initial review of the protocols. A feature of some of the protocols appeared to be the inclusion of statements relating to the moral issues involved in saving and losing lives, including such statements as 'there is a question of morality in this one really' or 'it's like playing God isn't it'. The same two judges were given the 24 protocols in a different random order and asked to underline each word or group of words indicating moral issues. There was a high level of agreement between the two judges (a total of four discrepancies) and following discussion between the judges these discrepancies were resolved. For version 1 of the problem just one example of moral principles was identified across the twelve protocols. For version 2, the protocols of five subjects contained moral issues with an average of 1.8 statements per protocol for these five subjects. While it is dangerous to infer too much on the basis of so few subjects, it does appear that version 2, highlighting loss of life, is more likely to induce subjects to include moral issues in their conceptualization of the problem. The importance of this element of the decision frame becomes clear in the next section concerned with individual differences.

Analysis of individual differences

A detailed analysis of the relationship between framing effects and choice behaviour was undertaken by examining the performance profiles for each subject. These profiles are illustrated in Table 3 giving details of the frame adopted by subjects and their choice behaviour for both versions of the problem. On the basis of the protocol analysis it was possible to classify the frames used by the subject into three categories:

G. Gain frames where the key words identified by judges were *only* words involving saving life and thereby the gains associated with the problem.
L. Loss frames where the key words identified by the judges were *only* words involving losing life and thereby the losses associated with the problem.

Table 3   A profile of performance for each subject across both versions of the Asian disease problem, including a classification of the frame adopted (G = gain frame, L = loss frame, B = frames showing evidence of both gains and losses), whether moral principles were identified (M where this was the case) and subject's choice behaviour (RA = choice of riskless alternative, RS = choice of risky alternative)

Subject	Version 1		Version 2	
	Frame	Choice	Frame	Choice
1	G	RA	L/M	RA
2	G	RA	L/M	RA
3	G	RA	L	RT
4	B/M	RT	B/M	RT
5	G	RA	L/M	RA
6	G	RA	B	RA
7	G	RA	L	RT
8	B	RA	L	RT
9	G	RA	B/M	RT
10	B	RT	B	RA
11	G	RA	L	RT
12	G	RA	L	RT

B. Frames where the key words identified by the judges were of *both* kinds, indicating that both gains and losses were features of the decision frame. It was sufficient that just one of each type of word(s) be present in the protocol for it to be classified in this way.

In addition, any one of these three types of frame could also include moral issues and these were indicated by the letter M. In appendix 1 are three protocols which illustrate the G, L, and B frames, with the B frame example also including evidence for moral principles. Table 3 also includes details of subject's choice behaviour in terms of whether they were risk averse (RA) or risk seeking (RS).

Reference to Table 3 shows that, for version 1 of the problem, the majority of the subjects (nine) adopted a G frame and were risk averse. This supports prospect theory in demonstrating that version 1 induced subjects to frame the problem in terms of gains and to choose the riskless alternative. The other three subjects adopted a B frame and two of these were risk seeking (choice behaviour inconsistent with prospect theory). It appears that a G frame is strongly associated with risk aversion, whereas a B frame is not strongly associated with either of the two alternatives.

Version 2 of the problem provides a more complicated performance profile. Only four subjects adopted an L frame as predicted by prospect theory and in each case they were risk seeking, as predicted by the theory. The other eight subjects adopted more elaborate frames by including moral issues in an L frame (three), adopting a B frame (three), or moral issues in a B frame (two). These frames were not apparently strongly associated with choice to one or other alternative. Thus when subjects adopted an L frame, unaffected by moral issues, both frame and choice behaviour was consistent with the theory. However, elaboration in terms of either moral issues or an appreciation of both gains and losses represents a more complex frame than that assumed by prospect theory, and choice behaviour does not show the strong tendency for risk seeking assumed by the theory.

The preceding analysis revealed many instances of subjects adopting frames and choosing alternatives that were inconsistent with the predictions of prospect theory. A different way of investigating these inconsistencies was considered in terms of how subjects justified their choices. Within each protocol it was possible to identify a statement or statements implying the moment of choice and some justification for that choice. These statements were identified by the experimenter and are listed in appendix 2 for those subjects who behaved inconsistently. While a full analysis of these statements is inappropriate, there do appear to be some interesting trends. For instance, if we consider version 1 of the problem for subject 10, the analysis of the complete protocol revealed that this subject adopted a B frame. However, the choice/justification part of the protocol presented in appendix 2 includes only L statements and the subject's choice behaviour was risk taking. Prospect theory assumes that framing in terms of loss is associated with risk taking and so this finding is consistent with the theory. A similar finding is evident for subjects 4, 6, 9, and 10 for version 2 of the problem. In each case the choice/justification part of the protocol is associated with either G or L statements alone, and choice behaviour risk averse or risk taking respectively. Appendix 2 also contains examples where this is not true, i.e. subjects 2 and 5 for version 2 (in each case L statements associated with risk seeking), and examples that are impossible to resolve (subjects 1 and 11 for version 2 of the problem).

While any further analysis of these data is inappropriate, it does highlight an important issue as to whether the whole or only part of the verbal protocol is more representative of the decision frame adopted by a subject. Most definitions of the decision frame imply that all the subject's conceptions of acts, outcomes, and contingencies are a vital feature of the frame (Tversky and Kahneman, 1981). However, a subject may transform, restructure, or simply forget some of the information and it may be that protocol statements closer in time to the moment of choice may more accurately reflect the kind of information that has informed that choice. At present it is impossible to resolve this issue and it seems more appropriate to base further discussion on an analysis of the complete protocol.

Of the 24 protocols generated across the two versions of the task, thirteen were classified as either L or G frames as predicted by prospect theory, and in all these cases choice behaviour was consistent with the predictions of theory. The major problem is that the other protocols (11 of the 24) indicate that the decision frames were more elaborate, either because they included both gains and losses or because moral principles were identified. In these cases the relation between task version, frame, and choice behaviour cannot be predicted by the theory. The implications of these and other findings are considered in the next section.

DISCUSSION

An important feature of the present study was the different ways in which decision-making behaviour was investigated, including an evaluation of choice behaviour, decision frames, and the relationship between these two. In terms of choice behaviour over all three decision problems, the present findings support previous research, and thereby prospect theory, in demonstrating that the majority of subjects were risk averse across the versions of the problems assumed to be framed in terms of gains, and risk seeking across the versions of the problems assumed to be framed in terms of losses. An alternative analysis was presented in terms of a within-subjects comparison. Rather than evaluating choice behaviour for the two versions independently, this analysis identified those subjects who showed the predicted reversal of preference across the two versions of a particular problem. This showed a lower level of support for the theory, though a majority of subjects demonstrated the reversals as predicted. Both the between- and within-subjects analysis provided support for prospect theory, given that decision frames can be inferred on the basis of choice behaviour. It was an evaluation of this inference which was the principle issue when analysing the verbal protocols.

A major aim of the present study was to analyse the verbal protocols so as to identifying the frames used when subjects were completing the Asian disease problem. In prospect theory it is argued that subjects frame one version of the problem in terms of gains, the other in terms of losses. The protocol analysis, summarized in Table 3, revealed that for the majority of the protocols (13 of the 24) the problem appeared to be framed in terms of either a gain or a loss. In these cases, framing in terms of gains only (i.e. G frames) occurred with version 1 of the problem and was always associated with choice of the riskless alternative. Framing in terms of losses only (i.e. L frames) occurred with version 2 of the problem and was always associated with choice of the risky alternative. This pattern of problem version, frame, and choice behaviour represents strong support for prospect theory.

However, the theory has difficulty in handling the remaining eleven protocols, where, in each case, the decision frame was more elaborate than a simple representation in terms of either gains or losses. In some instances the frames contain information in terms of both gains and losses (i.e. B frames), whereas in other cases the frames contain information relating to moral issues. Where subjects adopted these more elaborate frames the relation between version of the problem, frame, and choice behaviour cannot be explained in terms of prospect theory. These elaborated frames occur about equi-often in both versions of the problem and are associated with both risk-seeking and risk-averse behaviour. It appears that the nature of choice behaviour with elaborated decision frames requires an alternative explanation.

Previous research using the Asian disease problem has inferred the frame adopted by a subject on the basis of choice behaviour alone. The present study suggests that in just over half the cases, where subjects use a simple frame, this may be appropriate. However, in just under half the cases, subjects adopt a more complex frame and the relation between choice behaviour and frame is different. This suggests that using choice behaviour alone is misleading. If in the present study we had presented results in terms of a between-subjects analysis alone, the results would have been very supportive of prospect theory (on average, 71 per cent of subjects across both versions of the problem). However, using the protocols to determine the frames used by subjects reveals a lower level of support (50 per cent of subjects adopted the appropriate G or L frame and were risk averse or risk seeking respectively). Some of the subjects whose choices were consistent with the theory appear to have decision frames that are more elaborate than assumed by the theory. It was argued earlier that the relationship between the elaborated decision frames and choice behaviour is not accountable in terms of prospect theory.

The foregoing discussion raises the issue of the extent to which previous research, based on choice behaviour alone, is similarly overestimating the support for the theory. While the present study is limited in both the number of subjects used and the range of problems considered, it does nevertheless suggest an urgent need for further research which focuses directly on the decision frames used by subjects in a broader range of problems.

The preceding analysis is prefaced on the assumption that the verbal protocols provide an accurate way of determining the decision frames used by subjects. The relation between verbal protocols and underlying cognitive activity has been hotly debated, with some critics arguing that it is only the product of thought not the process of thought that is accessible to consciousness (Nisbett and Wilson, 1977). If such a criticism were true it would severely restrict the usefulness of protocols as a means for investigating underlying cognitive activity. Further, there is concern that the act of generating a verbal protocol, while engaging in a cognitive task, may crucially change the nature of the underlying cognitive activity. There has been some refutation of these criticisms (Smith and Miller, 1978; White, 1980; Ericsson and Simon, 1980). Perhaps the most extensive review was presented by Ericsson and Simon (1984), where it was argued that only information in focal attention can be verbalized and insofar as this is an important feature of a task, so a protocol analysis has some validity. Given that the Asian disease problem was unfamiliar to subjects and required them to manipulate very explicit sources of information, it seems likely that focal attention was an important component of choice, suggesting that protocol analysis is a valid method in the present research. However, there appears to be no objective criteria for identifying situations where focal attention is important and thereby where protocol analysis is appropriate.

An additional problem raised by the present study concerns the extent to which all or only part of the protocol is representative of the subject's decision frame. Definitions of the decision frame have been presented in very general terms and do not distinguish between sources of information which are addressed during the decision-making process and those that actually inform choice. In simple choice situations, like the Asian disease problem, this distinction may not be so important. However, it is likely to become more important in complex situations, since these are associated with much more information processing over long periods of time. Resolution of this issue demands a clarification at the theoretical level in terms of a more precise definition of the decision frame, as well as at the methodological level in terms of which part of the protocol should be analysed. There is a need for future research to address these issues.

In conclusion, the present study has provided some support for prospect theory in suggesting that the tendency for risk aversion in the domain of gains and risk seeking in the domain of losses is due to framing effects. In particular, the relation between problem version, frame, and choice behaviour was consistent with the theory in just over half the cases. However, this was not so in just under half the cases and these exceptions were associated with the subject adopting a more elaborate frame. It appears that it is not possible for prospect theory to predict subjects' choice behaviour in these cases. This conclusion must cast doubt on the generalizability of prospect theory to more complex everyday world decision situations, since the complexity of these might be expected to be associated with decision frames that are more elaborate than simple gains or losses.

In addition, the results do suggest that a direct evaluation of decision frames may be useful in understanding the differences between subjects who do and do not make decisions according to the predictions of prospect theory. The findings do suggest caution when interpreting the decision frame on the basis of choice behaviour alone, since, for some of the subjects in the present experiment, choice behaviour did not provide a reliable basis for determining the frame adopted. The present experiment does highlight the importance of considering and directly evaluating the frame used by decision makers, though the conclusions are limited by the small number of subjects tested.

REFERENCES

Ericsson, K. A., and Simon, H. A. (1980). Verbal reports as data, *Psychological Review*, **87**, 215–51.
Ericsson, K. A., and Simon, H. A. (1984). *Verbal Protocol Analysis*, MIT Press.
Kahneman, D., and Tversky, A. (1979). Prospect theory: an analysis of decision under risk, *Econometrica*, **47**, 263–91.
Kahneman, D., and Tversky, A. (1984). Choices, values, and frames, *American Psychologist*, **39**, 341–50.
Newell, A., and Simon, H. A. (1972). *Human Problem Solving*, Prentice-Hall.
Nisbett, R. E., and Wilson, T. D. (1977). Telling more than we can know: verbal reports on mental processes, *Psychological Review*, **84**, 231–59.
Smith, E. R., and Miller, F. D. (1978). Limits on perception of cognitive processes: a reply to Nisbett and Wilson, *Psychological Review*, **85**, 355–62.
Tversky, A., and Kahneman, D. (1981). The framing of decisions and the psychology of choice, *Science*, **211**, 453–8.
White, P. (1980). Limitations on verbal reports of internal events: a refutation of Nisbett and Wilson and of Bem, *Psychological Review*, **87**, 105–12.

APPENDIX 1

Subject 1

Well on program A 200 people will be saved whatever happens

but on B there's a one-third probability that they will be saved and two thirds probability that nobody will be saved

right well I think I would opt for program A

because definitely that way 200 will be saved

on program B you've only one-third chance that they all will be saved

but on B you've a two-thirds chance that nobody will be saved

so I would tend to play safe and at least be sure that some survived

Generated during version 1 of the problem

Frame classification: G (i.e. only saving statements)

Subject's choice behaviour: Riskless alternative

Number of words in protocol: 94

Subject 7

Well A there is a one-third probability that nobody will die

well I'd have to adopt program A

because at least you have a chance that nobody will die

in program B you're gambling with 400 people

I'd have to risk program A

I could be forgiven if I made a wrong decision

then my excuse would be that I was not sure that 600 people would die

Generated during version 2 of the problem

Frame classification: L (i.e. only losing statements)

Subject's choice behaviour: Risky alternative

Number of words in protocol: 82

Subject 9

Well I'd go for program A

because we are talking about peoples lives now

I think you just couldn't take an option where it is definitely known that 400 people will die

it would be much better if you could hopefully save all the people

the two-thirds probability that 600 people will die means that probably that 400 people will die

but at least you gave them a chance in program A hopefully

that is what it seems like to me in this question

Generated during version 2 of the problem

Frame classification: B (i.e. both saving and losing statements) and inclusion of moral principles

Subject's choice behaviour: Risky alternative

Number of words in protocol: 85

APPENDIX 2

The following are statements implying choice and justification for choice for those subjects whose framing and choice behaviour was inconsistent with prospect theory. All statements have been edited so that program A refers to the riskless alternative and program B the risky alternative.

Version 1 of the problem (domain of gains)

Sub 4 (B frame, risk-taking choice behaviour): 'I think I would go for program B and risk the one-third probability that you can save the whole 600.'

Sub 8 (B frame, risk-averse choice behaviour): 'I'd say program A was more of a safe bet .... That's it I'd choose program A.'

Sub 10 (B frame, risk-taking choice behaviour): 'You are definitely going to lose 400 so I'd go for program B.'

Version 2 of the problem (domain of losses)

Sub 1 (L/M frame, risk-averse choice behaviour): 'Well I'd have to choose A then because it's too high a risk is B really.'

Sub 2 (L/M frame, risk-averse choice behaviour): 'I think I'd choose A that 400 people will die.'

Sub 5 (L/M frame, risk-averse choice behaviour): 'Because it's dealing with human life I would have to choose program A because I wouldn't like it to be on my conscience that my gamble failed and more people died.'

Sub 6 (B frame, risk-averse choice behaviour): 'So I think I'd go for program A. At least you would know that you are definitely saving 200 people.'

Sub 10 (B frame, risk-averse choice behaviour): 'Well in this problem I would go for the sure gain of 200. Basically I see the problem as you've got a one-in-three chance of saving everyone or you can definitely save 200. In this situation I would go for the definite saving of 200 people. The one-third probability is not high enough to offset the chance of saving 200 people.'

Sub 11 (B frame, risk-taking choice behaviour): 'Well I think I'd choose program B. Go for the 600.'

Sub 4 (B/M frame, risk-taking choice behaviour): 'Still I'd probably take the risk of option B. I'd hope that nobody would die, though I couldn't live with my conscience if the other probability happened.'

Sub 9 (B/M frame, risk-taking choice behaviour): 'Well I'd go for program B because we are talking about people's lives now. I think I just couldn't take an option where it is definitely known that 400 people will die. It would be much better if you could hopefully save all the people . . . but at least you gave them a chance in program B hopefully. That is what it seems like to me.'

10

Preselection, uncertainty of preferences, and information processing in human decision making

TADEUSZ TYSZKA

INTRODUCTION

This paper summarizes findings of three experiments on information and evaluation processes in decision making. All three experiments addressed the question: how does a person who is to make a decision search the information on choice alternatives? Additionally, one of them was designed to trace how such a person processes both descriptive and evaluative information.

Several years ago, when describing the information search process in the postdecisional phase, Festinger (1957) contrasted it with the features of acquiring information in the predecisional phase. He wrote:

> ... One may further expect that such a person will search for information in an impartial way. He will not select one type of information in order to accept it and avoid information of another type. Rather he will be motivated to acquire knowledge about all aspects and all alternatives ... (Festinger, 1957, p. 127).

Such a view was commonly accepted by those who believed that human decision behaviour was fundamentally rational.

The concept of a decision maker's unbounded rationality and its implication for predecisional information acquisition has been called in question by Simon (1957). His concept of bounded rationality and satisficing principle implied, among other things, that the decision maker acquires a limited amount of

Process and Structure in Human Decision Making
Edited by H. Montgomery and O. Svenson. © 1989 John Wiley & Sons Ltd

information. Indeed, the satisficing principle requires that the decision maker examines alternatives one by one, whether a given alternative meets his/her requirements, and eliminates any alternative that is unsatisfactory in at least one respect; the first alternative that meets all the requirements is accepted. Such a strategy allows that some alternatives are eliminated quite early and hence that the decision maker has not to acquire information about all aspects and all alternatives.

More recently, Montgomery (1983; see also Chapter 2 in this volume) developed the concept, according to which the decision process starts from searching for a promising alternative (or alternatives). When such an alternative is found, the later phase of the decision process consists in testing whether it really dominates the others. Thus, a positive preselection among choice alternatives is postulated. Under these assumptions both information and evaluation processes in the second phase of decision making might reveal the same tendencies as in the postdecision phase: partiality and selectivity of information searching and a biased appraisal of choice alternatives.

As the evaluation process continues, every theory of choice assumes that decisions are based on preferences of the decision maker. Whatever has been postulated in various approaches on the shape of human preferences (the decision maker compares alternatives with each other or he/she evaluates an alternative according to some external standards), it is usually assumed that these preferences are certain, unambiguous, and consistent. In other words, it has been assumed that the decision maker knows what he/she wants and what he/she prizes more and what less, and that he/she can consistently compare various likes and dislikes.

Two objections have been raised against these assumptions. March (1978), when further developing the concept of bounded rationality, denies all these characteristics of human preferences in many contexts. He claims that people do not have very clear and consistent systems of value on which they base their preferences. Several observations on preference reversals as a result of only minor changes in the problem formulation or in the naming of the alternatives (Fischhoff, Slovic, and Lichtenstein, 1980) seem to support this claim.

Another objection may be raised against the assumption that the process of evaluation of alternatives is unbiased. Festinger (1957) observed that in the post-decisional phase people's opinions are hardly impartial. He stated that after making a choice, a person not only selectively receives information on choice alternatives but also begins to assess alternatives one-sidedly. After making a choice, the discrepancy in attractiveness grows between the chosen and the unchosen alternative. This takes place either through an increase in the attractiveness of the alternative choice, or through a decline in the attractiveness of the alternative rejected, or through both of these things at once.

Assuming a preselection process, as postulated by Montgomery (1983), implies that a biased appraisal of alternatives may occur prior to making an overt decision. Indeed, Montgomery (1983) mentions various forms which, on the one hand, lower the attractiveness of an alternative and, on the other, raise its attractiveness. For example, the decision maker can lower (or raise) the value of a certain attribute with respect to which a promising alternative is worse or better than some other alternative. He/she can reduce or exaggerate the difference between two alternatives on some attributes. (Even in the case of such an easily measurable attribute as money the difference of, say, $100 can be felt differently, depending on what we think we can acquire for this amount.) One can use arguments of the probabilistic type, e.g. that it is not certain whether a given negative consequence will occur at all. One can finally 'manufacture' additional positive or negative evaluations based on making inferences about some features based on other features.

The three experiments will be summarized here. They have been published separately, and will be referred to as experiment 1 (cf. Engländer and Tyszka, 1980), experiment 2 (cf. Tyszka, 1985), and experiment 3 (cf. Tyszka, 1986). All of them addressed the question of limited and selective information acquisition by the decision maker. Two mechanisms responsible for this selectivity have been traced: negative and positive preselection of alternatives. Experiment 1 was of an exploratory character. In experiment 2 a limited amount of available information was manipulated by the experimenter. This as well as the character of initial information about alternatives (negative, positive, and mixed) were two variables whose impact on selectivity of information acquisition was tested. Experiment 3 dealt with the familiarity of the decision maker with the decision task. Assuming that subjects unfamiliar with the decision task would display uncertain preferences, we aimed to check how this uncertainty influenced both information search and decision strategy. Because of the character of this book the applied process-tracing techniques will be described in some detail before summarizing the results.

METHOD

In all three experiments the information-search tracing technique was employed, and in one of them it was combined with the think-aloud technique. Two types of information-searching techniques were utilized. In two experiments (1 and 3) the subjects were confronted with the letter labels of the choice alternatives, and were simply allowed to ask any questions on each of the alternatives before making a decision among these alternatives. Thus, no attributes were imposed on the subjects. Instead, alternatives had been described in advance, in sufficient detail to meet any possible question asked by the subject. The experimenter was accompanied by an assistant (or assistants) whose task was to provide the subject with the required information according to prearranged descriptions. The subject then decided what and how many questions were answered. A session ended when the subject made his/her choice. All the subject's questions were tape recorded.

Additionally, in experiment 3 subjects were asked to 'think aloud', i.e. to say everything that came to their minds. Furthermore, after the assistant had answered each of their questions, the subjects were asked to evaluate the information supplied (if they did not happen to do so spontaneously).

In experiment 2 a totally different information-search technique was utilized. At first, unlike previous experiments, it was the experimenter who defined attributes on which the alternatives could be described. Thus the subject was given an information board, as shown in Table 1.

There were three sets of initial information on the choice alternatives:

Set p, denoted by circles in Table 1, contained information on some positive characteristics of the alternatives.

Set n, denoted by asterisks in Table 1, contained information on some negative characteristics of the alternatives.

Set pn contained both the information of set p and of set n.

The attributes 1 to 6 in Table 1 were arranged for each subject individually according to their order of importance for the respective subject, 1 being the most important attribute and 6 the least important one.

Faced with the given set of initial information, the subject was told to assume that he/she was going to make a choice among the six alternatives. Before doing this, however, he/she was permitted to learn about twelve further characteristics not given in the table. He/she was asked to indicate which twelve entries of the table he/she wanted to be shown. On completion he/she was given another sheet containing the same set of initial information and again asked to indicate some entries. This time, however, only six entries were allowed. Actually, no required information was given to the subject; instead, he/she was asked to make a tentative decision on the grounds of the limited initial information (Table 1).

In experiments 1 and 2, in which students of architecture served as subjects, two decision tasks were used in each experiment: (a) selection of one out of six jobs for architects and (b) selection of one out of six books in architecture to be published. In experiment 1 all the subjects attended two sessions, each containing one decision task. In experiment 2 the first session was only used for eliciting the subjects' rank order of importance of the attributes. In the second session the subjects were assigned to one of two groups. One group was given set n and then set pn in the editorial decision task and set p and pn in the task of job selection. The second group was given set p and set pn in the first decision task and sets n and pn in the second decision task.

Experiment 3 followed a 2×2 factorial design. The factors were the subject's profession—architect or engineer (car designer)—and type of task—choice of one of five flats versus choice of one of five cars. Thus, the independent variable

Table 1 Initial information on choice alternatives (Tyszka, 1985)

Alternatives	Attributes					
	1	2	3	4	5	6
A_1	Not fully satisfactory*		Satisfactory°		Very good°	
A_2	Very good°		Non-satisfactory*	Satisfactory°		
A_3		Satisfactory°		Not fully satisfactory*		
A_4	Non-satisfactory*		Very good°			
A_5				Good°		
A_6		Not fully satisfactory*			Satisfactory°	Very good°

Entries marked by * have been revealed in one experimental version while entries marked by °, in other experimental versions.

in this experiment was familiarity with the decision task, defined as correspondence between the subject's profession and the type of decision task.

RESULTS

Information search

In order to define how evenly subjects questions were distributed over choice alternatives, a special index of variability of this distribution was introduced. This index was defined as: $V = (\sigma/\bar{X}) \times 100$, where σ is the standard deviation and $\bar{X}$ is the mean of the distribution.[1] The lower the index, the more evenly distributed are the questions.

1. In all three experiments we found the average indices of variability to be rather high, which means that questions asked by the subjects were highly concentrated on a few alternatives only.
2. It was the chosen alternative which almost always attracted the greatest number of questions (experiments 1 and 3).
3. Similarly, in experiment 3 we found that subjects' descriptive and evaluative statements tended to focus on a few alternatives only.
4. Perhaps the most intriguing finding of experiment 1 was that subjects did not always asked about the same attributes of different alternatives. Instead, they asked different questions for different alternatives. (Imagine, for example, that someone choosing between two films asks whether film A contains elements of humour and whether film B contains erotic elements.) There were several subjects whose patterns of information searching consisted of such incomparable questions. Making a decision based on such unparallel information is evidently inconsistent with any model of rational behaviour. However, it makes sense when the decision maker already has some predetermined picture of the alternatives and is searching for additional information to supplement or confirm this picture.
5. In experiment 2 we found a significant effect of the type of initial information (positive versus negative) on the variability of distribution of questions over the alternatives. The variability increased noticeably, i.e. questions were concentrated on fewer numbers of alternatives, in situations where the initial information contained negative characteristics.
6. The variability of distributions of questions was also significantly higher under the condition of a smaller amount of available information (six questions allowed) than in the case of more (twelve) questions allowed. This means that a greater limitation in the amount of information available did

---

[1] An even better measure is simply the entropy of the distribution: $H = \Sigma^n - p \log p$. In experiment 3 we used this measure.

not simply cause the subjects to acquire proportionally less information about each alternative, but made them limit the number of alternatives examined, i.e. they concentrated on a smaller number of alternatives, presumably the most promising ones.

7. In experiment 3 an additional analysis of types of transitions between two successive questions was completed. These types have been distinguished by Jacoby *et al.* (1976) and Payne (1976):

Type 1. The next question concerns the same attribute as the previous one and is addressed to a different alternative; this corresponds to acquiring information by attributes.

Type 2. The next question concerns a different attribute than the previous one and is addressed to the same alternative as the previous one; this corresponds to acquiring information by alternatives.

Type 3. The next question concerns a different attribute than the previous one and is addressed to a different alternative than the previous one; such transitions, if they were numerous, would show lack of any orderliness in acquiring information.

Tables 2 and 3 show data from two subjects on the pattern of questions on alternatives A to E (F is the column designating questions concerning all alternatives at the same time). The numbers on the left side stand for the coded number of a question[2] and their sequence corresponds to the sequence of questions asked. Table 2 roughly corresponds to acquiring information by attributes while Table 3 corresponds almost ideally to acquiring information by alternatives. We found a distinct tendency for information acquisition by alternatives rather than by attributes. This tendency was stronger in the second half of questions asked.

8. The tendency to search information by alternatives rather than by attributes was stronger for subjects dealing with familiar tasks than for those facing unfamiliar decision tasks.

Descriptive and evaluative information processing

Using the verbal reports of experiment 3 we have classified various statements into several categories. First, we distinguished statements which referred to facts (descriptive statements) from those referred to evaluation (evaluative statements). Both categories were further classified according to whether the statement was absolute, i.e. describing or evaluating an alternative according to some external standard, or whether it was comparative, i.e. comparing it with some other alternative. The evaluative statements were classified further according to their evaluative sign: positive versus negative evaluation.

[2] The coded numbers concern various attributes. Successive digits indicate attributes of different levels of generality.

Table 2 Pattern of information searching of subject A–C1

Aspects	Alternatives					
	A	B	C	D	E	F
0060						×
0020						×
2020						×
3030						×
0030		×				
0070	×		×	×	×	
0130	×		×	×	×	
0132	×		×	×	×	
0132	×		×	×	×	
0040	×			×		
0060			×			
0060				×	×	
1010	×			×		
1020	×			×		
0020	×			×		
3020	×			×		
3020					×	
	9	1	5	10	6	4

9. It was found that the majority of descriptive and evaluative statements of the protocols were of the absolute rather than comparative type. Thus, information was processed for each alternative separately rather than by comparing alternatives with each other.

10. The ratio of comparative to absolute types of statements was higher for groups with unfamiliar tasks than for groups with familiar tasks.

11. Subjects facing less familiar tasks focused their evaluations on fewer alternatives than those familiar with the task. It may be suggested that they were more inclined to limit their evaluative judgements by concentrating on a few alternatives only.

12. The proportion of positive evaluations was higher in groups less familiar with their tasks than among those more acquainted with the task. Thus, those unfamiliar with the task were more positive about the choice alternatives.

13. In all experimental groups we found hints of biased appraisal of choice alternatives. Several protocols ended with the subject emphasizing the

Table 3 Pattern of information searching of subject I-C5

Aspects	A	B	C	D	E	F
			Alternatives			
1100	×					
3030	×					
0130	×					
0020	×					
0023	×					
0040	×					
1100		×				
3030		×				
1010		×				
0040		×				
0130		×				
0030	×					
3170		×				
1100			×			
3030			×			
0040			×			
0030			×			
3170			×			
0033			×			
0040			×			
3030			×			
0030				×		
3030				×		
0040				×		
3030					×	
0040					×	
0030					×	
0060			×		×	
0040					×	
2020					×	
0050						×
0050	×					
	7	7	9	3	6	1

advantages and positive evaluation of the alternative chosen. The ratio of positive to negative evaluations for the chosen alternative was higher in most instances for the second half of the decision process than for the first half. Explicit de-emphasizing of negative aspects of the chosen alternative was observed in some instances.

DISCUSSION

The findings listed above leave no doubt about the selective and unequal interest of the decision maker in various choice alternatives. Information search and processing in decision making is characterized and affected by the fact that there is a negative as well as a positive preselection of alternatives.

Findings 1 and 3 of our experiments demonstrate explicitly that Festinger's contrast quoted at the beginning of this chapter was completely amiss. Different choice alternatives are not investigated with the same care. Some are omitted from the very beginning, others are examined with a few questions only, and some are searched out quite thoroughly. This result has also been documented in many other experiments (cf. Dahlstrand and Montgomery, 1984; Payne, 1976) and is consistent with both mechanisms that were discussed in the introduction, i.e. elimination of alternatives that appear unsatisfactory in some moment of their examination and positive preselection of some promising alternative(s).

Our finding 5 explicitly demonstrates that knowledge of the negative characteristics of some choice alternatives increases the decision maker's concentration on a few alternatives. This is evidently due to negative preselection (elimination of some alternatives). Moreover, findings 7 and 9 fit well to the characteristics of the satisficing strategy: the subjects tended to acquire information by alternatives rather than by attributes, and they processed this information for each alternative separately rather than by comparing alternatives with each other.

On the other hand, the mechanism of positive preselection is suggested by finding 2, where subjects concentrate their attention on the finally chosen alternative, and by finding 6, where under a limited amount of available information they restrict the number of examined alternatives rather than the number of attributes.[3]

Additionally, finding 4, concerning incomparable information seeking, is also consistent with the concept of testing promising alternatives. Biased appraisal of the alternatives is indicated by finding 13.

The two identified mechanisms may very well be complementary. Either negative preselection may precede positive preselection, as suggested by Montgomery (1983), or both processes may be combined and hence may be

---

[3] However, finding 6 is in apparent disagreement with the experimental results reanalysed by Svenson (1983), who showed that the percentage of available information searched decreased with increasing numbers of alternatives and attributes, and that this decrease was more strongly affected by the increase in the number of attributes than by the increase in the number of attributes. This might be interpreted as higher utilization of the information on a large number of alternatives than on a large number of attributes. It is possible that the inconsistency is due to the fact that in our experiment the subjects were limited in the amount of information available while in experiments discussed by Svenson they could search all of the information provided.

difficult to separate during the process of decision making. Distinct hints of positive preselection were also present in experiment 3 in which the satisficing strategy seemed to dominate the whole process of decision making (cf. findings 7 and 9).

Concerning the evaluation processes our findings support both claims discussed at the beginning of this paper. Subjects' appraisal of the choice alternatives proved to be biased prior to making an overt decision (cf. finding 13). Like selectivity of information acquisition, this is apparently due to preselection of alternatives. We also found apparent evidence of uncertainty in human preferences; this uncertainty affects the decision strategy adopted by the decision maker.

As findings 8 and 10 show, the subjects more familiar with the decision task searched for and processed information consistently with the satisficing strategy, while those less familiar with the task did it to a significantly lesser extent. There are good reasons to attribute this difference to the lack of standards of evaluation in the latter group. This lack of standards of evaluation is probably also reflected by the fact that subjects less familiar with the task were using comparative judgements more often and were focusing their evaluation on fewer alternatives than those subjects more familiar with the task (cf. finding 11).

If this interpretation is correct it indicates that (a) human preferences may be uncertain (in this case due to unfamiliarity) and that (b) this uncertainty of preferences may influence the decision strategy. In particular, the difference in proportion of positive evaluations between our two groups (finding 12) (which is itself an interesting phenomenon) may have its implications for how the decision problem is experienced in the two groups. For those more familiar with the decision task the problem may consist in having to choose only among bad alternatives. Some of the subjects expressed such an opinion directly. For those less familiar with the task, it seemed like a choice among relatively positive alternatives. While the satisficing principle or some other strategy based on elimination of bad alternatives was quite appropriate for the former group, some strategy of comparing positive results could be useful for the latter group.

Two issues which were barely touched on in presented studies seem to be of great interest and worth further study.

One of them is how the preselection process takes place. According to Zajonc (1980), such a process is based on a minimal and very 'rough' global recognition only. In his opinion, this fact follows from the studies in which subjects preferred 'old' stimuli (exhibited earlier) to new ones, even when they were unable to recognize which stimuli were old and which were new. It also turns out that features used in discriminations among stimuli — discriminanda —e .g. brightness, tinge, and saturation in distinguishing colours, are not detectable as factors responsible for preferring — preferenda — colours. Unfortunately, neither Zajonc nor anyone else has been able to define more precisely which features would be responsible for these preferenda.

According to the more orthodox view, recognition precedes preferences. It is the advantage of one alternative over the others with respect to some attribute or attributes that makes this alternative promising. Experiment 2 demonstrated that subjects examined most extensively those alternatives that did not have any manifest negative features and were highly ranked with respect to the important attributes. These observations are in line with the strategies suggested by Montgomery (1983) that the decision maker may use to find a promising alternative.

So far there is no clear idea or empirical findings which would shed light on how this preselection process takes place. In particular, it is not known to what extent the preselection process is based on affect and to what extent it is controlled by cognitive–analytic processes. Perhaps there are situations in which one of these factors plays the dominant role. In this context Reykowski (personal communication) suggested that these two factors should result in a different degree of biased appraisal of a preselected alternative with affective preselection resulting in a more biased appraisal.

Two characteristics of the evaluation processes in decision making, that of biased appraisal of the choice alternatives and uncertainty of preferences, are perhaps interrelated. The most apparent relationship is that uncertainty of preferences should strengthen the tendency to biased appraisal of alternatives. Operations such as emphasizing, bolstering, etc., seem to be easier and more natural under ambiguous and uncertain preferences than under precise and certain ones. This hypothesis seems to be worth further study.

REFERENCES

Dahlstrand, U., and Montgomery, H. (1984). Information search and evaluative processes in decision making: a computer based process tracing study, *Acta Psychologica*, **56**, 113-23.

Engländer, T., and Tyszka, T. (1980). Information seeking in open decision situation, *Acta Psycholgica*, **45**, 169-76.

Festinger, L. (1957). *A theory of Cognitive Dissonance*, Row Peterson, Evanston.

Fischhoff, B., Slovic, P., and Lichtenstein, S. (1980). Knowing what you want: measuring labile values. In T. S. Wallsten (Ed.), *Cognitive Processes in Choice and Decision Behaviour*, Erlbaum, Hillsdale, N.J.

Jacoby, J., Chestnut, R. W., Weigl, K. C., and Fisher, (1976). Prepurchase information acquisition: description of a process methodology, research paradigm, and pilot investigation. In B. B. Anderson (Ed.), *Advances in Consumer Research*, Vol. 3, Association for Consumer Research, Chicago.

March, J. G. (1978). Bounded rationality, ambiguity, and the engineering of choice, *Bell Journal of Economics.* **9**, 587-608.

Montgomery, H. (1983). Decision rules and the search for a dominance structure: towards a process model of decision making. In P. Humphreys, O. Svenson, and A. Vari (Ed.), *Analysing and Aiding Decision Processes*, North-Holland, Amsterdam.

Payne, J. N. (1976). Task complexity and contingent processing in decision making: an information search and protocol analysis, *Organizational Behaviour and Human Performance*, **16**, 366-87.

Simon, H. A. (1957). *Models of Man*, Wiley, New York.

Svenson, O. (1983). Decision rules and information processing in decision making. In L. Sjöberg, T. Tyszka, and J.A. Wise (Eds.), *Human Decision Making*, Doxa, Lund.

Tyszka, T. (1985). Variability of predecisional information seeking behaviour, *Polish Psychological Bulletin*, **16**, 275-82.

Tyszka, T. (1986). Information and evaluation processes in decision making; the role of familiarity. In B. Brehmer, H. Jungerman, P. Lourens, and G. Sevón (Eds), *New Directions in Research on Decision Making*, North-Holland, Amsterdam.

Zajonc, R. B. (1980). Feeling and thinking: preferences need no inferences, *American Psychologist*, **35**, 151-75.

11

Structuring and evaluating simple monetary risks

ROB RANYARD

The way people evaluate monetary risks has traditionally been studied in the laboratory via the 'gamble paradigm'. Subjects are asked either to choose from or to evaluate simple gambles in which small amounts of money can be won or lost. The outcomes depend on a random event with known outcome probabilities. A convenient way to represent monetary risk options is by the decision tree, illustrated in Figure 1. This represents a problem of choice from two win/no-win gambles. Simple gambles like these have been used in a number of experiments. For any alternative, information concerning just two risk dimensions needs to be taken into account: the amount of money that can be won and the chance of winning it. Three of the tasks used in traditional studies are as follows: (a) the selling price task, where subjects are told they 'own' a gamble and they must state the minimum price for which they would sell the right to play it; (b) the binary choice task, where subjects have to choose from a pair the gamble they would rather play, as in Figure 1: (c) the multi-option choice task, in which subjects have to choose from three or more gambles.

Early gamble studies took a behavioural approach (Edwards, 1954, 1961: Tversky, 1969, 1972), empirically testing theories of risky judgement and choice solely in terms of final judgements and choices. In contrast, the analysis of monetary risks to be presented takes the 'cognitive process-tracing' perspective introduced in the landmark papers by Payne, Braunstein, and Carroll (1978) and Svenson (1979). A fundamental methodological assumption is that concurrent and retrospective verbal reports provide valid evidence of the important elements of cognitive activity involved in monetary risk tasks. This change in

Process and Structure in Human Decision Making
Edited by H. Montgomery and O. Svenson. © 1989 John Wiley & Sons Ltd

emphasis does not, however, imply that final judgements and choices are discarded. Verbal reports are used to supplement rather than replace these traditional data.

The theoretical goals of the cognitive process-tracing approach are to describe and explain cognitive processes underlying final judgements and choices. This paper will first describe some of the processes involved in simple monetary risk problems, mainly drawing on the author's own research (Ranyard, 1982, 1987, 1988: Ranyard and Crozier, 1984). It will be shown how people actively restructure the information presented to them in such tasks, and how they utilize an extensive repertoire of information-processing operators to construct their own individual evaluation strategies. The advantages of developing cognitive theory using the gamble paradigm stem from the existence of an extensive body of knowledge about final judgements and choices for gambles. Any new theory can be evaluated with respect to this empirical base and be compared to other theories which try to account for it.

Later sections of the paper will discuss factors which may help to explain why people use the structures and strategies observed in gamble studies, and the generality of the results obtained. These later sections are intentionally speculative, and are intended to suggest directions for future research. Specifically, the following issues will be explored:

(a) the extent to which the selection of information processing operators for structuring and evaluation are under the 'top down' control of task goals, or alternatively stimulus driven by properties of the configuration of information presented;

(b) the properties of simplicity and normative acceptability of problem structures and evaluation strategies, and their cognitive, communicative, and social functions;

(c) the extent to which the structuring plans and evaluation strategies observed in gamble studies are relevant to everyday monetary risk problems.

RESTRUCTURING THE TASK GOAL

Early studies using the gamble paradigm were based on the assumption that people adopt the goal set by the experimenter, i.e. to maximize. In the selling price task, for example, the subject was supposed to set the optimum price—that amount exactly equal to the expected value to him/her of the gamble to be sold. In the choice tasks, the optimal choice was the gamble with the greatest expected subjective value. The maximizing goals in these two tasks were assumed to be equivalent.

However, some evidence from one of our experiments showed how people may restructure the goals of decision or judgement tasks. Ranyard and Crozier

(1984) compared verbal reports in three tasks using simple gamble options as in Figure 1. They compared a binary choice, a multi-option choice, and a selling price task. In the latter, a number of statements people made involved strategic thinking, mainly anticipations of the transaction between the seller and the possible buyer. Subjects seemed to form a preliminary evaluation of the bet and then decide whether they wanted to play it or sell it. They then manipulated the selling price in an attempt to secure their preferred goal. For example, one subject said: 'A good chance here, not a bad payoff, so I'm going to ask quite a bit here because he should be keen to buy that.' Another subject said: 'Bad odds, would I go below £1? 3 to 17 odds, sell for 50p no 30p. I want to get rid, I don't like that one.' These examples show that even when people are urged to maximize they often restructure this goal and set a price directed towards alternative objectives: in the above examples, to either secure or avoid the opportunity to play. This can lead to different goals selected in the selling price task compared to the choice tasks. Such goal differences can lead to differences in information processing and consequently to differences in final choices and bids, perhaps to the extent of producing reversals of preferences (Lichtenstein and Slovic, 1971, 1973).

In fact, a number of writers have argued that people faced with experimental and real-world monetary risk problems are influenced by goals other than maximization. Simon (1955) pointed out that people will often be satisfied with an adequate rather than the best alternative, and he coined the term 'satisficing' for this goal of adequacy. This is related to the goal of reducing cognitive effort—satisficing requires less effort than maximizing. Finally, the goal of choosing an alternative for which a good justification can be made has been emphasized by some authors (for example, Montgomery, 1984, and Chapter 2 in this volume). Giving due consideration to the goals people select is important because as goals vary across individuals and situations, so will information processing.

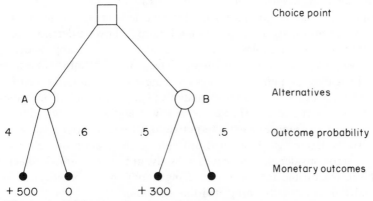

Fig. 1   A decision tree for choice from two win/no-win gambles.

RESTRUCTURING THE INFORMATION DISPLAYED

A number of aspects of the information displayed have been found to influence the kind of restructuring carried out. Huber (1980) showed some effects of both the number of alternatives presented and whether the displayed information was verbal or numerical. Our investigations have found that numerically presented information is routinely restructured by computational heuristics. For example, in the above-mentioned study (Ranyard and Crozier, 1984) three types of computation could be distinguished: rounding, a conversion, or simplification of values on the risk dimensions (as discussed by Kahneman and Tversky, 1979); difference computations, where differences between probability or pay-off values are calculated; and ratio computations, where a ratio of two values is estimated. The percentage of these three types of computations varied across the three tasks mentioned earlier. The selling price task was dominated by rounding, the multichoice task by both rounding and difference computations, and the binary choice task had frequent instances of all three types. The number of alternatives presented in each task was probably a determinant of this pattern of results. In addition, however, the task goal varied and was also likely to have been a factor. The way these two factors might determine how people restructure information using computational heuristics is discussed in a later section.

When more than two options are available, the displayed information can be described in terms of its similarity structure. For example, three simple gambles can be regularly spaced on both money and probability dimensions, or two can be close together but more distant from a third. The effect of similarity structure on preference and choice has been discussed a number of times (see Tversky, 1972, and a review in Payne, 1982). A study of verbal reports while choosing from sets of options with the above two similarity structures revealed a potentially important structuring technique. Quite simply, it was found that some people grouped similar alternatives together prior to evaluation, and this grouping determined subsequent evaluation (Ranyard, 1987).

A study using more complex gambles revealed further structuring plans used in choice problems (Ranyard, 1988). Figure 2 shows a decision tree for a pair of four-outcome gambles used in the study. The way subjects dealt with this relatively complex choice, involving sixteen pieces of information, was as follows. First they simplified the problem using an amalgamation heuristic, as illustrated in the figure. Amalgamation involved grouping similar outcomes (e.g. two wins, or a win and a zero, but never a win and a loss) and adding their probabilities. Thus reduces each alternative to a three or even a two-outcome gamble. In the latter case, illustrated in Figure 2, there are now eight pieces of information to consider, advantages and disadvantages on four risk dimensions. After this restructuring, a strategy comparing money and probability advantages and disadvantages usually completed the evaluation.

Less complex three-outcome gambles were also studied in this experiment.

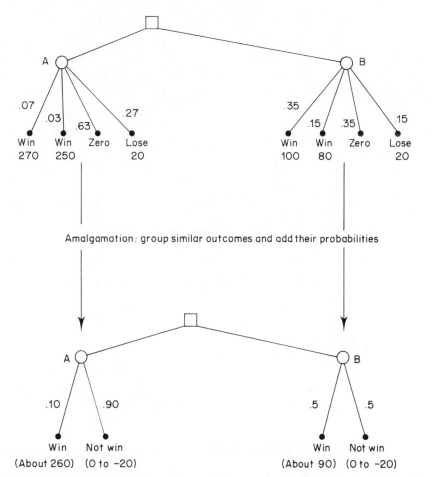

Fig. 2   The amalgamation heuristic applied to a pair of four-outcome gambles, simplifying them to two-outcome gambles.

Pairs as shown in Figure 3 were used, with common losing amounts and probabilities. Some subjects reduced these problems by applying a cancellation heuristic. This is illustrated in the figure, which shows how the common elements of the tree are cancelled and pruned from the tree, leaving it similar to the two-outcome tree of Figure 1.

EVALUATION STRATEGIES FOR CHOICE

Choices and reasons given for choices from pairs of simple gambles like those in Figure 1 revealed a basic evaluation strategy people use (Ranyard, 1982).

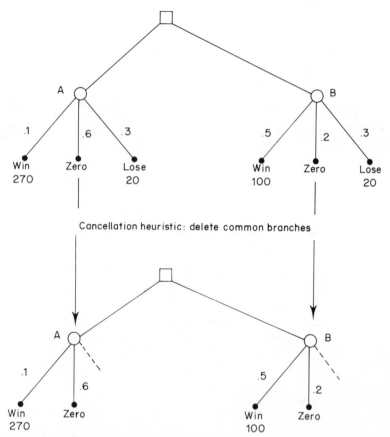

Fig. 3   The cancellation heuristic applied to two three-outcome gambles with common losses and loss probabilities.

This is the non-linear additive difference (NLAD) strategy discussed by Tversky (1969). In the simple context of Figure 1, this involves comparing the money advantage of one option with the probability advantage of the other. It is called non-linear because the subjective evaluations of these advantages are not linear functions of the objective dimensional differences. Intransitive preferences can result from this non-linearity in certain circumstances of NLAD use (Tversky, 1969; Ranyard, 1977). Even so it is a broadly rational strategy making full use of the information available, and may form the basis of evaluation strategies in a wider range of decision contexts.

In the multi-option choice study referred to earlier, two evaluation strategies depending on prior grouping were observed. Consider the example illustrated in Figure 4, in which four risky alternatives are first sorted into two groups of

Initial choice problem

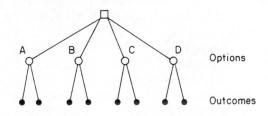

Options grouped by similarity

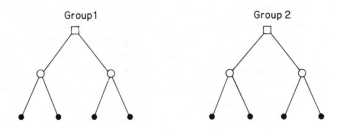

Evaluation round one: choose within each group

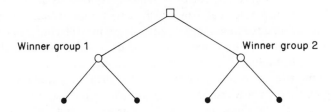

Evaluation round two: choose from round one winners

Fig. 4   The 'World Cup' evaluation strategy applied to choice from four simple gambles.

two similar options. Some subjects in the experiment used a strategy not illustrated in the figure. First they treated the similarity groups as single alternatives and compared them to each other using the NLAD strategy. They then applied the NLAD strategy again, this time to evaluate the alternatives within the group selected at the first stage.

Another subject used the strategy illustrated in Figure 4. It can be called the 'World Cup' strategy by analogy with the evaluation procedure of the soccer tournament (in which teams are put into groups, each team plays every other in the group, and the overall group winners go through to the next round). Having sorted the gambles according to their similarity, the subject chose the best from each group by applying the NLAD evaluation strategy. The group winners went forward to the next 'round' for the final evaluation, where the NLAD strategy was again used.

The function of grouping by similarity is simplification, or problem reduction, as are the previously discussed examples of structuring plans. In this case, it helps the decision maker to organize comparisons between alternatives, a major problem as the number of alternatives increases. Since similarity groupings are common in real-world risk problems, option grouping is likely to be a very useful and widely used problem-reduction technique.

Although the above study only scratches the surface of multioption choice issues, it does lend support to the idea that the NLAD strategy is a basic building block for evaluation in complex problems. The evidence suggests that a preferred structure for choice problems is one in which the advantages and disadvantages of pairs of alternatives can be compared successively. Such a process is only likely to come into its own in the later stages of the decision process. As Montgomery (1983) argues, with even moderately complex problems, many clearly inadequate alternatives may be eliminated early by simple, non-compensatory evaluation strategies. Once a set of promising alternatives remain, however, an efficient evaluation method making use of all the available information may be preferred.

However, the study of three-outcome gambles referred to above (Ranyard, 1988) produced some choice patterns which suggest that evaluation strategies based on comparing advantages and disadvantages may be context dependent. In this study, the common loss amount (see Figure 3) was systematically varied from trial to trial, and found to affect choice. Although some subjects appeared to cancel common losses as shown in Figure 3, and then compared the remaining probability and money advantages, the group choice data was not consistent with this structuring/evaluation model. For the group data, the probability advantage was preferred when common losses were low, but when they were high, preference switched to the money advantage. This suggests a limitation of the NLAD model of evaluation in binary choice. Although some subjects cancelled common losses and based their evaluation on NLAD, others noted the fact that losses were common but took the level of loss into account when comparing advantages. For them, the NLAD strategy was context dependent. This aspect of choice deserves further investigation.

THE CONTROL OF STRUCTURING PLANS

Having illustrated some of the structuring plans and evaluation strategies people employ in simple monetary risk problems, we can now turn to issues regarding their explanation. With respect to structuring plans, an important issue is the extent to which they are under the 'top-down' control of the person's goals or the 'bottom-up' control of properties of the displayed information. The importance of understanding the person's goals in judgement and choice tasks was discussed earlier. The issue of control can be illustrated by considering one interpretation of our findings on the way that the use of computational heuristics varied from task to task (Ranyard and Crozier, 1984). The way the selection of three possible computational heuristics might be controlled, by the basic task goal or by one property of the displayed information, is illustrated in Figure 5. One of the tasks involved the goal of choosing an option. In the selling price task, only one option was presented; in the binary choice task, by definition two options were presented (although they did not in fact have to be presented simultaneously); and in the multi-option choice task three or more options were presented. The arrows in the figure represent how alternative task goals and stimulus conditions might have controlled which computational heuristic was selected in different situations.

The arrows at the top of the figure represent the view that, generally, rounding is selected by the selling price goal and the computations involving more than one option are selected by the choice goal. Additionally, however, it is suggested that rounding may play some role in the choice tasks. This is consistent with the basic finding that the computations involving two options (difference and ratio computations) were not observed in the selling price task, although that involving just one option, rounding, was observed in the choice tasks. Apart from the latter point, the proposed control structure relates to the congruence between the absolute judgement goal of setting a selling price and the relative judgement goal of the choice tasks, and whether the computations involve one or more than one option. The role of rounding in choice tasks requires further investigation.

The arrows at the bottom of the figure represent the view that (a) the presence of a single option triggers rounding, but not computations involving more than one option, (b) the presence of two options triggers the computations involving two options, and (c) the presence of more than two options still triggers the difference computation although the ratio computation is inhibited somewhat.

The particular pattern of control illustrated is consistent with the results of the above-mentioned study. To examine the issue further, task goals and the number of options presented would need to be independently manipulated. For example, the number of gambles presented simultaneously in a selling price task could be systematically varied. If control of structuring was partly under the control of stimulus conditions the hypothesis of Figure 5 leads to the prediction that difference and ratio computations would emerge when two gambles were presented, even though the task was to set a selling price for each separately. Similarly, in choice tasks, gambles could be presented either simultaneously or sequentially. Again this keeps the task goal constant while varying the stimulus

Task goal

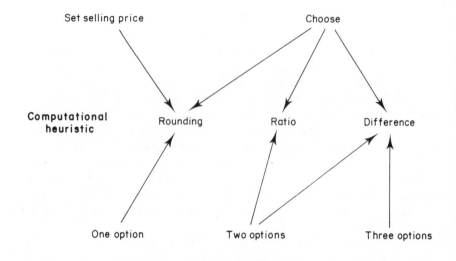

Stimulus condition

Fig. 5   An example of top-down and bottom-up control structuring with computational heuristics.

conditions. If control were to some extent stimulus driven one would predict from the hypothesis of Figure 5 that rounding might increase in the sequential condition at the expense of the other two computational heuristics. Alongside empirical investigations such as this, future research needs to be directed towards the development of more precise, testable theories of control.

SIMPLICITY, NORMATIVE ACCEPTABILITY, AND JUSTIFICATION

Structuring plans applied to choice problems serve cognitive, communicative, and social functions. The same is true of evaluation strategies. As suggested earlier, the specific function of structuring plans is problem reduction or simplification. The cognitive effect of this is that the reduced problem requires less memory load and cognitive effort when it is processed. The communicative function is similar. Any third party who is told about the problem by the decision maker will find the reduced problem easier to comprehend than the unstructured problem. Evaluation strategies are similarly preferred by decision makers if the cognitive effort they require is not too great, and an easy-to-use decision strategy is also easy to communicate. The social function of structuring plans and evaluation strategies relates to the problem of persuading third parties that one's decision is the right one. A simplified problem structure and a simple evaluation strategy can be incorporated into an argument in support of the preferred alternative, helping to make the argument more comprehensible. There are a number of studies which suggest that a comprehensible argument is more persuasive than one that is not (Eagly, 1974; Petty and Caccioppi, 1981, Ch. 3). Thus, three types of benefit can arise from a good choice of structuring plan and evaluation strategy: you can reduce the mental effort you need in making the decision; you can help others to understand your choice; you can improve your chances of persuading people that you have made the right choice. The idea that people might use simple evaluation strategies because they facilitate the justification of choice was first discussed by Slovic (1972, 1975), and also by Tversky (1972). Simplicity, however, does not of itself guarantee the justifiability of an evaluation strategy.

The other important attribute of cognitively and socially useful structures and strategies is normative acceptability. The basic normative requirement for a problem structure is that it is not oversimplified to the extent that important advantages and disadvantages are missed. For an evaluation strategy, the basic normative requirement is that all important advantages and disadvantages are taken into account. The decision maker, therefore, wants to choose a structure and strategy that strikes a balance between normative acceptability and simplicity. This must also be the case if third parties are to be persuaded that one's decision is a good one. However simple a problem structure or evaluation strategy might be, they will not be persuasive unless they are also normatively acceptable. The above considerations point towards an explanation of the use of NLAD-based evaluation strategies in the gamble studies reported above. The multi-option choice example (Figure 4) of grouping by similarity, selection of pairs for comparison by the World Cup method, plus NLAD for specific comparisons, is a good example of a balance between simplicity and normative acceptability of structure and strategy. The grouping structure simplifies the problem yet ensures that no important advantages and disadvantages are missed; the World Cup selection of pairs is efficient in memory requirements and at the same time ensures all options are processed; the NLAD comparison method pays attention to all advantages and disadvantages without, in this context, overloading working memory. Therefore, the processing system facilitates the work involved in making the decision in a normatively acceptable way, and it therefore serves important communicative and persuasive functions as well.

OVERVIEW AND CONCLUDING REMARKS

This paper has illustrated how people actively restructure the task goals and displayed information of simple monetary risk problems. Details of the following specific structuring plans for numerical information were illustrated: rounding, difference, and ratio computations; grouping options by similarity; the amalgamation of similar outcomes; and the cancellation of common outcomes. It was also noted that in choice problems, people often structure the advantages and disadvantages of options relative to each other. This is a prerequisite of the NLAD evaluation strategy commonly observed in gamble choice tasks. The process of restructuring displayed information in the above ways had the following characteristic: although it generally simplified the problem presented, it did not lead to oversimplification and consequent loss of important information. Further research, using cognitive process-tracing techniques and studying real-world monetary risk problems, would usefully extend our knowledge of the structuring plans people apply and the characteristics of such plans.

As indicated above, the common evaluation strategy observed in choice tasks was the NLAD strategy, based on comparing the advantages and disadvantages of alternatives. The strategy was observed in binary and multi-option choice tasks with simple two-outcome gambles and binary choice tasks with three or four possible outcomes. The appraisal of NLAD presented in this paper made the following main points: (a) the strategy has sufficient normative acceptability and simplicity for it to serve a number of useful functions: (b) it may play an important role in complex choice problems; and (c) the evaluation of advantages and disadvantages it involves are likely to be context dependent.

In addition to describing structuring plans and evaluation strategies employed in monetary risk problems, the paper considered two important explanatory issues. The first was the issue of the control of structuring plans: the extent to which they are under the top-down control of task goals or, alternatively, are stimulus drive. Possible control structures were illustrated by an interpretation of some results on computational heuristics (see Figure 5). The second explanatory issue concerned the role of two properties of problem structures and evaluation strategies: their simplicity and their normative acceptability. The cognitive, communicative, and social functions of these properties were illustrated with reference to the World Cup strategy shown in Figure 4. The discussion of these two factors leads to the general conclusion that both need to be incorporated into any thorough-going explanation of the structuring plans and evaluation strategies employed in complex, real-world monetary risk problems.

REFERENCES

Eagly, A. H. (1974). Comprehensibility of persuasive arguments as a determinant of opinion change. *Journal of Personality and Social Psychology*, **29**, 758–73.
Edwards, W. (1954). The theory of decision making, *Psychological Bulletin*, **51**, 380–417.
Edwards, W. (1961). Behavioral decision theory, *Annual Review of Psychology*, **12**, 473–98.
Huber, O. (1980). The influence of some task variables on cognitive operators in an information-processing decision model, *Acta Psychologica*, **45**, 187–96.

Kahneman, D., and Tversky, A. (1979). Prospect theory, *Econometrica*, **47**, 263–80.

Lichtenstein, S. C., and Slovic, P. (1971). Reversals of preference between bids and choices in gambling decisions, *Journal of Experimental Psychology*, **89**, 46–55.

Lichtenstein, S. C., and Slovic, P. (1973). Response-induced reversals of preference in gambling: an extended replication in Las Vegas, *Journal of Experimental Psychology*, **101**, 16–20.

Montgomery, H. (1983). Decision rules and the search for a dominance structure: towards a process model of decision making. In P. C. Humphreys, O. Svenson, and A. Vari (Eds), *Analyzing and Aiding Decision Processes*, North-Holland and Akadémiai Kradó, Amsterdam/Budapest.

Payne, J. W. (1982). Contingent decision behaviour, *Psychological Bulletin*, **92**, 382–402.

Payne, J. W., Braunstein, M.L., and Carroll, J.S. (1978). Exploring predecisional behaviour: an alternative approach to decision research, *Organisational Behaviour and Human Performance*, **22**, 17–44.

Petty, R. E., and Caccioppi, J. T. (1981). *Attitudes and Persuasion: Classic and Contemporary Approaches*, William C. Brown, Dubuque, Ioha.

Ranyard, R. H. (1977). Risky decisions which violate transitivity and double cancellation, *Acta Psychologica*, **41**, 449–59.

Ranyard, R. H. (1982). Binary choice patterns and reasons given for simple risky choice, *Acta Psychologica*, **52**, 125–35.

Ranyard, R. H. (1987). Cognitive processes underlying similarity effects in risky choice, *Acta Psychologica*, **64**, 25–38.

Ranyard, R. (1988). An empirical evaluation of some information processing models of risky decision making (submitted for publication).

Ranyard, R. H., and Crozier, W. R. (1984). Reasons given for risky judgement and choice: a comparison of three tasks. In P. C. Humphreys, O. Svenson, and A. Vari (Eds), *Analysing and Aiding Decision Processes*, North-Holland, Utrecht.

Simon, H. A. (1955). A behavioral model of rational choice, *Quarterly Journal of Economics*, **59**, 99–118.

Slovic, P. (1972). *From Shakespeare to Simon: Speculations—and Some Evidence—about Man's Ability to Process Information*, ORI Research Monograph 12(2), Oregon Research Institute, Eugene.

Slovic, P. (1975). Choice between equally valued alternatives, *Journal of Experimental Psychology: Human Performance and Perception*, **1**, 280–7.

Svenson, O. (1979). Process descriptions of decison making, *Organizational Behaviour and Human Performance*, **23**, 86–112.

Tversky, A. (1969). Intransitivity of preferences, *Psychological Review*, **76**, 31–48.

Tversky, A. (1972). Elimination by aspects: a theory of choice, *Psychological Review*, **79**, 281–99.

12

Information search and decision making: The effects of information displays

GUNILLA A. SUNDSTROEM

A central assumption underlying most process-oriented research on decision making is that the way information is acquired indicates which decision rules are used (Olshavsky, 1979; Payne, Braunstein, and Carroll, 1978; Svenson, 1979). In general, two main techniques are used in process-tracing research: verbal reports (as, for instance, used by Payne, 1976a) and/or information display boards (Herstein, 1981; Van Raaij, 1977, 1983, among others). Verbal reports have been discussed extensively by Nisbett and Wilson (1977), Ericsson and Simon (1984), and Payne (1980). This chapter makes use of different information display boards and considers the effect of these and task complexity on choice behaviour. First, a brief description of the technique and an account of relevant results reported in the literature are provided. The results of a study using information boards are then reported and are compared with earlier findings.

INFORMATION BOARDS

Generally, information boards display decision alternatives in an alternative × attribute matrix (Jacoby et al., 1976; Payne, 1976a). Typically, alternatives constitute the rows and attributes the columns of the matrix. The specific information (e.g. aspect of a decision alternative) is usually typed on a card enclosed in an envelope. The decision makers are instructed to use as much information as they need to make a decision. Common experimental manipulations are variation in the number of alternatives and attributes and changes in

Process and Structure in Human Decision Making
Edited by H. Montgomery and O. Svenson 1989 Published by John Wiley & Sons Ltd

the design of the information display board. Another possible experimental manipulation, mentioned by Jacoby *et al.* (1976), is variation in the way alternatives are labelled, for instance use of both real and artificial product names (e.g. Van Raaij, 1977, 1983).

Both Svenson (1979) and Aschenbrenner (1978) reviewed results from studies using information display boards. A common finding in this work is that as the total amount of information available is increased the proportion of information used becomes smaller. Specifically, an increase in the number of alternatives and in the number of attributes results in the use of a smaller proportion of information available (Aschenbrenner, 1978; Svenson, 1979).

A central aspect of the data analysed in process studies concerns the sequence in which information is acquired during the decision process. Use is often made of an index proposed by Payne (1976b), the Payne index (PI). This takes account of the total number of transitions ('paths' from one piece of information to the next), defined as $n - 1$, where n equals the total number of pieces of information acquired. A transition is considered interdimensional if two aspects of the same alternative are examined sequentially (Ta) and intradimensional if the transition is from one value level of an attribute to another level of the same attribute (Td). The index PI integrates these two types of transitions as follows: $(Ta - Td)/(Ta + Td)$. A negative PI indicates the predominance of intradimensional search and a positive index the predominance of interdimensional search. Svenson (1979) and Aschenbrenner (1978) indicate that intradimensional search strategies are those most frequently reported in studies in the field.

The effect of the design of information display boards has been investigated in a few studies. Bettman and Kakkar (1977) used both a setting in which aspects were organized by alternative (alternative-salient format) and a setting in which aspects were structured by attributes (attribute-salient format). They found subjects to process information interdimensionally when the format was alternative salient and intradimensionally when it was attribute salient. Herstein (1981), investigating a binary choice situation, found that when alternatives were displayed attribute saliently information was searched for intradimensionally. When they were displayed alternative saliently, it was also typically searched for intradimensionally, but to a much lesser extent.

DECISION RULES AND INFORMATION ACQUISITION

The main purpose of process-tracing studies is to relate characteristics of information-search patterns to the use of specific decision rules. Payne (1976b) suggested that both variability of information search across alternatives and PI can be used to characterize information-search patterns. Klayman (1984) and Dahlstrand and Montgomery (1984) correctly point out that a single information-search pattern might be compatible with more than one rule. Moreover, decision makers can use more than one rule during a single decision process (Montgomery, 1984; Pras and Summers, 1975). Consequently, the classification of just one rule to an information-search pattern merely indicates which strategy could have dominated throughout the decision process.

In general, decision rules are classified as being either compensatory or non-compensatory. A decision strategy is compensatory when trade-offs between high and low values across attributes are possible. When such trade-offs are not possible, a strategy is considered non-compensatory.

Use of a compensatory rule implies that an equal number of aspects are considered for each decision alternative. If the alternatives differ in the number of different aspects the decision maker considers during the choice process, the use of a non-compensatory rule is inferred.

In the following, the characteristics of the information search patterns likely to be associated with four different decision rules are described (cf. Billings and Marcus, 1983).

Additive linear (AL) rule

According to this rule the subjective worth of each aspect is assessed for each of the alternatives. The assessments for a given alternative are added so as to obtain the alternative's overall subjective worth. A decision is based on an ordinal comparison of overall subjective worths. Application of this rule implies a uniform pattern of interdimensional search, i.e. that an equal number of aspects is considered for each alternative and that alternatives are evaluated sequentially. Consequently the search pattern is dominated by Ta and the variability of the proportion of information searched for across alternatives is zero.

Additive difference (AD) rule

Tversky (1969) described this rule, which involves a pairwise comparison of alternatives. The difference between two alternatives is defined as the sum of differences obtained in the pairwise comparisons. Application of this rule is inferred when a decision maker considers an equal number of aspects for each alternative and information is searched for intradimensionally. In this case Td dominates and the variability across alternatives of the proportion of information search for is zero.

Conjunctive (CON) rule

The decision maker using a conjunctive rule defines cut-off values which the aspects of an alternative must equal or exceed. If an aspect of a given alternative does not meet all the cut-off values adopted, the alternative is eliminated from the choice set. The amount of information examined for different alternatives varies and the search strategy is interdimensional: Ta dominates. The satisficing principle, described by Simon (1955), is a conjunctive rule with the addition to choose the first alternative satisfying all adopted cut-off values.

Elimination by aspects (EBA) rule

Tversky (1972) described this rule, which involves the successive elimination of alternatives. The attributes describing the alternatives are ordered in terms of importance. The most important attribute is chosen and a cut-off value is determined for this attribute. Aspects of alternatives are compared with the chosen cut-off values, alternatives that do not satisfy this cut-off value being eliminated. The decision maker then repeats this process with the remaining attributes, processing them in their order of importance. Use of this strategy implies intradimensional search and thus Td dominates. Since alternatives are successively eliminated, the proportion of information utilized varies across alternatives.

Surprisingly few studies have examined the conditions leading to a change of information-search strategy. In most studies the focus has been on the effect of the number of alternatives and the number of attributes on the information-search pattern. In this way task complexity or information load has been manipulated (Billings and Marcus, 1983; Jacoby *et al.*, 1976; Olshavsky, 1979; Payne, 1976a). Generally, a greater number of alternatives results in a change from compensatory to non-compensatory strategies. A similar effect of the number of attributes has not been reported. The effect of variation of the design of the information display on decision strategies has not been the main focus of studies using different designs of the information display board. Moreover, the significance of the necessity for repeated information retrieval has frequently been neglected. It is possible to classify decision situations according to the need for information retrieval and the type of information retrieval available. At least three situations can be distinguished: (a) information does not have to be externally retrieved once acquired, (b) information has to be externally retrieved each time the decision maker is not able to retrieve the information from memory, and (c) external information retrieval is not possible.

Any given set of instructions used in a process study tends to create one of these situations. For example, subjects in the study reported by Payne (1976a) were allowed to keep a piece of information available once they had acquired it. In contrast, the subjects in the study by Herstein (1981) could only look at one piece of information at a time. The experimental setting determines the relation between the decision process and information search (cf. Aschenbrenner, 1978). Payne, Braunstein, and Carroll (1978) pointed out that the situation in which external information retrieval is unnecessary allows the decision maker to employ a strategy of acquiring the necessary information first and then proceeding to the decision process.

The present study was undertaken in order to assess more precisely the effect on the choice of decision strategy of manipulating the design of the information board and of task complexity. Because of an interest in the role of information retrieval, an experimental situation was chosen in which external information retrieval was possible when called for (situation (b) as described above).

THE EXPERIMENT

Method

Subjects

The subjects were 96 students of the University of Mannheim, recruited via campus-wide ads and paid-for participation.

Design

A $3 \times 2 \times 2$ between-subjects design. Subjects were randomly assigned to one of the 12 experimental conditions.

Decision alternatives

A set of eight decision alternatives (one-bedroom apartments) were constructed with eight attributes, each of these described in terms of four different aspects. The attributes were: type of heating, kitchen facilities, sanitary facilities, size, neighbours, distance to store, distance to the University, and inconvenience due to noise and industrial pollution. The aspects represented partly good qualities (e.g. close to the University) and partly bad (e.g. noisy).

Four sets of alternatives were presented: (a) four alternatives with four attributes, (b) eight alternatives with four attributes, (c) four alternatives with eight attributes, and (d) eight alternatives with eight attributes. Attributes commonly used in newspaper ads, i.e. type of heating, kitchen facilities, sanitary facilities, and size, were used in the sets with four attributes (a,b). Rent was assumed not to differ for the decision alternatives, and was not included in the attribute set. Each subject in a particular experimental condition received the same set of decision alternatives.

Information boards

Three types of information boards were employed: alternative salient, attribute salient, and the standard matrix format.

The alternative-salient board had labels of the apartments (W_1, W_2, ..., W_n) at the top of each column, indicating the alternatives. Each piece of information was typed on an index card and enclosed in an envelope labelled with the name of the attribute (for instance 'distance to the University'). In order to inhibit intradimensional and enhance interdimensional search, aspects of alternatives were randomly assigned to board positions, For example, the aspects '5 minutes to the University' was positioned in the first row for the first decision alternative, and the aspect '15 minutes to the University' was positioned in the second, third, or fourth row for the second decision alternative.

The attribute-salient board had labels of the attributes at the top of each column, envelopes being labelled by apartment number. The principle for positioning specific aspects of alternatives was the same as just described for the alternative-salient information board. For exaniple, if the first aspect of apartment W_1 was in the first row for the first attribute, the second aspect for W_1 was not positioned in the first row of the second column. The attribute-salient board was thus designed to inhibit interdimensional and enhance intradimensional search.

The matrix format corresponded to information boards commonly used: alternatives formed the columns and attributes the rows. The envelopes were not labelled in this condition.

All three types of information boards thus allowed both inter-and intradimensional search. Each subject was presented with one of the three types of information boards.

Procedure

Subjects were seated at a table placed in front of the information board. The way in which the information board was designed was explained to the subjects. They were asked to take a careful look at the board before starting their information search. The general instructions stressed the following: Your task is to choose one of the apartments displayed on the board. You may examine as many pieces of information as you wish, for as long as you wish. However, you are restricted in that you may only examine one piece of information at a time. Subjects were then allowed to examine one index card at a time, and were required to give it back to the experimenter before picking up the next one. After choosing one of the apartments, subjects were asked to write down all the information they could recall about the apartments they had examined. Finally, subjects were to rank-order in terms of importance the attributes describing the decision alternatives, as well as the decision alternatives themselves.

Analysis

All analyses of variance reported below were performed using a $3 \times 2 \times 2$ design with eight subjects per cell. The independent variables were: design of the information board (three levels as described in the method section), the number of alternatives (four and eight), and the number of attributes (four and eight). In all analyses, the three factors were treated as between-group factors. In order to meet the formal requirements for the analyses of variances, raw proportions were subjected to an arcsine transformation.

RESULTS

In the following only data concerning information search will be reported. To enhance the interpretation of results, data in the tables refer to the untransformed data.

Proportion of information used

An ANOVA was performed, using the arcsine-transformed proportion of different pieces of information searched for as the dependent variable. The effect both of a change in the number of alternatives ($F(1, 84) = 4.35$, $p < 0.05$) and of a change in the number of attributes was significant ($F(1, 84) = 7.70$, $p < 0.01$). The mean and the corresponding absolute numbers are displayed in Table 1. Clearly, the condition that encouraged the use of the greatest proportion of the information available was four alternatives displayed with four attributes.

A larger number of attributes and alternatives increases information load. The design of the information board did not have any significant impact on the overall proportion of information used. The obtained proportions are similar to those reported by Payne (1976a).

The relative number of pieces of information searched for more than once (number of pieces of information picked at least twice/total number of pieces investigated) was computed, arcsine-transformed, and served as a dependent

Table 1 Overall proportion of different pieces of information searched for. The numbers in parentheses represent the corresponding absolute numbers. Total number of pieces of information available was: 16, 32, 32, and 64

Number of alternatives	Number of attributes		Mean
	4	8	
4	0.86(13.8)	0.53(17.0)	0.70
8	0.58(18.6)	0.42(26.9)	0.50
Mean	0.72	0.48	

Note. Overall $n = 96$; *per column* $n = 48$; *per cell* $n = 24$.

measure in an ANOVA. The main effect of number of attributes was significant $(F(1, 84) = 8.35\ p < 0.01)$. When the decision alternatives were described by four attributes, 10 per cent of the information was searched for more than once. When they were described by eight attributes only 4 per cent of the information was used more than once. Neither the number of alternatives nor the design of the information board produced a corresponding effect.

Does higher information load lead to fewer attributes being used or to fewer decision alternatives being examined? Two ANOVAs were performed with the arcsine-transformed proportion of displayed alternatives examined and the arcsine-transformed proportion of available attributes used serving as dependent measures. In the first of these two ANOVAs the effect on the relative number of alternatives examined of increasing the number of attributes was significant $(F(1, 84) = 4.54,\ p < 0.05)$. Subjects choosing between alternatives with four attributes averaged 0.97, i.e. almost all alternatives were investigated. Subjects with eight attribute alternatives averaged 0.89. The proportion available of alternatives examined also decreased as a function of the number of alternatives in the choice set $(F(1, 84) = 7.30,\ p < 0.01)$. When choosing between four alternatives subjects averaged 0.96, whereas subjects choosing between eight alternatives averaged 0.89. A non-significant interaction of alternatives indicates that subjects choosing from the alternative-salient board did not reduce the number of alternatives examined when the choice set contained eight alternatives $(F(2, 84) = 2.35,\ p < 0.10)$.

The other ANOVA employing the arcsine-transformed proportion of available attributes used as the dependent measure showed a two-way interaction between the design of the information board and the number of attributes available $(F(2, 84) = 3.07,\ p < 0.05)$; the respective means are displayed in Table 2. As is evident, when decision alternatives are displayed in an attribute-salient

Table 2   Proportion of attributes included in the decision process. Numbers in parentheses represent the corresponding absolute numbers

Information board	Number of attributes	
	4	8
Alternative salient	0.98(3.9)	0.75(6.0)
Attribute salient	0.91(3.6)	0.90(7.2)
Matrix format	0.98(3.9)	0.81(6.5)

Note. Overall $n = 96$; per cell $n = 16$.

way, the number of attributes had no impact on the proportion of attributes used.

The three types of information boards all differed from one another when either four or eight alternatives were displayed, with eight attributes being available (Scheffé, $p < 0.01$). The smallest proportion of attributes was utilized in the alternative-salient condition, the highest in the attribute-salient condition. In general, results are compatible with those reported by Olshavsky (1979) who also noted the exclusion of attributes as their number was increased.

In summary, a higher information load resulted in a general decrease in the relative proportion of information used. The greater the number of attributes, the smaller was the proportion of information examined more than once. A larger number of both attributes and alternatives results in alternatives examined during the decision process was not influenced by the design of the information board; however, the relative number of attributes used was. The attribute-salient information board facilitated the decision maker in using a uniform number of attributes. The matrix format and the alternative-salient display did not have a corresponding effect.

Variability of search and the Payne index

As indicated above, both PI and the variability of search are frequently employed to relate the information-search pattern to a specific decision rule. Two ANOVAs using PI and variability of search (the standard deviation across alternatives of the proportion of information searched for across alternatives) respectively as dependent variables were carried out. A significant effect of the number of attributes on both PI ($F(1, 84) = 11.58$, $p < 0.001$) and the variability of search ($F(1, 84) = 6.20$, $p < 0.05$) was found, whereas the number of alternatives did not have an effect on any of the two dependent measures. The means are displayed in Table 3.

Table 3 Standard deviation (SD) of the proportion of information searched for across alternatives and the Payne index (PI) as a function of the number of attributes available[a]

	Number of attributes	
	4	8
PI	−0.13	0.30
SD	0.34	0.27

[a] See text for explanation of PI.
Note. Overall $n = 96$; *per cell* $n = 24$.

When subjects choose between alternatives described by eight attributes, information search is dominated by interdimensional search; i.e. subjects search information within alternatives but across attributes. The variability of search decreases when eight attribute alternatives are in the choice set. The lack of an effect of number of alternatives on the variability of search contrasts with results reported by Payne (1976a), who found that variability of search increased when subjects had to choose from a larger set of alternatives. In the present study, the design of the information board had no significant effect on either PI or variability of search, which is in contrast with results reported by Herstein (1981) and Bettman and Kakkar (1977). The present results suggest that the decision strategy, and not the design of the information board, is a major determinant of information-search behaviour as characterized by SD and PI.

Decision rule used

As already mentioned, the classification of information search patterns to one of the decision rules described above (AL, AD, CON, EBA) merely indicates which strategy could have dominated throughout the decision process. It does not follow that the search was used consistently throughout the whole decision process.

Subjects were classified as using one of the rules described above (AL, AD, CON, EBA). The classification was done as suggested by Payne (1976b) and by Billings and Marcus (1983). If PI was positive and an equal proportion of information was searched for across alternatives (SD across alternatives of the proportion information searched for equals zero), the pattern was classified as being compatible with AL. If PI was negative and variability of search was zero, use of AD was assumed. When the proportion of information searched for across alternatives differed and PI was positive, use of CON was inferred. Finally, if PI was negative and variability of search was not zero, use of EBA was assumed. For example, if PI for a subject was -0.75 and SD was greater than zero, the information search pattern was classified as being compatible with EBA. All information search patterns except four could be classified. These four patterns had to be excluded since their PI did not differ from zero. The results are displayed in Table 4.

All subjects except six used a variable amount of information across alternatives, i.e. the majority of search patterns were compatible with a non-compensatory decision rule. The literature suggests a preference for decision rules involving intradimensional search, i.e. use of either AD or EBA. The overall proportion of AD + EBA was 0.44, implying an almost equal distribution of inter- and intradimensional search strategies. An ANOVA was performed with the relative proportion of AD + EBA used as a dependent measure. A zero three-way interaction between the independent variables (the number of alternatives, the number of attributes, and the design of the information board)

Table 4 Classification of information-search patterns as being consistent with the additive linear (AL) model, the additive difference (AD) rule, the conjunctive (CON) rule or with the elimination by aspects (EBA) rule. See text for explanation

	Number of alternatives			
	4		8	
Number of attributes	4	8	4	8
Information boards	1 2 3	1 2 3	1 2 3	1 2 3
AL	2a			1
AD	2	1		
CON	2 3 1b	4 6a 4	2 5 2	6 6a 7
EBA	3 3 5	3 1 4	6 3 6	1 1 1

Note. Overall $n = 92$, per cell, see below.
1: alternative-salient board
2: attribute-salient board
3: matrix format
a: one subject unclassified per column
b: two subjects unclassified per column

had to be assumed in order to obtain an error term. The effect of the number of attributes was significant ($F(1, 2) = 22.24$, $p < 0.05$). When the decision alternatives were displayed with four attributes, subjects averaged 0.63, which implies that intradimensional search dominated in these conditions. When the decision alternatives were displayed with eight attributes, the relative proportion of AD + EB was 0.26. Clearly, then, as the choice set consisted of eight attribute decision alternatives, subjects more often searched for information interdimensionally. This indicates that a change in choice strategy is a function of the number of attributes. The change is from patterns being compatible with EBA to patterns being associated with CON. This finding is in contrast with Payne (1976b), who reported an increase of EBA when a larger number of attributes described the decision alternatives. One possible explanation for the difference between the present results and results reported by Payne (1976b) might be the fact that subjects in the study by Payne were allowed to keep information once acquired, whereas subjects in the present study had to acquire the information again once they could not remember it.

Importance of attributes

Data were collapsed across information-board conditions in computing the mean importance ranking for each attribute. On the basis of these computed means a new rank order was constructed which is displayed in Table 5. Under all the conditions, size was the most important attribute.

When the alternatives were characterized by four attributes, the least important attribute was kitchen facilities. When the alternatives were described by eight attributes, regardless of the number of alternatives, distance to store was the least important attribute.

DISCUSSION

In comparing the results above with major findings in the literature, both similarities and differences are evident. With regard to the factors influencing the amount of available information used, the results are consistent with earlier findings. Both the number of attributes and the number of alternatives have an impact on the proportion of information used. However, the design of the information board did not have a corresponding effect. The relative number of alternatives examined was dependent upon the number of attributes available, suggesting that the different levels of an attribute are represented as aspects in memory, i.e. in direct relation to a specific alternative. The role of the information

Table 5 Rank order of attributes based on the rank orders constructed by subjects. Data are collapsed across information-board conditions

Number of alternatives	Number of attributes	
	4	8
4	4 3 1 2a	4 8 1 7
		3 2 5 6
8	4 3 2 1	4 7 8 3
		1 2 5 6

Note. Overall $n = 96$; per cell $n = 24$.
a 1: heating 2: kitchen 3: sanitary facilities 4: size 5: neighbours 6: distance/store 7: distance/university 8: pollution + noise
Read. The most important attribute is to the left in the first row.

board as an external structuring device was evident in the fact that, in the more complex decision situation, use of the attribute-salient board increased the number of attributes that were considered.

In contrast with the findings reported by Bettman and Kakkar (1977) and by Herstein (1981), the type of information board was not found to have a significant effect on information-search patterns.

With respect to factors influencing the choice of decision strategy, some interesting differences compared with earlier results reported in the literature emerged. First, the predominance reported earlier of strategies involving intradimensional information search (Aschenbrenner, 1978; Svenson, 1979) was not replicated. In the present study, subjects used about an equal number of strategies involving inter- and intradimensional search. This differs from results of Payne (1976a, 1976b), who reported a dominance of strategies involving intradimensional search (AD and EBA).

In the present study the factor having an impact on most of the dependent measures was the number of attributes. In contrast, in the studies of Payne (1976a, 1976b) and Olshavsky (1979), the number of alternatives was the strongest determinant of decision-making behaviour. When alternatives in the present study were described by eight attributes, information-search patterns were consistent with use of the CON rule. Except in the binary choice situation, Payne (1976b) reports a dominance of EBA.

One possible explanation for this major discrepancy between the present results and those previously reported in the literature may be differences in the instructions given. In the present study, subjects were not allowed to keep the recorded information available once acquired, as was the case in the studies reported by Payne. In those studies, subjects did not need to memorize information in relation to a specific alternative. An index card once examined could be used as an external memory device. In the present study subjects had to retrieve the information externally if they were unable to remember it. Why should this generally result in search patterns being compatible with CON instead of EBA? In a situation in which decision makers are forced to memorize information in order to make adequate decisions, it is likely that they will choose a search strategy allowing for as effective memorization as possible. The smaller proportion of repeated search for information when eight attributes described decision alternatives suggests that interdimensional search is more effective for memorization than is intradimensional search.

The findings suggest that the necessity for information retrieval and the type of information retrieval available are crucial aspects in a decision situation. Thus, task complexity is not *per se* the major determinants of information-search patterns. It would appear that in process-oriented decision research involving complex decision situations, greater attention should be given to the aspect of information retrieval.

REFERENCES

Aschenbrenner, K.-M. (1978). Komplexes Wahlverhalten als Problem de Informations-verarbeitung. In H. Ueckert and D. Rhenius (Eds), *Komplexe menschliche Informations-verarbeitung. Beitraege zur Tagung 'Kognitive Psychologie' in Hamburg*, Huber, Bern.

Bettman, J. R., and Kakkar, P. (1977). Effects of information presentation format on consumer information acquisition strategies, *Journal of Consumer Research*, **3**, 233-40.

Billings, R. S., and Marcus, S. (1983). Measures of compensatory and noncompensatory models of decision behavior: process tracing versus policy making, *Organizational Behavior and Human Performance*, **31**, 331-52.

Dahlstrand, U., and Montgomery, H. (1984). Information search and evaluative processes in decision making: a computer based process tracing study, *Acta Psychologica*, **56**, 113-23.

Ericsson, K. A., and Simon, H. A. (1984). *Protocol Analysis. Verbal Reports as Data*, MIT Press, Cambridge, Mass.

Herstein, J. A. (1981). Keeping the voter's limit in mind: a cognitive processing analysis of decision making in voting, *Journal of Personality and Social Psychology*, **40**, 843-61.

Jacoby, J., Chestnut, R. W., Weigl, K. C., and Fischer, W. (1976). Prepurchase information acquisition: description of a process methodology, research paradigm, and a pilot investigation. In B. B. Andersson (Ed.), *Advances in Consumer Research*, Vol. 3, Association for Consumer Research, Chicago, Ill., pp. 321-7.

Klayman, J. (1984). Analysis of predecisional information search patterns. In P.C. Humphreys, O. Svenson, and A. Vari (Eds), *Analysing and Aiding Decision Processes*, North-Holland and Akademiai Kiado, Amsterdam/Budapest.

Montgomery, H. (1984). Decision rules and the search for a dominance structure: towards a process model of decision making. In P. C. Humphreys, O. Svenson, and A. Vari (Eds), *Analysing and Aiding Decision Processes*, North-Holland and Akademiai Kiado, Amsterdam/Budapest.

Nisbett, R. E., and Wilson, T. D. (1977). Telling more than we know: verbal reports on mental processes, *Psychological Review*, **84**, 231-59.

Olshavsky, R. W. (1979). Task complexity and contingent processing in decision making: a replication and extension, *Organizational Behavior and Human Performance*, **24**, 300-16.

Payne, J. W. (1976a). Task complexity and contingent and protocol analysis. *Organizational Behaviour and Human Performance*, **16**, 366-87.

Payne, J. W. (1976b). Heuristic search processes in decision making. In B.B. Andersson (Ed.), *Advances in Consumer Research*, Vol 3, Association for Consumer Research, Chicago, Ill., pp. 321-27.

Payne, J. W. (1980). Information processing theory: some concepts and methods applied to decision research. In T. S. Wallsten (Ed.), *Cognitive Processes in Choice and Decision Behavior*, Erlbaum, Hillsdale.

Payne, J. W., Braunstein, M. L., and Carroll, J. S. (1978). Exploring predecisional behavior: an alternative approach to decision research, *Organizational Behavior and Human Performance*, **22**, 17-44.

Pras, B., and Summers, J. (1975). A comparison of linear and nonlinear evaluation process models, *Journal of Marketing Research*, **12**, 276-81.

Simon, H. A. (1955). A behavioral model of rational choice, *Quarterly Journal of Economics*, **69**, 99-118.

Svenson, O. (1979). Process descriptions of decision making, *Organisational Behavior and Human Performance*, **23**, 86-112.

Tversky, A. (1969). Intransitivity of preferences, *Psychological Review*, **76**, 31-48.

Tversky, A. (1972). Elimination of aspects: a theory of choice, *Psychological Review,* **79**, 281–99.

Van Raaij, W. F. (1977). Consumer information processing for different information structures and formats. In W. D. Perreault (Ed.), *Advances in Consumer Research,* Vol 4, Association for Consumer Research, Chicago, Ill., pp. 176–84.

Van Raaij, W. F. (1983). Techniques for process tracing in decision making. In L. Sjöberg, T. Tyszka, and J. A. Wise (Eds), *Human Decision Making,* Bokförlaget Doxa, Bodafors.

ACKNOWLEDGEMENTS

This chapter is reprinted from *Acta Psychologica* (1987), **65**, 165–79.

13

Change of preferences under time pressure: Choices and judgements

OLA SVENSON

and

ANNE EDLAND

Time is a precious commodity in our lives. The faster things can be done the better it is. This is one of the maxims that seems to be underlying much of contemporary thinking. However, if the time available for a person for the completion of a given task is too short this may be associated with negative consequences both for the person him/herself and for the quality of the performance.

When the time available for a given task is initially unrestricted but is then decreased gradually, this may first lead to increased focusing and mobilization of more resources for performing the task. If the time available is restricted even further this may lead to feelings of time pressure. It seems reasonable to assume that as time becomes shorter this experience becomes more intense, transforming itself into what may be called time stress.

When a discrepancy appears between, on the one hand, what a person would like to do or feels he/she should do and, on the other hand, what he/she actually finds time to do, then feelings of time stress seem likely to appear. It is clear that time stress is not only a matter of the time available but also of, for example, the importance and complexity of the task that has to be processed in relation to other psychological and physiological variables (e.g. Holsti, 1971). Thus, time

Process and Structure in Human Decision Making
Edited by H. Montgomery and O. Svenson 1989 Published by John Wiley & Sons Ltd

stress is a subjective phenomenon which may be associated with high levels of arousal and which may be compared with other types of stress, in particular regarding effects on cognitive processes.

The effects of stress on social, psychological and physiological variables have been a constant research topic for many years. Researchers focusing on the task performed under stress instead of the human reaction in other aspects have typically used relatively simple types of performance tasks such as multiple choice reaction time tasks (Goldberger and Breznitz, 1982).

Easterbrook (1959) reviewed studies of the effects of emotion on cue utilization. The important empirically derived conclusion from such research is that 'when the direction of behavior is constant, increase in drive is associated with a reduction in the range of cue use ...'. The term 'drive' refers to a dimension of emotional arousal or general overexcitement (Easterbrook, 1959, pp.183–4). As mentioned above, time stress may both be assumed to lead to emotional arousal and to less time per information unit processed. Therefore similar effects in terms of reduction in utilization could appear under time stress just as under emotional arousal in general.

Relatively little research has inquired about how stress affects more complex cognitive activities such as choosing among multiattribute alternatives. Several researches claim that psychological stress may influence decision effectiveness, suggesting that cognitive functioning and decision making deteriorate (e.g. 'tunnel vision' and the like) under stress (e.g. Smock, 1955; Broadbent, 1971; Holsti, 1971; Janis and Mann, 1977). However, many of these claims were based on surprisingly little well-controlled empirical results. One of the few studies of judgement and decision making under time pressure was published by Wright (1974), who found that subjects tended to place greater weight on the negative aspects of alternatives when under time pressure. In another study, Ben Zur and Breznitz (1981) asked subjects to choose between two gambles characterized by both positive attributes (amount and probability of winning) and negative attributes (amount and probability of losing). Under time pressure their subjects dwelled more on negative factors, possibly indicating a strategy of avoiding the negative aspects. Zakay and Wooler (1984) studied time pressure, training, and decision effectiveness. For the task they investigated (a multiattribute utility task) training was effective only if decisions were not made under time pressure.

Christensen-Szalanski (1980) studied the effects of time restrictions on the choice of decision strategies and found that simpler strategies were used under time pressure. Zakay's (1985) results similarly indicated that the conjunctive decision rule tended to be used more often under time pressure. Smith, Mitchell, and Beach (1982) investigated the effects of time constraints on the choice between five decision strategies given by the experimenter. The results indicated that for complex processes confidence in the decisions made decreased with time pressure and that when under time pressure moderately complex decision strategies were preferred.

Wright and Weitz (1977) studied the effects of time horizon and time for a decision. They found that subjects who made quicker decisions were more loss averse and used more one-dimensional types of strategies in comparison with those working without any time pressure. In a study of voting behaviour (Hansson, Keating, and Terry, 1974) it was found that time pressure induced more conservative voting as compared to the relatively more liberal voting behaviour of both liberals and conservatives under no time pressure.

Time restrictions may lead to several possible effects on the cognitive processing of a task (cf. Miller 1960). First the process may be speeded up so that the result will be the same (although feelings of time stress may lead to psychological and somatic reactions in the individual). Second, the process may not be speeded up but left when time has run out. In this case the response will be based on the state of the process when interrupted. However, interpretations of data along this line are dependent on specific knowledge or assumptions about the process that is interrupted. Third, the cognitive processes may be altered as a result of the time pressure which will be of primary interest in the present study.

One aim of the study is to find out in detail how the utilization of different attributes is changed under time pressure. In parallel with a general change in weights of the attributes there may be a change of use of specific aspects on the attributes, as Wright (1974) demonstrated. Therefore, a second aim is to investigate whether negative aspects play a greater role under time pressure than they do when there is plenty of time for completing the task. Furthermore, the study aims at testing whether time-pressure effects may be so strong that the majority of a group of decision makers indicates preference for one alternative when given ample time but switch to preference for the other alternative under time pressure. Such a preference-reversal phenomenon would have both theoretical and practical implications.

In the first experiment below subjects were asked to construct pairs of equally valued decision alternatives (student apartments). Using these pairs the effect of time pressure on choices could be investigated in the second experiment. In the third experiment attractiveness judgements of student apartments were related to the changes in choice frequency found in the second experiment.

EXPERIMENT 1

Method

Subjects

Nineteen students of psychology at the University of Stockholm served as subjects in the experiment.

Stimuli

The choice alternatives were student apartments characterized by three attributes: size, travelling time to the University, and housing standard (cf. Svenson and Karlsson, 1986). Size was expressed in square metres, travelling time in minutes for a single trip to the University, and housing standard by the adjectives 'old' or 'modern'.

The choice alternatives were presented in pairs in which one complete alternative was characterized on all attributes whereas information about size was lacking on the other. Table 1 shows a sample stimulus.

In all, 24 pairs of alternatives were presented to the subjects. Table 1 shows the stimuli used as well as the results which will be commented on later. The values in parentheses were determined from the subjects' responses, as described below.

Procedure

Subjects received the paired alternatives of Table 1 in a random order, each appearing on a separate page in a stimulus booklet. The subjects worked at their own pace in a group session. Their task was to fill in a missing value (viz. size) for the incomplete apartment that would make the two apartments equally attractive. They were told that the student apartments to be presented were intended for one person and that they should base their judgements on their own values, imagining that they were single (if this was not the case).

Results

The mean judgements of equivalent size were computed across subjects and appear in Table 2. When plotting the difference in travelling time in a pair (t) against the difference in size (s) chosen to compensate for the difference and creating equally valued pairs, this relation was approximately described by a linear relation: $t = 0.4\ s$ ($r^2 = 0.6$). The effect of standard was not strong enough to warrant separate functions for the old and modern standards respectively.

Table 1 An example of a stimulus in Experiment 1 where subjects were asked to fill ou the open space to make the alternatives equally attractive

A		B	
Size	25 m^2	Size	—
Travelling time	14 min	Travelling time	22min
Standard	Old	Standard	Modern

Table 2 Stimuli used in Experiment 2. Size for constructed alternative indicates means of the judgements inserted in the open alternative to make the alternatives in a pair equally attractive

Complete alternative		Constructed alternative	
Travelling time (min)	Size (m²) Standard	Travelling time (min)	Size (m²) Standard
14	15 Old	22	(20) Modern
14	15 Old	30	(23) Modern
14	15 Old	43	(29) Modern
14	25 Old	22	(26) Modern
14	25 Old	30	(32) Modern
14	25 Old	43	(37) Modern
22	15 Old	30	(19) Modern
22	15 Old	43	(25) Modern
22	25 Old	30	(27) Modern
22	25 Old	43	(32) Modern
22	35 Modern	14	(31) Old
22	48 Modern	14	(41) Old
30	15 Old	43	(20) Modern
30	25 Old	43	(30) Modern
30	35 Modern	14	(28) Old
30	35 Modern	22	(32) Old
30	48 Modern	14	(38) Old
30	48 Modern	22	(41) Old
43	15 Modern	22	(17) Old
43	25 Modern	22	(22) Old
43	35 Modern	14	(25) Old
43	35 Modern	30	(32) Old
43	48 Modern	14	(34) Old
43	48 Modern	30	(41) Old

Thus, the results indicate that in order to tolerate 10 min more travelling time to the University the students wanted on the average 4 more square metres of area in their flats. Only one case (which was eliminated before computing the regression) gave an answer differing from this trend (the first pair with travelling time 43 min for the complete alternative in Table 2).

The equally valued pairs in Experiment 1 were used in the following experiment, which explored the effects of variations of the time available for each decision.

EXPERIMENT 2

Method

Subjects

Sixteen psychology students at the University of Stockholm served as subjects. No one in this group had participated in Experiment 1 but the students were recruited in the same way as those of that experiment.

Stimuli

This experiment used the alternatives produced in Experiment 1. Each pair consisted of one 'complete' and one 'constructed' alternative. The reason for using approximately equally attractive alternatives is that in this way no 'floor' or 'ceiling' effects (e.g. the majority choosing one alternative in a pair) could decrease the power of the experimental design. The full set of 24 pairs of decision alternatives was presented twice. For the first presentation the attribute of travelling time was presented on the top line, size in the middle, and standard on the bottom line; for the second set of 24 pairs, the information was presented in the reverse order. Each pair was printed on a slide for projection onto a screen. The position of the two alternatives (left or right) was randomized as well as the order of presentation of the alternatives.

Procedure

As in Experiment 1 subjects were instructed to make their choices according to their own values, imagining (if necessary) that they were single without any children. When each slide was projected the experimenter announced the number of that pair. The subjects circled the alternative (A or B) that they preferred on the response sheet. The exposure time for each slide was controlled automatically by a timer connected to the projector. Because another slide followed automatically after the preceding one, the subjects were requested to provide their answers within the exposure time available.

A pretest was performed to determine one exposure time that would induce no time stress at all and another time that was sufficient for processing the information but would be associated with feelings of time stress. A separate group of six students was used with eight different exposure times: 3, 5, 7, 9, 11, 13, 15, and 17 seconds. The students were asked to rate the extent to which they felt that they were stressed by the different exposure times. Five seconds was chosen as a stressful exposure time because it allowed reading and processing the material but with feelings of time stress. Fifteen seconds was chosen as a non-stressful exposure time, which generally was not associated with feelings of time stress. Consequently, the sixteen subjects in Experiment 2 were exposed to the stimuli for 5 or 15 s.

Results

Table 3 indicates the differences in experienced stress. The difference before and after the experiment was not significant for the long exposure time group but highly significant for the short exposure time group ($t = 5.977$, d.f. $= 15$, $p < 0.01$)

The order in which the attributes were presented had no effect on the choice of alternative in a pair. This was tested by transforming the choice proportions to Φ (cf. Cohen, 1969) and then applying t-tests for (across stimuli) correlated samples. More constructed alternatives were chosen for both exposure times: (225/384) being chosen in the time stress group ($z = 3.44$, $p \geqslant 0.01$) and (206/384) in the no time stress group (this last ratio was too close to one to be significant in itself, $z = 1.42$). A chi-square test indicated no interaction between complete or constructed alternative and exposure time on choice frequency (chi square $= 1.713$, d.f. $= 1$).

In each pair, one of the alternatives had the better (shorter) travelling time and the other one the better (bigger) size (with one exception mentioned earlier), which was used when describing the subjects' choice behaviour in Experiment 2. The frequency of choosing the alternative with the shorter travelling time was computed for each pair for each of the two conditions (stress and no stress). These proportions were then transformed to Φ which were subsequently used in t-tests. The alternative with the shorter travelling time was chosen in 36 per cent of the choices in the no-stress condition and in 64 per cent (by coincidence adding to 1.0) for the stress condition. Simple t-tests for correlated samples (again across pairs) indicated that this difference in proportions was highly significant ($t = 9.16$, d.f. $= 22$, $p < 0.001$). Thus, under no time stress subjects tended to prefer the apartment with the greater size in a pair and under time

Table 3 Mean ratings of stress levels before and after experiment for two groups of subjects

	Time for each choice	
	5 seconds	15 seconds
Before experiment	48	30
After experiment	115	27

stress the apartment with the shorter travelling time. Both these variables were presented quantitatively so the results do not reflect differences between quantitative and verbal information.

To summarize, the results indicate the following. First the alternative that was 'constructed' (through the subjects' judgements in Experiment 1) to be equally attractive as the complete alternative in a pair was preferred more often than the latter in choices. Second, in the no time stress condition the alternative with the better size and poorer travelling time was preferred most often and the reverse was true in the time-pressure condition, indicating that systematic choice reversals can be induced by time pressure.

EXPERIMENT 3

The difference in choice proportions in Experiment 2 do not give very detailed information about actual differences in the evaluations of the alternatives. One may, for example, ask whether time stress leads subjects to change their evaluations so that a short travelling time looks more favourable or so that a smaller size seems less negative. Experiment 3 elucidates this problem.

In this experiment, attractiveness judgements were collected for single-choice alternatives under time stress and no time stress conditions. A very brief account of the results was presented in another context (Svenson, Edland, and Karlsson, 1985) and full details will therefore be given below in the present study.

Method

Subjects

Thirty-two psychology students of the University of Stockholm participated in the experiment.

Stimuli

This time, apartments were presented one at a time on slides and the levels on the attributes were on travelling time 16, 34, or 64 minutes to the University, on apartment size 21, 31, or 46 m², and the standard was modern, average, or old. In all, 27 different apartments were created by factorially combining the three levels of the three attributes. For half of the group in each condition travelling time was characterized verbally (short, average, or long) and for the other half numerically, with numbers equivalent to the verbal labels (Svenson and Karlsson, 1986).

Procedure

In a pretest it was found that an exposure time of 4 seconds for each apartment allowed subjects to be able to process the information and make their judgements and yet experience time stress. An exposure time of 14 seconds was used for the non-stress condition. Sixteen of the subjects were given 4 seconds and sixteen 14 seconds for their judgement.

In the experiment proper, the random sequence of stimuli was projected onto a screen, each with a constant exposure time determined by a timer connected to the projector. the subjects answered in booklets by marking the attractiveness of each apartment on a horizontal response line. The line was 160 mm long and marked 'very poor' above the extreme left and 'very good' above the extreme right of the line.

As in Experiment 2 the subjects were administered a questionnaire before the session and after it.

Results

As in Experiment 2 there was a significant difference in reported time stress before and after the experiment for the group with the short exposure time ($t = 3.4$, d.f. $= 15$, $p < 0.01$).

The results indicated an overall tendency for the 4 second condition to produce less positive judgements of attractiveness but an analysis of variance (exposure time × numerical–verbal presentation × apartments) showed only a rather weak effect ($F = 3.11$, d.f. $= 1/104$, $p = 0.07$). In Experiment 2 it was clear that alternatives with long travelling times and big size were preferred less frequently under time pressure. Alternatives with either of these characteristics will be analysed first. Thus, an analysis of variance was performed for alternatives with a long travelling time only (exposure time × numerical–verbal presentation × apartments). In the 4 second condition the mean attractiveness judgements of alternatives with long travelling times were significantly lower than in the no-stress condition ($F = 12.58$, d.f. $= 1/28$, $P < 0.01$). A corresponding analysis of alternatives with big size only also indicated a significant effect of time pressure ($F = 10.55$, d.f. $= 1/28$, $P < 0.01$), rending big apartments less attractive under time pressure. This was also the case for apartments with the modern standard only ($F = 11.15$, d.f. $= 1/28$, $P < 0.01$). Following the logic of the design, statistical tests of the differences for small size, short travelling time and old standard were performed but they were not significant ($p < 0.05$). Figure 1 shows the means for apartments with extreme values on the three attributes. For example, the left hand end of the top line indicates the arithmetic mean of all apartments with a long travelling time under no timepress condition. The figure illustrates the above mentioned significant changes but it also provides information about the average effect of varying each of the attributes from one extreme to the

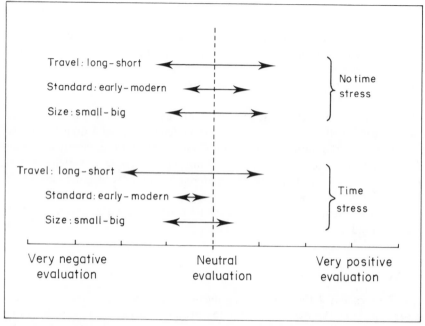

Fig. 1   Arithmetic means across stimuli with the less valued (to the left on each line) or the most valued (to the right) aspect on each attribute for time pressure and no time pressure condition.

other. Thus, under time pressure the effect of varying travelling time increases while the effect of standard becomes very small.

DISCUSSION

The present study has demonstrated that decisions and choices can be affected by time pressure. This effect was strong enough to affect the majority of subjects so that one type of alternative was preferred under time pressure and another type when decision time was unlimited. This change of preference seemed to be the result of subjects becoming more influenced by negative aspects on the most important attribute (travelling time). Another factor that contributed seemed to be the smaller importance given initially to less important attributes (cf. Figure 1) and the increasing importance given to the already initially most important attribute. This is in line with Easterbrook's (1959) findings cited in the introduction.

It was interesting to find that alternatives that were constructed as equally attractive as their counterpart in a pair were on the average chosen more frequently. Differences between ratings and actual choices have been reported before (e.g. Lichtenstein and Slovic, 1971). It is hard to explain this difference in a satisfactory manner with the data available here. There may be purely statistical effects and/or more fundamental psychological processes which could produce this effect.

Although it is unwise to draw any definite conclusions from the results reported here to a wider range of tasks, the effects of time pressure are quite compelling both from an applied and a theoretical perspective. In the applied perspective there are numerous cases in, for example, man–machine interactions where the time available for certain operations plays a crucial role. This holds for rapid decisions and actions like flying an aircraft, as well as for decisions in more slowly reacting systems such as a nuclear power plant. Theoretically, time pressure is related to the use of available resources and stress. Issues such as priorities made between goals and decision rules under time pressure seem to be likely research topics for the future.

REFERENCES

Ben Zur, H., and Breznitz, S. J. (1981). the effect of time pressure on risky choice behaviour, *Acta Psychologica*, **47**, 89-104.
Broadbent, D. E. (1971). *Decision and Stress*, Academic Press, London.
Christensen-Szalanski, J. (1980). A further examination of the selection of problem solving strategies: the effects of deadlines and analytic aptitudes, *Organizational Behaviour and Human Performance*, **25**, 107-22.
Cohen, J. (1969). *Statistical Power Analysis for the Behavioral Sciences*, Academic Press, London.
Easterbrook, J. A. (1959). The effect of emotion on cue utilization and the organizationn of behavior, *Psychological Review*, **66**, 183-201.
Goldberger, L., and Breznitz, S. (1982). *The Handbook of Stress. Theoretical and Clinical Aspects*, The Free Press, New York.
Hansson, R. O., Keating, J. P., and Terry, C. (1974). The effects of mandatory time limits in the voting booth on liberal–conservative voting patterns, *Journal of Applied Social Psychology*, **4**, 336-42.
Holsti, O. R. (1971). Crisis, stress and decision making, *International Social Science Journal*, **23**, 53-67.
Janis. I. L., and Mann, L. (1977). *Decision Making*, Free Press, New York.
Lichtenstein, S., and Slovic, P. (1971). Reversals of preference between bids and choice in gambling decisions, *Journal of Experimental Psychology* **89**, 46-55.
Miller, J. G. (1960). Information input overload and psychopathology, *American Journal of Psychiatry*, **116**, 695-704.
Smith, J. F., Mitchell, T. R., and Beach, L. R. (1982). A cost–benefit mechanism for selecting problem-solving strategies: some extensions and empirical tests, *Organizational Behavior and Human Performance*, **29**, 370-96.
Smock, C. D. (1955). The influence of psychological stress on the intolerance of ambiguity, *Journal of Abnormal Psychology*, **59**, 177-88.
Svenson, O., Edland, A., and Karlsson, G. (1985). The effect of numerical and verbal information and time stress on judgments of the attractiveness of decision alternatives.

In L. B. Methlie and R. H. Sprague (Eds), *Knowledge Representation for Decision Support Systems*, North-Holland, Amsterdam, pp. 133–44.

Svenson, O., and Karlsson, G. (1986). Attractiveness of decision alternatives characterized by numerical and non-numerical information, *Scandinavian Journal of Psychology*, **27**, 74-84.

Wright, P. (1974). The harassed decision maker: time pressures, distraction, and the use of evidence, *Journal of Applied Psychology*, **59**, 555-61.

Wright, P., and Weitz, B. (1977). Time horizon effects on product evaluation strategies, *Journal of Marketing Research*, **16**, 429-43.

Zakay, D. (1985). Post-decisional confidence and conflict experienced in a choice process, *Acta Psychologica*, **58**, 75-80.

Zakay, D., and Wooler, S. (1984). Time pressure, training and decision effectiveness, *Ergonomics*, **27**, 273-84.

ACKNOWLEDGEMENTS

This chapter is reprinted from *Scandinavian Journal of Psychology* (1987), **28**, 322-30.

It was supported by grants from the Bank of Sweden Tercentenary Foundation, the Swedish Council for Research in the Humanities and Social Sciences, and the Swedish fund for Workers' Protection and by grants from the US National Science Foundation to Decision Research. Part of this study was made while the first author was a visiting researcher at Decision Research. The authors wish to thank Baruch Fischhoff, Kerstin Meyerhöffer, Mari Ward, Vivianne Runske, Leisha Sanders, and Paul Slovic for their valuable contributions to this chapter.

Part IV
Societal decision making

Introduction

OLA SVENSON

and

HENRY MONTGOMERY

This part includes applications of decision theoretic approaches to societal decision making. Societal decision making processes are hard to study for several well-known reasons, such as lack of experimental control and difficulties in obtaining relevant data. Often, interesting societal problems are initially ill-structured and the situation is further complicated by the fact that several actors simultaneously are engaged in structuring and restructuring the evolving problem. Thus, the societal decision-making *process* is difficult to study. It is also difficult to find out how societal decision makers *structure* information during the decision-making process. However, as a rule, it is easier to study the structure of a societal decision after the decision process is finished. For example, it is possible to analyse written documents in which decisions are explained and/or justified. This approach is exemplified in three of the contributions to this section (Biel and Montgomery, Crozier, and Gallhofer and Saris). Another *post hoc* approach is illustrated in Biel and Montgomery's chapter, namely to interview politicians and other actors on how they structure a given decision problem in which they have decided for a certain line of action.

An alternative to the *post hoc* approach for studying decision structures is to elicit judgements in a non-decisional setting about components which potentially will be available during the process of making a decision. This approach is illustrated in Nilsson's contribution.

Thus, with an exception for Nilsson's chapter, the data in the present part reflect how decision makers structure information *after* the decision is made. Obviously, such data only give indirect and partial information about how the decisions actually were made. Still, the *post hoc* decision structure will have

Process and Structure in Human Decision Making
Edited by H. Montgomery and O. Svenson. © 1989 John Wiley & Sons Ltd

links back to the actual decision-making process if it is assumed that the structure results from the preceding decision process. Data on *post hoc* structures plus theories about the nature of the links back to the actual decision-making process may provide knowledge about processes and structures leading to the decision. This is a major theme in the present section.

The structuring of a decision problem implies that a cognitive representation of the problem is constructed (cf. Huber, Chapter 1 in this volume; Montgomery, Chapter 2 in this volume). It is typically assumed that elements of this representation provide input to processes or operations that are executed by the individual in order to attain certain goals or subgoals (e.g. the goal to find the best alternative) (cf. Huber, Chapter 1 in this volume; Maule, Chapter 9 in this volume; Payne, 1982). It may now be asked whether or not the representation of the problem changes as a result of processing operations.

In early process-tracing research of decision it was often taken for granted that the structure of the cognitive representation of a decision problem was reasonably stable throughout the process (e.g. Bettman, 1979; Svenson, 1979; Payne, Bettman, and Johnson, 1987). To the extent that this is true, *post hoc* data on decision structures are unlikely to provide any unique information in comparison with data on the psychological predecisional representation of the decision problem. The reason is that in this case, the postdecisional structure has not emerged as a result of the preceding decision-making process but rather reflects a static psychological mental representation. More recently, Montgomery (1983; Chapter 2 in this volume) claimed that decision makers attempt to restructure their initial representation in such a way that one alternative can be seen as dominant and, hence, emerge as the obvious choice. The extent to which *post hoc* decision structures include dominant alternatives may then be used as a verification of the dominance-search model. Moreover, the manner in which a dominance structure has been constructed may give more detailed information about the decision maker's thought processes. (Another and more direct way of testing the model would be to investigate if the cognitive processes preceding a decision, such as information-search patterns and changes of attractiveness judgements, are in line with a process leading to a dominance structure; cf. Montgomery and Svenson, Chapter 7 in this volume.) It should be noted, however, that the dominance-search model is hard to falsify since there are many possibilities of interpreting given data as being in line with a dominance structure (see Montgomery, Chapter 2 in this volume).

Cognitive representations of decisions after they are made also serve the functions of justifying the decision for the decision maker him/herself and to others and of providing arguments for convincing other people to make the same decision.

The Biel and Montgomery chapter illustrates this function of a *post hoc* representation. Here the cognitive representations of decision problems were inferred from interviews and debates about alternative ways of producing energy.

Thus, the decisions were already made by the officials and politicians providing the material. In addition to a representation of the decision problem in terms of alternatives and attributes, Biel and Montgomery introduced causal chains or scenarios comprising instrumental attributes (means) and, at the end of a scenario, goal attributes. The results indicate agreement about goals but disagreement about means in comparisons of politicians and officials with opposed opinions about energy policy. Independently of which energy policy was preferred the scenarios were compatible with dominance for each actor's preferred alternative.

Nilsson also studied causal cognitive representations, in this case between economic variables related to expected inflation (e.g. increased price of raw materials leads to increased wages which leads to increased inflation). Comparing the plausibility of such chains or scenarios of different lengths, he found that longer scenarios were most frequently rates as equally plausible as shorter ones. This contrasts with findings in similar fields where longer scenarios have been found to be more plausible than shorter ones, as pointed out in the chapter.

The structure of a decision or rather a series of decisions after they were made was studied in the chapter by Crozier. In 1978 the British Government decided to invest in the De Lorean sports car. This decision, which was made under tremendous time pressure and involved almost 80 million pounds and a prospect of 2000 jobs in Belfast, turned out to be disastrous. Crozier analysed the Minutes of Evidence issued in 1984 by the House of Commons Select Committee. Here, arguments are made by the civil servants to justify and explain why this very poor decision was made.

The analysis was made using a decision-tree representation, the empirical decision analysis method (cf. Gallhofer and Saris, Chapter 6 in this volume), and organizational decision models. In particular, the arguments for the need to make such a quick decision were analysed. The justification was made possible through a simplified representation of the problem. For example, it is reasonable to assume that De Lorean could not have obtained another offer of support for the factory if the decision had been delayed. This assumption seems to follow from the fact that De Lorean did not consider Northern Ireland with the specific problems in the area at the time. However, this plausible conclusion is not represented in the *post hoc* representation of the problem. The justification is quite compatible with dominance structuring.

When giving reasons for political decisions Crozier claims that political leaders and civil servants are under pressure to present the simplest argument that is acceptable for many audiences, namely that there is no alternative to the course of action recommended. However, this justification may be unacceptable for some kinds of audiences and the second most simple argument for having acted correctly has to be used. In routine decisions this is to refer to the fact that the correct procedure was followed but in more complex situations the rationality of the process has to be demonstrated. The simplest form of rationality is dominance and only if this is not sufficient do more sophisticated reasons have to be given in the process of justification according to Crozier.

The chapter by Gallhofer and Saris presents an analysis of Dutch foreign policy decisions during the period from 1900 to 1955, including classified material. These decisions were analysed through the application of decision trees and exploration of the cognitive represenation of the decision problems as reflected in the documents. In particular, the metric sophistication of this representation was investigated as well as the decision rules used in arriving at the decisions. Thus, although this analysis was *post hoc*, because the data were documents such as telegrams and letters sent during the process of making a decision, this study also provides some insights into the actual decision processes taking place.

The results validated the decision-tree method and indicated that decision rules requiring no metric representation at all occurred most frequently while rules requiring higher metric representations of probabilities and utilities (such as the expected utility rule) were quite infrequent (3 out of 235 cases). Argumentation structures involving metric representations of probabilities were more frequent than such representations for utilities.

Most of the studies in this book analyse decision making as a process monitored by one decision maker. In the field of societal decision making it may also be fruitful to look at societal decision processes as the result of an initial structuring of the problem and determination of preferences followed by a dialogue (cf. Svenson, Chapter 5 in this volume) that determines the final decision. Gallhofer and Saris provide structural representations of this dialogue and Crozier presents data relevant for understanding this process. If data covering this process are unavailable retrospective data giving arguments for different decisions may be of great help, as illustrated in the Montgomery and Biel chapter. Common to the chapters in this part on societal decision making is their strong coupling of theory and data. This is a strength when such difficult problems as societal decision-making processes are studied.

REFERENCES

Bettman, J. R. (1979). *An Information Processing Theory of Consumer Choice*, Addison-Wesley, London.
Montgomery, H. (1983). Decision rules and the search for a dominance structure: towards a process model of decision making. In P. C. Humphreys, O. Svenson, and A. Vari (Eds), *Analyzing and Aiding Decision Processes*, North Holland and Akadémiai Kiado, Amsterdam/Budapest.
Payne, J. (1982). Contingent decision behavior, *Psychological Bulletin*, **92**, 382–402.
Payne, J., Bettman, J. R., and Johnson, E. (1987). Adaptive strategy selection in decision making (unpublished manuscript).
Svenson, O. (1979). Process descriptions of decision making, *Organizational Behavior and Human Performance*, **23**, 86–112.

14

Scenario analysis and energy politics: The disclosure of causal structures in decision making

ANDERS BIEL

and

HENRY MONTGOMERY

The scenario concept has been widely used in discussions about the future during the past decades. At least two different meanings of the concept can be found: an 'external' and an 'internal' sense. Scenarios in the external sense refer to derivations by means of agreed-upon models and are meant to be accurate, complete, and consistent (Norman, 1984). External scenarios are often used in formal planning procedures where they are intended to propose the ranges of possible future developments and outcomes. Scenarios in the internal sense relates to one person's anticipations of future states of the world (Kahneman and Tversky, 1982; Tversky and Kahneman, 1983; Thüring and Jungermann, 1986) and are based on the person's own experiences from the past. Internal scenarios could be expected to be less complete than external scenarios but they are, as we will show, internally consistent.

Along with Axelrod (1976) and Kahneman and Tversky (1982) we believe that people often explore a decision situation by generating causal chains of events that may result from different alternatives. We propose that scenarios could be used to conceptualize how decision makers represent decision alternatives and in particular that they may be employed for analysing causal beliefs held by political decision makers.

Process and Structure in Human Decision Making
Edited by H. Montgomery and O. Svenson. © 1989 John Wiley & Sons Ltd

Below, we first describe a conceptual framework to be used for analysing internal scenarios. The framework is explained in terms of concepts that we have found in previous analyses of data related to decision making in energy politics. The presentation following next supplements and earlier study (Biel and Montgomery, 1986a). Here, we will show in detail how the coding procedure works. The reliability of the coding procedure is checked for two types of data, viz. written speeches and notes from interviews. Thereafter, we show how scenario analysis could shed light on the reasons for disagreements between different parties. Finally, we present a case study purporting to validate scenarios as conceptualizations of how a decision maker represents decision alternatives.

CONCEPTUAL FRAMEWORK

Imagine a hypothetical town where the officials at the municipal energy works, together with leading social democrats, have proposed that present local oil plants should be substituted by one district heating system. The conservatives are not too happy with the suggestion since they would rather extend the use of electricity for heating purposes. The town is faced with two possible *alternatives* or options for its future heating supply. Alternatives are not always mutually exclusive. The problem confronting decision makers may rather be to find the right mixture of alternatives that will contribute to energy production.

For each alternative there are a number of beliefs concerning the outcomes of that alternative. The outcomes could occur at different points in time and could be related to each other in causal chains. The entire set of causal chains that a person expects to result from the implementation of a given alternative is called a *scenario*. According to this definition, a scenario could be structured in many ways. It may consist of only one chain, or of several chains, each of which may split up into different chains. Moreover, the chains in a scenario may be interconnected with each other.

In order to illustrate the concepts in a scenario, some of the consequences anticipated by the social democrats in our hypothetical case are presented in Figure 1.

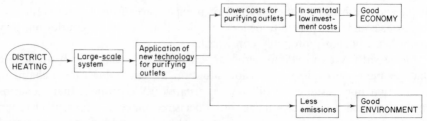

Fig. 1 A scenario showing some consequences of a choice of a district heating system.

The outcomes of the choice of an alternative could be described in terms of a set of *attributes* (e.g. economy and environment). Attributes could take on different values (e.g. good or bad economy) and it should be possible to compare different alternatives on the same attributes.

The attributes are of two types, viz. *goal attributes* and *instrumental attributes*. The goal attributes describe the goals of the decision maker. As a rule, they correspond to the last event in the causal chains of a scenario. The instrumental attributes (underlined in Figure 1) correspond to outcomes that are means for attaining the goals of a given alternative. Thus, instrumental attributes always precede goal attributes in a scenario.

Goal attributes are manifested at different levels of specification. For instance, statements about various types of investment costs, such as costs for purifying outlets, could be regarded as subattributes of the attribute 'investment costs', which in turn is a subattribute of the goal attribute 'economy'. Table 1 gives examples of subattributes which were grouped into particular goal attributes in our analyses.

A subattribute is assumed to be a conceptual specification of a particular goal attribute, and a given subattribute is assumed to be subordinate to one, and only one, goal attribute. This is in contrast to instrumental attributes, which can be combined with several goal attributes. Table 2 lists the instrumental attributes that were indentified in energy politics.

Invariant relations between instrumental attributes and goal attributes are called *causal models* (e.g. large scale leads to good economy). Variations in different persons' causal models are assumed to reflect fundamental differences in their belief systems.

To affect an alternative on a particular attribute the decision maker may take different *policy measures*, such as giving subsidies, raising or lowering taxes or fees, making laws, or taking organizational measures. Policy measures are less pronounced on the local level but were frequent in a study of speeches given by the Swedish Minister of Energy (Montgomery and Biel, 1984).

Table 1 Goal attributes and examples of accompanying sub-attributes reported by Biel and Montgomery (1986a)

Economy	Balance of trade, investment costs, fuel costs, costs for consumers and producers
Environment	Effects on the environment of emissions and waste products
Flexibility	Possibility of using various fuels, possibility of combining one alternative with other alternatives
Safety/vulnerability	Safety in supply of fuel, stability of fuel market, reliability of energy production
Employment	Employment in different regions or sectors
Energy production	Possibility of attaining a desired level of energy production
Freedom of choice	Possibility for the consumer to choose heating system

Table 2 Identified instrumental attributes. The questions examplify under what circumstances the instrumental attributes are recognized

Technology	How well do technical components of an energy system work? What possibilities are there to develop technical components?
Scale	How large is the scale of the constructions associated with a given alternative?
Size of venture	How large are the commitments to a certain alternative?
Domestic industry	To what extent is domestic industry utilized?
Domestic fuel	To what extent is domestic fuel utilized?
Local industry	To what extent is local industry utilized?
Local fuel	To what extent is local fuel utilized?
Location	How good is the location of power plants and other constructions in relation to different goal attributes?
Offer of energy sources	How does the possibility of using various fuels affect different goal attributes?
Offer of production plants	How does the possibility of using various production plants within the system affect different goal attributes?
Solid fuel	What effects do the use of solid fuel have on different goal attributes?
Monopoly	How does monopoly on energy production and energy distribution affect different goal attributes?

In sum, we assume that causal thinking is important when alternatives are evaluated. The decision maker conceives of causal chains—scenarios—which result from the implementation of particular alternatives. A standard form for a causal chain is that the choice of a given alternative leads to a certain level of an instrumental attribute (e.g. the introduction of district heating leads to large-scale constructions), which in turn is followed by one or two subattributes (possibilities for future back-pressure plants leading to revenues from electricity production), and ending by a positive or negative value on a goal attribute (in this particular case good economy).

We also assume that for a specific decision area there exists a restricted number of goals around which the anticipation of possible outcomes are concentrated. Instrumental attributes are characteristics associated with several goal attributes whereas subattributes are conceptual specifications of single goal attributes.

DATA COLLECTION

Two sets of data are used in the present study. One set is written speeches held by the Swedish Minister of Energy in various public appearances. These data were mainly used to develop the conceptual framework presented above

(Montgomery and Biel, 1984). This framework guided the collection of the second set of data, the main set of data in this study. These data were obtained by interviewing politicians and officials at the municipal energy works in ten Swedish towns about current alternatives for supplying heat in their own town (see Biel and Montgomery, 1986b). In seven of the ten towns the key issue was whether a district heating system should be built, or in some cases enlarged, at the expense of other systems such as electrical heating or a combination of local plants. In the remaining three towns all interviewees agreed that a district heating system should be built. The towns varied with respect to size, location, and whether there was access to local fuel (peat or wood) or not. A total of 45 subjects were interviewed. The subjects were chosen so that different opinions in each town should be represented. However, a majority of the subjects were in favour of district heating (32 persons).

All subjects were first asked about which alternatives were discussed for supplying heat in the town. The interviewee was then asked to describe the alternatives with regard to each of the goal attributes presented earlier. Examples of questions are: 'How do you judge the alternatives with respect to environmental effects' and 'How do the alternatives affect the safety of the heating system?'

Some time after the interview each subject answered a second round of questions by telephone or by mail. In this interview the subject was confronted with arguments given by persons who favoured another solution. The questions concerned those points on which the subjects disagreed or talked at cross-purposes in the first interview.

The first round of interviews were conducted by two interviewers. One of them asked the questions and the other wrote down the answers.

CODING PROCEDURE

The following steps were used when analysing written texts as well as the interviews. A short example of the procedure will be given directly after the presentation of the steps.

1. Identify all possible alternatives. This step requires a good knowledge of the particular topic at hand.
2. Note in the text where statements about an alternative start and end. Passages with no recognizable alternative are omitted.
3. Identify goal attributes within each passage. Sometimes goal attributes are not explicitly mentioned and must be inferred from subattributes.
4. For each goal attribute and alternative, indentify the causal chains that lead to the goal attributes from the alternatives.
5. Demarcate each causal step/attribute.

6. Where applicable, policy measures are also coded.
7. Label each attribute and write down each step in the causal chain, starting from the alternative and ending with the goal attribute.
8. Identify, across all alternatives, attributes that are part of chains leading to more than one goal attribute. Attributes combined with more than one goal attribute are called instrumental attributes.
9. Across the whole material, check for each alternative and goal attribute if there are partly overlapping chains. Include only the most detailed chain.
10. Construct one scenario for each person and alternative.

Below is given a short text to give an idea of how the procedure works. The text is taken from a speech given by the Swedish Energy Minister. Causal attributes and policy measures are underlined and explained within brackets.

I would like to say some words about environmental technology. The government will continue to demand very strict environmental *regulations* (policy measure) for the use of *coal* (alternative). It is therefore of importance to press for good *technology* (instrumental attribute) in this field. That is why we support this development by generous *subsidiaries* (policy measure) of 75 per cent of the surplus costs for the advanced environmental *technology* (instrumental attribute) during this period of development. Due to our strict environmental *regulations* (policy measure) and economic *subsidiaries* (policy measure) a very interesting development of *new methods* (instrumental attribute) for burning fuel and of filters for purifying the outlets (inferred to affect *emission* as subattribute to goal attribute *environment*). Also, a development (support for earlier instrumental attribute technology) is taking place within the *Swedish industry* (instrumental attribute: domestic industry). I am fully convinced that Swedish industry will have a very successful *export* (subattribute, inferred to affect *economy for domestic industry*, new subattribute, ending with the goal attribute *economy*) commodity in this area.

Table 3 shows causal chains indentified in the text. These causal chains result in a scenario which is shown in Figure 2.

RESULTS

Reliability

Two independent coders analysed notes from four interviews in the municipalities as well as three written speeches presented by the Swedish Energy Minister. Reliabilities were calculated for two occasions, before and after a discussion in which the codings were compared and where attempts were made to reach general agreement. The reliabilities were calculated as two times the number of codings in common for both coders divided by the total number of codings. The reliabilities were computed for three different levels. *First*, it was checked whether the two coders extracted the same alternatives or not. *Second*, the

Table 3 Causal chains depicting some of the consequences, expected by the Swedish Energy Minister, of introducing coal in the Swedish energy system. Causality is indicated by adjustment to the right in the left column and the chains are read from bottom up to the goal attribute

	COAL (alternative)
ECONOMY (goal attribute)	Inferred.
Economy for domestic industry (subattribute)	Inferred.
Export (subattribute)	Swedish industry will have a very successful export commodity in this area.
Technology (instrumental attribute)	This very interesting development concerns advanced technology for burning fuel and of filters for purifying emissions.
Domestic industry (instrumental attribute)	Due to our ... (see the two policy measures below), a development is taking place within the Swedish industry.
Regulation (policy measure)	The government will continue to demand very strict environmental regulations.
Subsidiary (policy measure)	The development of advanced environmental technology is supported by generous subsidiaries of 75 per cent of the surplus costs,
ENVIRONMENT (goal attribute)	Inferred.
Emission (subattribute)	Inferred.
Technology (instrumental attribute)	See above under economy for the rest of the causal chain.

agreement on causal chains was examined. At least one subattribute and the corresponding goal attribute should agree between the two coders.

However, it was sufficient if a more elaborated chain included a less developed one. Thus, omission of an event on behalf of one of the coders did not affect the reliability on this level. Order of events or omission of events in a chain were reflected on the *third* level—agreement about events.

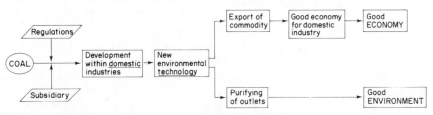

Fig. 2 A scenario showing some of the expected consequences of using coal in Sweden's future energy system according to the Swedish energy minister.

Agreement about events were at hand when the coders extracted the same events in the causal chain and derived the same order between these events.

It should be noted that disagreements on a higher level affect the reliability on a lower level. Chains that are left out due to missing alternatives are considered as disagreements on the chain level. Also, chains omitted by one of the coders for a given alternative lower the reliability on the event level.

As can be seen in Table 4, the reliability scores for the two types of material are approximately on the same level. The only clear difference is that the reliability for alternatives is higher for the interview data, which indicates that the alternatives are more distinctly defined in the interviews. This is hardly surprising, since the interviewer and the interviewee agreed upon relevant alternatives for the municipality's heating supply before the alternatives were judged. Although the interviews in this way were characterized by an imposed structure, they also had some drawbacks as a means to get information about scenarios. In interviews, as compared to written documents, the thoughts are less clearly expressed. Thus, the causal structure is more difficult to find.

The following explanations can be given for the more common disagreements between the coders. That the score for interview and alternative before discussion did not reach 1 is attributed to the fact that our respondents sometimes during the interview recalled alternatives that were not of immediate interest but well worth considering in the near future. These alternatives were considered by only one of the coders. The fact that one of the coders did not notice a consequence, and thus omitted a causal chain, accounts for approximately one-third of disagreements for causal chains. Other disagreements were due to over-interpretation of something that was not a consequence, a failure to recognize that the subject him/herself rejected the consequence, coding the consequence as an advantage with one alternative rather than a disadvantage with another alternative, or assigning a consequence to the wrong goal attribute.

Table 4 Reliability scores for analysis of scenarios from written speeches and from interveiws

Level	Written speeches		Interviews	
	Before discussion	After discussion	Before discussion	After discussion
Alternative	0.83	1.0	0.93	1.0
Causal chain	0.77	0.98	0.73	0.97
Event	0.66	0.95	0.64	0.94

On the event level, the most common disagreement was whether a particular statement included one event or two separate events. This type of disagreement accounted for more than half of the errors on the event level. Omissions of a subattribute in immediate association with the goal attribute also occurred.

Some general features of the scenarios

In order to make the following presentation more comprehensive the options have been reduced to district heating as one alternative and alternatives to district heating as the other alternative (e.g. electricity and/or local plants). Similarly, the subjects are divided into two groups: those in favour of district heating and those in favour of alternatives to district heating. The presentation is based on scenarios identified after the first round of interviews.

Agreement about goals

Table 5 shows to what degree different goal attributes were attended to. For district heating, almost all proponents imagined consequences related

Table 5 Number of causal chains for each goal attribute that according to proponents and opponents of district heating (d.h.) results in positive or negative consequences

Party Consequence	Econ	Envir	Flex	Safe	Empl	Eprod	Freed
				Goal attribute			
			District heating				
Proponents of d.h.							
Positive	54	33	32	48	16	11	
Negative	3	4	2	3			4
Opponents of d.h.							
Positive		2	3	4	2		
Negative	34	6	7	4		4	5
			Alternative choices				
Opponents of d.h.							
Positive	27	18	10	11	6		2
Negative	1	2				2	
Proponents of d.h.							
Positive	9	3					
Negative	17	1	3	1		5	1

to economy, environment, flexibility, and safety. Half of the proponents touched upon aspects related to employment and energy production. The opponents concentrated on consequences related to economy, environment, and safety where almost all subjects had something to say. Half of the opponents also remarked on flexibility and energy production. For alternatives to district heating, almost all proponents imagined consequences related to economy, environment, flexibility, and safety, and half of the proponents commented on employment. The opponents focused on negative aspects of economy.

Each entry in the table indicates the number of causal chains across all subjects between a given alternative and a given goal attribute. The column sums may be interpreted as a measure of the importance of the attributes in question. It can be seen that the sums exhibit approximately the same rank order across different alternatives and parties. Economy always receives most attention; safety/vulnerability, environment, and flexibility occupy a medium position, whereas employment, energy production, and freedom of choice seems to be of little importance in most cases.

Disagreements about means

The results with respect to instrumental attributes are similar to those for goal attributes in that the relative importance by and large is the same across parties and alternatives. By far the most attended to instrumental attributes included aspects of size, i.e. scale size and size of venture. For advocates of district heating 50 per cent of the causal chains included aspects of size. The corresponding percentage for opponents was 72 per cent. For alternatives to district heating advocates referred to aspects of size in 33 per cent of the causal chains, while the opponents' scenarios contained aspects of size in 50 per cent of the chains.

Although the parties referred to the same instrumental and goal attributes they disagreed almost completely about the relations between the two types of attributes (see Table 6). The most striking differences are found in how large-scale systems are viewed. To the advocates of district heating, big is beautiful. In the opponents' scenarios, big is evil. Among other things the advocates asserted that large-scale systems give possibilities to use different kinds of fuels, which implies that cheap fuels could be used, which in turn leads to good economy. Large-scale systems also make it possible to use back-pressure production, which gives revenues to the producers and, hence, contributes to good economy. The advocates also emphasized that a large-scale system leads to a decrease in the number of plants. This results in less emission and hence in a better environment. The opponents imagine totally different consequences of large-scale systems. High investment costs, energy losses in culverts, and monopoly on heating distribution contribute to bad economy. The choice of particular fuels in large-scale plants leads to more pollution, and so on.

Table 6 Number of causal chains between instrumental attributes and goal attributes in the scenarios of district heating (d.h.) for each party. The + and − signs indicate positive and negative consequences respectively

Party	Goal attribute						
	Econ + −	Envir + −	Flex + −	Safe + −	Empl + −	Eprod + −	Freed + −
Proponents of d.h.							
Scale (large)	23	14 2	14 2	15 2	1	9	
Size of venture (large)	11	3	1	1	1		
Size of venture (limited)	3		1				
Local fuel	3			15	11		
Domestic fuel	1		1	3	1	1	
Technology	1 3	4 1	4				
Location	3	2		1			
Offer of energy sources	5		9	3	1		
Offer of production plants	1		2				
Solid fuel	3	4	1				
No instrumental attributes		6 1	11		1	1	4
Opponents of d.h.							
Scale (large)	7	1 3	1 3	1 2		1	3
Size of venture (large)	13	1 3	4	2		3	1
Size of venture (small)	1		1				
Local fuel	7			2	2		
Domestic fuel	2			1			
Offer of energy sources			1				
Monopoly	1						
No instrumental attributes	3						1

Dominance

Table 5 shows that there was a strong tendency for both parties to express positive consequences of introducing the favoured alternative and negative consequences of introducing a non-favoured alternative. In other words, violations of dominance were rare. In particular, negative consequences of favoured alternatives were seldom expressed (7 per cent of all chains to goal attributes for these alternatives). The other type of violation, positive consequences of non-favoured alternatives, were slightly more common (1.6 per cent of relevant chains).

In sum, the following general trends were found through a comparison of scenarios from the two parties.

(a) By and large the parties agreed about the importance of the same set of goal attributes.
(b) Divergences in the views held by different parties could be traced back to different beliefs about causal relations between one or two instrumental attributes and the goal attributes.
(c) Independently of which alternative was favoured, the scenarios implied that each subject viewed his/her favoured alternative as largely dominant (i.e. only advantages, no disadvantages); i.e. both parties represented the alternatives in line with a 'dominance structure' (Montgomery, 1983).

Economy scenarios — a more detailed view

In order to gain a deeper understanding of the disagreements between the two parties, we examined the alternative district heating and the goal attribute economy in some detail. This combination was usually the most elaborated part of the scenarios. For each party (proponents and opponents) scenarios within each group were merged into one scenario. Only causal chains derived from at least three persons from two different municipalities were included in the merged scenarios. The chains that were merged had to be in exact agreement, not only partly overlapping. These restrictions were imposed in order to avoid idiosyncratic views.

The economy scenarios were used for facilitating a comparison of the respondents' answers to the questions in the second interview. These questions concerned those points on which the parties disagreed or talked at cross-purposes in the first interview. Remaining evident disagreements after the second interview are commented upon below while minor ones are left open. The causal links corresponding to the disagreements are denoted by arabic numbers in the scenarios.

We think that the disagreements shown in Figures 3 and 4 can be explained in terms of a few principles. One principle concerns the relation between large scale (or size of venture) and economy. To the proponents a large size of venture results in an increased basis for heat supply leading to low energy costs and a good economy. The opponents imagine a causal link from large scale and a large size of venture leading to monopoly. Less competition for heat supply and increased costs will follow. This disagreement seems to result from a difference in perspective taken by the two

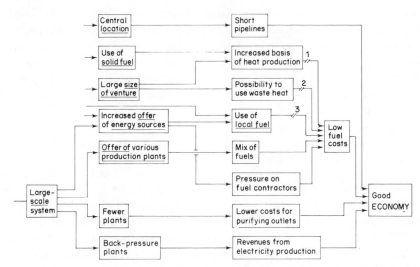

Fig. 3 Scenario of district heating supporters for expected economic consequences of introducing district heating. Divergent views between parties concerning expected consequences are marked by // in the causal chains. Arabic numbers refer to comments in the text.

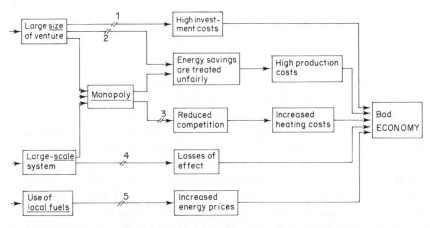

Fig. 4 Scenario of district heating opponents for expected economic consequences of introducing district heating. Divergent views between parties concerning expected consequences are marked by // in the causal chains. Arabic numbers refer to comments in the text.

parties. Those in favour of the district heating view it 'from the inside' and focus on positive consequences that are directly linked to district heating. The opponents, on the other hand, concentrate on aspects outside the district heating system (energy savings, competition from alternatives) that will not be realized if district heating is introduced. The causal links denoted as 1 and 2 in Figure 3 and as 2 and 3 in Figure 4 are examples of disagreements due to different perspectives.

A second principle underlying some disagreements is the possibility of control. Both proponents and opponents expect that local fuels will be exploited in district heating plants. However, whereas the proponents imagine low energy costs the opponents claim the opposite (see 3 in Figure 3 and 5 in Figure 4). This controversy results from different views with respect to the possibility of controlling the fuel price. The proponents believe that the use of local fuels gives the opportunity to control and exert an influence on the price level. To the opponents the price trend is doomed to be negative since an increase in demand, due to an introduction of local fuels in nearby municipalities, will raise the prices.

A third principle related to disagreements is the use of different subattributes. Links 1 and 2 in Figure 4 are examples of this principle. In the first case high investment costs were rebutted by introducing energy costs. In the second case energy savings were redefined. While opponents referred to the consumer's possibilities to save energy, and hence money, the proponents talked about savings in the production system.

All the above disagreements are related to the fact that the two parties introduce or focus on different   aspects or events in their scenarios. The 'inside' versus 'outside' perspectives imply that different instrumental attributes are focused (although these different attributes are all linked to size of scale or size of venture). Similarly, the different views with respect to the possibility of control start out from different aspects (own power versus external forces). These aspects were not classified as instrumental or subattributes since they were not part of the original scenarios. Finally, the use of different subattributes obviously implies that the parties consider different events in their scenarios.

In only two cases of disagreements were the views held by each party directly comparable (i.e. the disagreement concerned relationships between the same aspects or events). Thus, the proponents of district heating claim that losses of effect are small in large-scale systems (4 in Figure 4) and they also deny that there is a short supply of local fuels (5 in Figure 4).

We hope that the above rather detailed analysis of the disagreements between the two parties shows how scenario analysis may be used to pin-point the structure and the sources of different disagreements. It is interesting to note that there are so few cases of directly comparable controversies. By applying different perspectives (inside–outside) as well as different time perspectives (not exemplified above), by imagining different opportunities to control future outcomes, and by introducing new subattributes a dominance structure is upheld and defended against counterarguments.

DISCUSSION

In the present study we have attempted to shed some light on the belief systems underlying political decision makers' conceptions of the consequences of different choice alternatives. We find it important to scrutinize these causal beliefs. Unless the causal beliefs underlying a decision process are valid the end result is likely to be poor. Furthermore, causal beliefs are expressed in the political debate and capture the official position of the althority. In this way the politicians commit themselves to act in line with their beliefs.

Below, we discuss how the present method, which we will refer to as scenario analysis (SA), relates to other methods proposed to analyse individual decision makers in politics (Gallhofer, Saris, and Melman, 1986). Among those other methods there are mainly three that we have in mind: cognitive mapping (CM), empirical decision analysis (EDA) procedure, and multiple paths to choice (MPC). The CM approach seeks to represent assertions used by a decision maker in a specific situation. The cognitive map is a structural model of a person's beliefs and values that can be derived from these assertions (Shapiro and Bonham, 1973; Axelrod, 1976). The EDA procedure was developed to determine the decision rules used by the decision maker when choosing between options (e.g. Gallhofer and Saris, 1979; Gallhofer, Saris, and Melman, 1986). The MPC method tries to describe the decision-making process by applying conceptual models and related decision rules that may account for different stages in the decision process (Maoz, 1981, 1986). For a more detailed description of the methods, see Gallhofer, Saris and Melman (1986).

As for the *reliability* of SA it can be noted that the interjudge reliability is satisfactory as compared to the other methods. The reliability scores for these other methods fall somewhere between 0.60 and 1.0 depending on the level of detail (Gallhofer, Saris, and Melman, 1986; Maoz, 1981). However, the somewhat large discrepancy of the reliability scores in our material before and after agreement was searched between coders indicates that the coding procedure can be refined.

Concerning the *validity* of SA as compared to the other methods, it should be noted that the SA and CM methods are similar to each other inasmuch as both methods focus on the decision maker's causal beliefs rather than on decision rules and information integration, as is the case in the other two methods. We think that the present data speak in favour of the SA and CM methods since the views held by the parties clearly were due to different causal beliefs. On the other hand, both parties integrated the information in line with a dominance structure and hence their decisions followed a dominance rule. Thus, using the EDA or MPC methods to analyse the parties' decision rules will not shed light on divergences between the parties. In order to reveal differences between the parties it is necessary to focus on their causal beliefs and such an analysis could be conducted by using the SA or the CM method.

However, there are a number of important differences between the SA and CM methods that we have to consider in order to find out which of the two methods is more suitable for analysing causal beliefs in a decision situation. First, in SA each scenario is restricted to one option as viewed by one actor. In CM several scenarios are merged into one cognitive map. The conceptualization of a decision maker's belief system in a number of separate 'maps' makes each one of them easier to survey than a complete cognitive map. Second, in order to facilitate comparisons between parties with different views the SA method makes some assumptions about the structure in terms of attributes. Third, the denotation of the nature of causal relationships differs in scenarios and in cognitive maps. Both CM and SA denote causal linkages between concepts/attributes as arrows, but in a cognitive map signs on the arrows identify the nature of the causal linkage. If a concept is perceived to increase or promote another concept, a positive sign is used while a negative sign indicates an inverse relationship (e.g. use of local fuel increases/decreases energy prices). In a scenario the nature of the causal relationship is spelled out in the description of the effect in a given cause–effect link (e.g. use of local fuel leads to increased/ decreased energy prices). Lastly, in CM the final events are grouped into very broad categories, such as Swedish utility, whereas in SA more specific categories are used for grouping the final events (e.g. good/bad economy for Sweden). We think that all these special features of SA yield a better overview of the structure in people's representation of causally related events in a decision situation.

Support for the potential usefulness of scenario analysis was obtained in an extended case study (Biel and Montgomery, 1986b). In this study, respondents were asked to comment upon their own scenarios as well as scenarios for the same choice alternatives as viewed by the other party. Respondents agreed that scenarios presented them with a good structure of their views. The scenarios were easy to interpret and comment upon. The respondents' positive attitudes are probably attributed to the fact that the decision maker's own causal beliefs are used to express his/her view. Since the method is straightforward it can be used by the decision maker to externalize his/her own causal beliefs. By constructing scenarios the line of thought must be made explicit. This should make it easier to find weak links. Thus, experts could be consulted about the likelihood of anticipated events and previously missing information regarding salient goal attributes can be added.

In the extended case study, respondents were also asked to imagine how the opponent viewed the choice alternatives. It was found that these imagined scenarios were close to the opponent's own views. Thus, the respondents seemed to know where they had each other's views. However, this was not apparent to themselves. It was only after they had seen the scenarios that they became aware of this fact. Yet, one important deviation between 'own' and 'other's' scenarios should be mentioned. There was a tendency to see one's own position as based on facts whereas the opponent's position to some extent is seen as influenced by private interests rather than the benefit of the energy consumer. These divergent perspectives are much in line with Heider's (1958) distinction between the perceiver and the other, a distinction which is a cornerstone in one of the most influential modern social psychological theories: attribution theory (see, for example, Hewstone, 1983). Due to different states of awareness within the individual about him/herself and the other, the perceiver tends to overemphasize dispositional qualities (such as promoting self-interest) rather than situational factors (environmental constraints) when accounting for the other person's actions—the so-called fundamental attribution error.

Generally, however, the present data suggest that decision makers can take advantage of scenario analysis. Not only can decision makers externalize their own views in scenarios but also use the method to systematically represent the views of other actors. These scenarios can be scrutinized in the same way as their own scenarios. Also, scenarios could be applied by a third party in conflict resolution. However, before scenario analysis is recommended for more general practical use, it is necessary to explore how the method applies to other domains. The question is whether or not different views about future expectations can be represented in such a clear-cut structure as was the case for the domain of energy politics.

REFERENCES

Axelrod, R. (1976). The cognitive mapping approach. In R. Axelrod (Ed), *Structure of Decision*, Princeton University Press, Princeton, N.J.

Biel, A., and Montgomery, H. (1986a). Scenarios in energy planning. In B. Brehmer, H. Jungermann, P. Lourens, and G. Sevón (Eds), *New Directions in Research on Decision Making*, Elsevier Amsterdam.

Biel, A., and Montgomery, H. (1986b). Kommunerna och värmeförsörjningen — föreställningar bakom energipolitiska ställningstaganden (In Swedish) (unpublished manuscript).

Gallhofer, I., and Saris, W. (1979). Strategy choices of foreign policy decision makers: The Netherlands 1914, *Journal of Conflict Resolution*, **23**, 425–45.

Gallhofer, I., Saris, W., and Melman, M. (Eds) (1986). *Different Text Analysis Procedures for the Study of Decision Making*, Sociometric Research Foundation, Amsterdam.

Heider, F. (1958). *The Psychology of Interpersonal Relations*, Wiley, New York.

Hewstone, M. (Ed.) (1983). *Attribution Theory. Social and Functional Extensions*, Basil Blackwell, Oxford.

Kahneman, D., and Tversky, A. (1982). The simulation heuristic. In D. Kahneman, P. Slovic, and A. Tversky (Eds), *Judgement under Uncertainty: Heuristics and Biases,* Cambridge University Press, Cambridge.

Maoz, Z. (1981). The decision to raid Entebbe: decision analysis applied to crisis behaviour, *Journal of Conflict Resolution,* **25,** 677–707.

Maoz, Z. (1986). Multiple paths to choice: an approach for the analysis of foreign policy decisions. In I. Gallhofer, W. Saris, and M. Melman (Eds), *Different Text Analysis Procedures for the Study of Decision Making,* Sociometric Research Foundation, Amsterdam.

Montgomery, H. (1983). Decision rules and the search for a dominance structure: towards a process model of decision making. In P. C. Humphreys, O. Svenson, and A. Vari (Eds), *Analyzing and Aiding Decision Processes,* North-Holland, Amsterdam.

Montgomery, H., and Biel, A. (1984). *Scenarios and Causal Models in Political Decision Making,* Paper presented at the Annual Conference of the British Psychological Society, Warwick.

Norman, D. A. (1984). Some observations on mental models. In D. Gentner and A. L. Stevens (Eds) *Mental Models,* Erlbaum, Hillsdale, N.J.

Shapiro, M., and Bonham, M. (1973). Cognitive processes and foreign policy decision making, *International Studies Quarterly,* **17,** 147–74.

Thüring, M., and Jungermann, H. (1986). Constructing and running mental models for inferences about the future. In B. Brehmer, H. Jungermann, P. Lourens, and G. Sevón (Eds), *New Directions in Research on Decision Making,* Elsevier, Amsterdam.

Tversky, A., and Kahneman, D. (1983). Extensional versus intuitive reasoning: the conjunction fallacy in probability judgment, *Psychological Review,* **90,** 293–315.

ACKNOWLEDGEMENTS

This chapter was supported by a grant from the Swedish Council for Energy Research.

The authors wish to thank Ola Svenson and an anonymous reviewer for their comments on an earlier draft of the chapter.

15

The credibility of inflation-related scenarios of different lengths

GÖRAN NILSSON

Economists have proposed a variety of models of people's predictions of future rates of inflation. One group of models typically assumes that people weigh past inflation rates in order to predict the future rate of inflation (see, for example, Batchelor, 1980). In these models, inflation rates for previous years are assumed to be the only information people use when making their predictions. Other models assume that people integrate current economic information when making their predictions. In this approach, subjects are assumed to integrate information until the marginal benefit of more information equals the marginal cost of being incorrect (Wallis, 1979). A third appraoch proposed by economists is to assume perfect foresight, i.e. the rational expectations hypothesis (cf. Maddock and Carter, 1982). It is assumed in this approach that people act as if they have an unbiased model of the economy as a cognitive representation.

There are a few studies which deal with subjective perceptions of past inflation rates (Jonung, 1981, 1985). These studies support the hypothesis that people use mainly past inflation rates to predict future rates of inflation (e.g. Wärneryd and Wahlund, 1986). Keren (1983) studied predictions of future rates of inflation in different economic cultures, i.e. Canada and Israel. People were asked to extrapolate past inflation rates into the future in order to make their predictions. The results indicated that subjects in an economy of higher rates of inflation are better at predicting the future rate of inflation as compared to subjects living in an economy with a more modest rate of inflation. Beherend (e.g. 1966, 1977, 1984) studied what people think is a reasonable price for certain commodities as well as the learning and relearning of the price of goods. Her data suggest

Process and Structure in Human Decision Making
Edited by H. Montgomery and O. Svenson. © 1989 John Wiley & Sons Ltd

that people use information from only a few commodities to make judgements of perceived inflation.

Some studies have been made on what people think are the causes of inflation. Nilsson (1985) and Svenson and Nilsson (1986) showed that people can differentiate between the effects of changes in current economic variables on the inflation rate. A few researchers have been concerned with how causes of inflation seem to be interrelated in causal chains. Thus, this research deals with cognitive representations of the causes of inflation. Sevon (1984) showed that subjects' cognitive representation is much simpler when predicting the future rate of inflation as compared to the presentation used when explaining the causes of inflation. In line with Sevon's findings, Svenson and Nilsson (1986) showed that the cognitive representations for the causes of inflation could contain more links between variables than the cognitive representations of the effects of inflation.

The data in the above studies correspond to what has been called 'cognitive maps' (cf. Axelrod, 1976; Eden, Jones, and Sims, 1979). A cognitive map describes beliefs about causal relations between sets of variables. According to this theory, causal relationships can either be positive or negative. Thus, a positive causal relationship means that changes of two variables occur in the same direction; e.g. an increase in the causing variable will cause an increase in the affected variable. A causal relationship can also be negative—an increase in the causing variable will cause a decrease in the affected variable. Furthermore, a cognitive map may contain closed cycles or loops. Axelrod (1976) presented a method for revealing cognitive maps using questionnaires as well as verbal documents. Roberts (1976) presented the variable indentification as a three-step procedure when using the questionnaire method. First, the potential variables that could make up a cognitive map should be identified. Second, the importance of the potential variables obtained in step 1 should be estimated. Third, the potential variables should be reduced to a set of basic variables that must be included in the cognitive map. Relationships between the variables in the cognitive map are estimated by using paired comparisons. Furthermore, the importance ratings can be made quantitatively, allowing for identification of the most important relationships in the cognitive map. Finally, a procedure for reaching consensus among the subjects should be applied.

Svenson and Nilsson (1986) used a similar technique to reveal cognitive maps. The subjects were presented with a set of variables that in earlier studies had been found to be important for the changes in the inflation rate. Each variable in turn was presented as an 'affected' variable while the rest of the variables in the set were presented as causal variables leading to changes in the 'affected' variable. To clarify, the 'affected' variable (dependent variable) was presented to the right of the causal variables (independent variables). The subjects were then asked to focus on the presented dependent variable and asked to estimate the effects of changing each one of the independent variables. Thus, subjects were asked to judge the effect of a change in one of the independent variables on the dependent variable. By altering the dependent variable, all variables will be dependent and causal variables when not dependent. Furthermore, the subjects were asked to assign the rank 'one' to the most important variable, rank 'two' to the second most important, and so forth, until no more relations between the independent and dependent variables were perceived. The direction of the change (causal relationship—increase/decrease) of the dependent variable was indicated by the subjects as well. A matrix was then created in which each cell represented the number of subjects indicating the relationship from the causal variable to the dependent variable. By using these frequencies for each of the relations it is possible to unfold a tree of causal relationships between the variables. It is thus possible to create a cognitive map based on importance ratings as well as on the number of subjects having expressed a relationship between the causal and dependent variables.

A scenario describes one path through a cognitive map. Thus, one can easily generate scenarios out of a cognitive map (see, for example, Montgomery and Biel, 1984; Biel and Montgomery, 1985). Ducot and Lubben (1980) have pointed out that the term 'scenario' is not a well-defined concept. Jungerman (1986) proposed that the existing interpretations of scenario share some common features. First, a scenario might be conceived of as a chain of causally related events extended over a period of time. Thus, scenarios are hypothetical and describe potential futures. They include an initial state and a terminal state given a fixed time horizon. Furthermore, scenario elements are judged with respect to their importance, desirability, or probability. According to this conceptualization scenarios correspond to paths in decision trees. A second possibility is to conceive of a scenario as a net of causally related events that can exist in different states, allowing for interactions among scenario variables (see, for example, Montgomery and Biel, 1984).

As mentioned above, scenario elements are judged with respect to importance, desirability, or probability. Tversky and Kahneman (1982, 1983) showed that people use a number of heuristics and exhibit several biases in estimating the likelihood of different scenarios. To exemplify this, Tversky and Kahneman asked one group of subjects to judge the probability of an earthquake in California causing a flood where more than a thousand people would drown. This is an example of a 'conjunction' of two events. Another group of subjects judged the probability of a flood where a thousand people would drown—a probability with no conjunction. The estimated probability of the conjunction event was significantly higher as compared to the event with only a flood. Tversky and Kahneman suggested that a scenario that includes a possible cause and an outcome could be perceived as more probable than merely the outcome itself. Thus, subjects rate the conjunction of two events as more likely than one of the constituent events. Tversky and Kahneman argued that subjects make the conjunction fallacy because they use a representative heuristic to arrive at their judgement. However, they proposed that the conjunction fallacy is only present when the scenarios are plausible to the subjects. They have also shown that people assign higher probabilities to events when it is easier to construct scenarios leading to the event as compared to when it is more difficult (Tversky and Kahneman, 1982). Furthermore, they argued that it is natural for the probability of an event to be evaluated by the degree to which that event is representative for an appropriate mental model. Clearly, empirical research on categorization of objects has shown that information is commonly stored in memory and processed in relation to mental models in the way that Tversky and Kahneman have proposed (Smith and Medin, 1981; Mervis and Rosch, 1981).

The scenarios presented by Tversky and Kahneman are distinct from the scenarios embedded in the cognitive model described by Svenson and Nilsson. In the Tversky and Kahneman case, only one scenario was judged by one subject at the time, either the outcome or the cause and the outcome. Thus, the authors analyse only the probabilities of different scenarios, focusing on only one plausible scenario; i.e. where only the plausible scenario has an effect on the outcome. Svenson and Nilsson, on the other hand, mapped a set of plausible scenarios, where a number of scenarios all ended in the rate of inflation. Thus, several scenarios were plausible at the same time for the subjects.

The results of Svenson and Nilsson (1986) showed that a specific variable may have a direct effect on the rate of inflation as well as indirect effects through intervening variables. Paralleling the thoughts of Tversky and Kahneman, longer causal chains leading to the inflation rate might correspond to a greater trust in these longer chains as compared to shorter chains without intervening variables when focusing on only one scenario leading to changes in the inflation rate. Hence, a longer story (longer link scenario) is more 'trustworthy', i.e. judged as more important, than a shorter link scenario. Plausible scenarios leading to inflation, linking a causal variable to inflation through intervening variables, should therefore be judged as more important for the rate of inflation as compared to the direct effect of the causing variable. For example, the international inflation rate will be more important for the rate of inflation when linked in a scenario with one or two intervening variables than when it is presented as a direct effect on the rate of inflation. On the other hand, a significant decrease in the importance of longer scenarios (as compared to a shorter one) ought to be interpreted as a disbelief in the longer scenario.

The purpose of this chapter is to analyse whether longer scenarios describing the causes of inflation are more plausible than shorter scenarios. Another purpose of this paper is to describe a methodology that can be used for deriving scenarios which are experienced as plausible by subjects.

METHOD

The experiment was performed in group sessions with subjects working with paper and pencil tasks.

Subjects

Thirty-two students were recruited through the University of Stockholm. The students attended various courses at the University. Nobody had participated in a similiar experiment before. Five subjects had formal training in economics. The students were paid 30 SEK to participate (about US $4).

Judgement task

Subjects were instructed to judge the importance of different scenarios for the future rate of inflation. The variables that could be included in a scenario were the following: (a) prices of raw materials and oil, (b) international rate of inflation, (c) business cycle in Sweden, and (d) nominal wages. All possible combinations of these four variables occurred in the scenarios with one, two, and three variables besides inflation, where inflation was the affected variable. Hence, there were three types of scenarios, viz. (a) scenarios with variables having only a direct effect on the rate of inflation, e.g. the price of raw materials and oil having a direct effect on the Swedish rate of inflation; (b) scenarios with variables having an indirect effect on the rate of inflation through one intervening variable, e.g. the price of raw materials and oil affecting the international rate of inflation which in turn affects the rate of inflation; and (c) variables having an indirect effect on the rate of inflation through two intervening variables, e.g. the price of raw materials and oil affecting international inflation which in turn affects the rate of inflation.

For each scenario, the subjects were asked to judge the importance of the presented scenarios by the following question: how important do you think each of the following sequences of events are for the Swedish rate of inflation within twelve months? The subjects made their judgements on a ten-point scale where zero indicated no effect on the rate of inflation. Figure 1 presents the scenarios which the subjects were asked to judge.

As indicated in Figure 1, the subjects were asked to judge each of the direct effects of the four variables on the rate of inflation and the indirect effects on the rate of inflation through one intervening variable (in total $4 \times 3 = 12$ indirect effects). The subjects were also asked to judge the effects of the four variables on the rate of inflation through two intervening variables (in total $4 \times 3 \times 2 = 24$ indirect effects).

Procedure

The experimental material was presented in booklets. The order of presented scenarios was randomized. Half the subjects judged the scenarios according to one randomized order of scenarios, the other half judged the scenarios in a reversed order. The judgements of the direct effects and the effects through one intervening variable were replicated by each subject. The experiment was

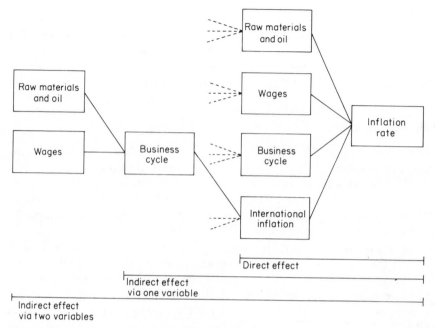

Fig. 1   The scenarios presented in the experiment.

conducted as a group experiment with five to eight subjects participating on each occasion. The experiment required, on the average, about one hour for a subject to complete.

RESULTS

The data were analysed on the group level and were aggregated in the following way. First, the means of each replicated scenario were computed for each subject (direct effects and the effects through one intervening variable). Second, the means of each variable in each of the different positions in the scenarios were computed for each subject.

Position in a scenario corresponds to direct effect, indirect effect through one intervening variable, and indirect effect through two intervening variables. In this way, the means of the variables having a direct effect were based on one scenario. The means of the variables having indirect effects through one intervening variable were based on three scenarios, and the means of the variables having indirect effects through two intervening variables were based on six scenarios for each variable. Finally, the overall means and variances were computed for each variable and position in a scenario across subjects.

The effect of positions in scenarios was, for each variable, tested by a one-way ANOVA. Thus, four analyses were made, one for each variable. The results are presented in Table. 1.

As indicated in Table 1 the judged importance of the variables affecting the rate of inflation decreases with the length of the scenarios. Thus, the variables are judged as most important when they have a direct effect on the rate of inflation. This relationship is highly significant for all variables except for international inflation ($F = 26.34$, d.f. $= 2/62$, $p < 0.01$; $F = 6.08$, d.f. $= 2/62$, $p < 0.01$; $F = 50.25$, d.f. $= 2/62$, $p < 0.01$; $F = 2.80$, d.f. $= 2/62$, $p = 0.15$ for raw materials and oil, Swedish business cycle, nominal wages, and international inflation respectively).

To test the difference between direct effects and indirect effects through one intervening variable and between indirect effects through one and two intervening variables, a *post hoc* analysis according to Scheffé was performed. The difference between direct effects and indirect effects via one intervening variable was significant for the price of raw materials and oil and for nominal wages ($\psi = 1.77$, $\psi = 2.48$, $p < 0.05$). The difference was not significant for the business cycle and international inflation ($\psi = 0.45$, $\psi = 0.59$, $p > 0.05$). The difference between indirect effects via one intervening variable and two intervening variables was not significant for any variable ($\psi = 0.60$, $\psi = 0.13$, $\psi = 0.81$, $\psi = 0.36$, $p > 0.05$ for business cycle, international inflation, wages, raw materials and oil respectively).

To sum up, the analysis showed that, generally, the importance of variables concerning their effect on the rate of inflation decreased with the number of intervening variables. Variables were judged as most important when they have a direct effect on the rate of inflation. A significant difference between the means

Table 1 Means of variables in different positions in the scenarios

Causing variable connected to inflation	Levels of effect on inflation			F ratio
	Direct	Indirect via one intervening variables	Indirect via two intervening variables	
Prices of raw materials and oil	7.28	5.52	5.15	26.34[a]
Swedish business cycle	6.06	5.61	5.01	6.08[a]
Nominal wages	7.77	5.27	4.47	50.25[a]
International inflation	6.39	5.80	5.66	2.80

[a] Significant at the 5 per cent level.

generally showed a disbelief in the scenario. Thus, the subjects' judgements about the effects of inflation-related variables were negatively correlated with the length of the scenario, rather than positively related, as would be expected in parallel with Tversky and Kahneman's findings of the conjunction fallacy for plausible scenarios. Despite a general disbelief in longer scenarios, some scenarios could be plausible and therefore they should be judged as more important than a shorter link scenario. The mean importance rating of each scenario computed across subjects is shown in Table 2. The difference between the means for scenarios of different lengths was tested by *t*-tests in the following way.

Indirect effects to inflation via one intervening variable were compared to the direct effects between the variable and inflation. Indirect effects via one intervening variable were compared to the corresponding scenario with two intervening variables. As an example, consider the relation between the price of raw materials and oil and inflation. The mean of the direct effect is, as indicated

Table 2   Mean judged importance of variables in different length scenarios

Direct effect/ effect through one variable		Second intervening variable in scenario		
	Wages	Business cycle	International inflation	Oil
Oil	7.28			
Oil — International inflation	6.25[a]	6.41	5.25[a]	
Oil — wages	6.02[a]		4.78[a,b]	5.19[a]
Oil — business	4.28[a]	4.93[a]		4.34[a]
Business	6.06			
Business — International inflation	4.89[a]	5.53		5.13[a]
Business — Oil	5.56	5.47	4.65[a,b]	
Business — wages	6.39		4.89[a,b]	4.44[a,b]
International inflation	6.39			
International inflation — Oil	6.33	7.00	5.38	
International inflation — business	5.53	5.44		5.59
International inflation — wages	5.55		5.53	5.06[a]
Wages	7.77			
Wages — International inflation	4.92[a]		4.31[a]	4.59[a]
Wages — Oil	5.25[a]	4.81[a]	4.22[a,b]	
Wages — business	5.66[a]		4.59[a,b]	4.31[a,b]

[a] Significant difference between direct and indirect effects at the 5 per cent level.
[b] Significant difference between indirect effects through one and two variables at the 5 per cent level.

in Table 2, 7.28. This mean was compared to the means of the indirect scenarios through international inflation, wages, and business cycle. The means are 6.25, 6.02, and 4.28 respectively. The means of the indirect effects through one intervening variable were compared to the corresponding scenarios with two intervening variables. For example, the scenario with the price of raw materials and oil affecting the international inflation which finally affects the rate of inflation was compared to the corresponding scenarios where wages and business cycle were the second intervening variables. Thus, the mean 6.25 was compared to the means 6.41 and 5.25 respectively.

Table 3 shows the number of scenarios where the judged importance of variables having a direct effect is significantly higher as compared to the effect through one intervening variable ($p < 0.05$, two-tail test). As indicated in the table, all scenarios with one intervening variable were judged as significantly less important as compared to direct effects of price of raw materials and oil and wages. For the Swedish business cycle, one scenario was judged as significantly less important, and for international inflation no scenario deviates significantly from direct effects. Returning to the hypothesis formulated in parallel with Tversky and Kahneman's (1983) conjunction fallacy phenomena, the results suggest that international inflation and business cycle are plausible variables in inflation-related scenarios when incorporated into two link scenarios.

Table 3 also shows the number of links where the judged importance of the shorter length scenario is significantly higher as compared to the longer length scenario. As indicated in the table, 7 out of 24 scenarios through one intervening

Table 3 Number of cases where the importance ratings for the shorter length link scenario were judged significantly higher as compared to the longer link scenario. The number of insignificant cases are shown in parantheses

causing variable connected to inflation	Number of scenarios where		
	Direct effect > indirect effect via one variable	Indirect effect via one variable > indirect effect via two variables	Direct effect > indirect effect via two variables
Prices of raw materials and oil	3 (0)	1 (5)	5 (1)
Swedish business cycle	1 (2)	3 (3)	4 (2)
Nominal wages	3 (0)	3 (3)	6 (0)
International inflation	0 (3)	0 (6)	1 (5)
Total	7 (5)	7 (17)	16 (8)

variable had significantly higher importance ratings as compared to the links with two intervening variables. Sixteen out of 24 different effects had significantly higher importance ratings as compared to the links with two intervening variables.

To sum up, the results showed that some scenarios with intervening variables seem plausible to the subjects, i.e. were not judged as less important as compared to the shorter scenario. However, the longer plausible scenarios were not judged as more important than the shorter scenario, as would be expected from the results of Tversky and Kahneman.

Based on the insignificant scenarios presented in Table 2, which thus are plausible to the subjects, a cognitive representation can be constructed using the non-significant two- and three-link scenarios only. The results are shown in Figures 2, 3, and 4. Figure 2 shows the insignificant two-link scenarios and Figure 3 shows the non-significant three-link scenarios. Figure 4 combines the

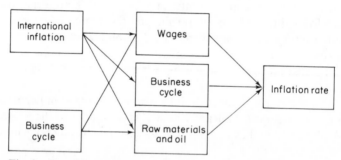

Fig. 2   Cognitive representations of plausible two-link scenarios.

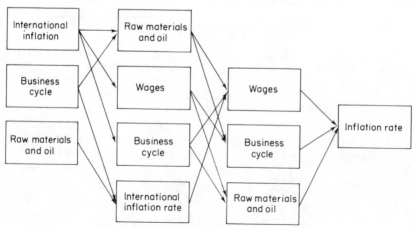

Fig. 3   Cognitive representation of plausible three-link scenarios.

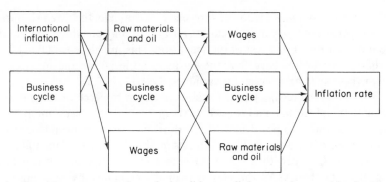

Fig. 4 Cognitive representation of plausible two-link scenarios combined with the three-link scenarios.

scenarios in Figure 2 with the non-significant scenarios found when comparing the indirect effects through one intervening variable with the indirect effects through two intervening variables.

DISCUSSION

This chapter has presented a method for representing economic variables in cognitive representations. Generally, methods presented for representing information in cognitive maps (e.g. Sevon, 1984; Svenson and Nilsson, 1986) deduce a set of hypothetical scenarios. However, the deduced scenarios do not need to have a psychological reality because they are in part dependent on the method applied. Clearly, the scenarios are at least to some extent constructions by the researcher. The method used in this chapter allows for an analysis of the plausibility of individual scenarios in the cognitive representation. It is possible to analyse each scenario by its intervening variables to find out which scenarios seem plausible to subjects. The presently elucidated scenarios can therefore be said to have a deeper cognitive meaning as compared to the representations obtained by the method used by Svenson and Nilsson (1986).

The results of the present study suggest that the judged importance of inflation-related variables does not increase, i.e. become more important, when linked into causal chains of scenarios. On the contrary, variables were judged to be more important if they are seen to have a direct effect on the rate of inflation as compared to indirect effects through one or two intervening variables. However, a few multilink scenarios seemed to be as plausible to the subjects as the comparable single-link scenarios, and in those cases one can interpret the results in line with Tversky and Kahneman's interpretation of the conjunction fallacy. It seems that subjects are able to evaluate the scenarios according to mental images in such a way that only a few of the links building up the complete set of scenarios are plausible to the subjects. For example, the Swedish business cycle was perceived as a plausible causal variable in only one three-link scenario while not plausible in the rest of the scenarios. This might be explained by the fact that subjects disbelieve that the business cycle affects the inflation rate through these specific intervening variables.

To speculate, the results parallel the results from research on psychological learning theory. Erickson and Jones (1978) suggested that subjects interpret new situations according to past learning and thus retrieve cognitive images to deal with situations of the present. Thus, subjects might have access to mental models of economics. One can then make inferences and evaluations of causes and effects of basic changes of the variables of the economy by referring to the appropriate mental model of the economy.

Finally, it is important to stress that cognitive representations of economic actors are important for changes in the economy at large. The collective actions of consumers, which affect the sales of specific commodities, the negotiations and agreement about wages in the labour market, and executive decisions in companies, are examples of situations where mental models are part of the decision process. In markets with independent economic agents, mental models certainly emphasize the function of the market, thus supplementing the idea of a free market with independent actors.

REFERENCES

Axelrod, R. (1976). *Structure of Decision: The Cognitive Maps of Political Elites*, Princeton University Press, Princeton, N.J.

Batchelor, R. (1980). Rational expectations, efficient markets and economic policy, *Annual Monetary Review*, **December** 15–25.

Biel, A. and Montgomery, H. (1985). *Scenarios in Energy Planning*. In B. Brehmner, H. Jungerman, P. Lourens, and G. Sevón (Eds), *New Directions in Research on Decision Making*, North-Holland, Amsterdam.

Beherend, H. (1966). Price images, inflation and national incomes policy, *Scottish Journal of Political Economy*, **13**, 273–96.

Beherend, H. (1977). Research into inflation and conceptions of earnings, *Journal of Occupational Psychology*, **50**, 169–76.

Beherend, H. (1984). *Problems of Labour and Inflation*, Croom Helm, London.

Ducot, C., and Lubben, G. J. (1980). A typology of scenarios, *Futures*, **12**, 51–7.

Eden, C., Jones, S. and Sims, D. (1979). *Thinking in Organizations*, Macmillan, London.

Erickson, J. R., and Jones, M. R. (1978). Thinking, *Annual Review of Psychology*, **29**, 61—90.

Jonung, L. (1981). Perceived and expected rates of inflation in Sweden, *American Economic Review*, **71**, 961–8.

Jonung, L. (1985). *Which Model Do People Carry in Their Minds When Forecasting Inflation Rates?*, Seminar Paper 1, National Institute of Economic Research, Stockholm, Sweden.

Jungerman, H. V. (1986). Inferential processes in the construction of scenarios, *Journal of Forecasting*, **4**, 321–7.

Keren, G. (1983). Cultural differences in the misperception of exponential growth, *Perception and Psychophysics*, **34**(3), 289–93.

Maddock, R., and Carter, S. (1982). A child guide to rational expectations, *Journal of Economic Literature*, **20**, 39–51.

Mervis, C. B., and Rosch, E. (1981). Categorization of natural objects, *Annual Review of Psychology*, **32**, 89–115.

Montgomery, H., and Biel, A. (1984). Scenarios and causal models in political decision making, *Proceedings of the Annual Conference of the British Psychological Society*, Warwick, 30 March to 2 April 1984.

Nilsson, G. (1985). *The Formation of Expected Rate of Inflation and Its Cognitive Relation to Perceived Related Economic Variables*, Cognition and Decision Research Unit Report, Department of Psychology, University of Stockholm, (in press).

Roberts, F. S. (1976). The questionnaire method. In R. Axelrod (Ed.), *Structure of Decisions: The Cognitive Maps of Political Elites*, Princeton University Press, Princeton, N.J.

Sevon, G. (1984). Cognitive maps of past and future economic events, *Acta Psychologica*, **56**, 71–9.

Smith, E. E., and Medin, D.L. (1981). *Categories and Concepts*, Harvard University Press, Cambridge, Mass.

Svenson, O., and Nilsson, G. (1986). Mental economics: subjective representations of factors related to expected inflation, *Journal of Economic Psychology*, **7** 327–49.

Tversky, A., and D. Kahneman, (1982). The simulation heuristic. In D. Kahneman, P. Slovic, and A. Tversky (Eds), *Judgements under Uncertainty: Heuristics and Biases*, Cambridge University Press, Cambridge, Mass.

Tversky, A., and Kahneman, D. (1983). Extensional versus intuitive reasoning: the conjunction fallacy in probability judgement, *Psychological Review*, **90**, 293–315.

Wallis, K. F. (1979). Econometric implications, rational expectations, *Econometrica*, **48**(1), 49–73.

Wärneryd, K. E., and Wahlund, R. (1986). Inflationary expectations. In H. Brandstätter and E. Kirchler (Eds), *Economic Psychology*, Trauner, Linz, pp. 327–35.

ACKNOWLEDGEMENTS

This study was supported by a grant from The Bank of Sweden Tercentenary Foundation to Ola Svenson. The author wishes to thank Henry Montgomery, Ola Svenson, Gunnar Karlsson, Jennifer Bullington, and one anonymous reviewer for their comments on an earlier draft of the chapter. Kerstin Meyerhöffer provided necessary assistance for the work reported here.

16

Postdecisional justification: The case of De Lorean

RAY CROZIER

The concept of justifiability has played a part in the study of decision processes since Shepard (1964) suggested that when faced with a decision problem where no alternative is better than every other in all respects people may 'try out various frames of mind until they find one whose associated subjective weights give one alternative the clearest advantage'. Hogarth (1980) has described a justifiability bias as a bias towards using a decision rule if the individual can find a rationale to justify it, a point similar to that made by Slovic (1975), who suggested that the ease with which a rule may be justified may be an important factor in determining the selection of the rule.

Decision researchers have used the concept of justification to refer primarily to the arguments for the course of action that one is considering; it can also refer to the account that one offers for an action that has already been taken, but postdecision justification has been little studied.

There is a substantial social psychological literature on dissonance which deals with the arguments that may be made about rejected alternatives in order to justify to oneself the particular choice that one has made. There is also relevant work by Fischhoff (1980) on 'hindsight bias' and by Nisbett and Wilson (1977) on biases in recalling how decisions were actually made, but this research has not usually analysed the justifications offered.

This chapter is concerned with the arguments that are presented in justification of a decision that has already been taken and whose outcome is known. It considers the nature of those arguments and the possible relationships between justifications and the cognitive processes that preceded the decision. The first

Process and Structure in Human Decision Making
Edited by H. Montgomery and O. Svenson. © 1989 John Wiley & Sons Ltd

part of the chapter focuses on one particular economic decision—the decision of the British Government to invest in the De Lorean sports car in 1978. The transcript of evidence presented in justification of that decision was coded and analysed in terms of categories derived from research into the identification of decision rules in verbal protocols and text instigated by Svenson (1979) and Saris and Gallhofer (1984). The second part of the chapter deals with more general issues arising out of this analysis and offers some suggestions towards the development of a theory of justification processes.

First we need to consider briefly the kinds of justification of a decision that could be offered. In decisions of a routine nature that involve following some established procedure it will be sufficient to argue that the procedure was correctly carried out. However, in more problematic cases a person is obliged to present some account of his/her decision. Scott and Lyman (1968) distinguish among explanations, excuses, and justifications in classifying the accounts that people can present for their actions. An account is a statement made by a social actor to explain unanticipated or untoward behaviour, whether of oneself or others, while an explanation is offered where the action is not untoward. Austin (1961) makes a distinction between excuses and justifications. In making an excuse one admits that the act was wrong or inappropriate but denies that one is responsible for it. In offering a justification one accepts responsibility for the action but denies that the act was wrong or inappropriate. Semin and Manstead (1983) provide an integration of several different typologies of accounts.

While such typologies are potentially useful in suggesting how accounts of decisions might be coded these schemes have been developed to classify actions in an interpersonal context and many categories are not relevant to decisions. We have also to consider that we might be called on to justify two elements in the decision situation—the decision and its outcome. Hence the outcome might be unfortunate but in our account we justify the decision—it was the right decision to take even though it turned out wrong. In general we do seem to talk of justifying decisions rather than excusing them, but we can imagine many contexts in which we would make an excuse for our decisions: we neglected important information, we did not pay sufficient attention, and so on.

We can also account for our decisions by explaining them in terms of a causal model that links the option we have chosen with its outcome and by arguing that this particular option leads to better or at least equivalent outcomes in comparison with the other options. Montgomery (1983) and Biel and Montgomery (1986a) draw upon the concepts of a scenario and a dominance structure to show how a causal model might be used to justify a decision. According to Montgomery (1983) decision making is 'a search for good arguments', and in justification one can set out to show that one has picked a dominant alternative by, for example, referring to a causal model which has a dominance structure. To argue this may involve techniques of dominance structuring like de-emphasizing or bolstering; one plays down or ignores causal models that produce non-attractive outcomes for the preferred alternative or one produces supporting arguments for that alternative. A similar position has been adopted by Axelrod (1976) with his concept of a balanced cognitive map.

It is of value to study empirically the arguments that are produced when accounting for a decision and we have chosen to examine in some detail one particular decision that has been taken where the outcome is known and where the outcome was, to put it mildly, unfortunate. This decision also has the advantage from our point of view that those who made it were called to account for it, and we have a written record of that account.

THE DE LOREAN DECISION

We focus on the decision of the British Government through its agents, the Northern Ireland Department of Commerce (DOC) and the Northern Ireland Development Agency (NIDA), to provide 60.62 million pounds in grants, loans, and share purchases to De Lorean Motor Cars Limited (DMCL) (which incidentally contributed only 0.5 million pounds to the project) in order to employ 2000 workers in Belfast to produce a new sports car. This is an interesting decision to study for a number of reasons:

(a) The decision was made under enormous time pressure. De Lorean met the DOC on 12 June 1978 and asked for a decision in principle by 28 June! DOC accepted this time scale (for reasons which will be clear from their account). 'Heads of Agreement' between the parties were drawn up on 21 June and the master agreement signed on 28 June 1978.
(b) The decision led to unfortunate consequences. In total the DOC and NIDA contributed nearly 77 million pounds but the project went bankrupt and the company was placed in receivership within four years (in February 1982) and the workforce was made redundant. There may have been serious financial irregularities in the administration of the project, and these have been the subject of police investigations in Britain (*Hansard*, 1985) and of legal proceedings in USA (see *The Observer*, 5 October 1986 for details of the case, and *The Belfast Telegraph*, 18 December 1986 for an account of De Lorean's acquittal in the United States on a charge of embezzlement).
(c) Even though the decision was made in only a few weeks the DOC did have time to commission a report from a firm of management consultants, McKinsey & Co. The concluded that 'the Department is being asked to fund an extraordinarily risky venture' and 'the chances of the project succeeding as planned are remote'. Yet these stern warnings made by one of Britain's leading management companies were not heeded nor indeed were other signs that were fundamental flaws in the proposal.
(d) In hindsight the decision is widely regarded as having been a very poor one. The House of Commons Committee which investigated it called it 'one of

the gravest cases of the misuse of public resources for many years', and concluded, 'the prospect of creating large scale employment in West Belfast proved so irresistible to DOC as to diminish its sensitivity to the commercial risk involved, impair its judgment and lead to the wrong decision made—a decision which has cost to date some £70m' (House of Commons, 1984). Commentators have used the failure of the project to argue more generally against the intervention of the state in promoting private industry (*The Times*, 19 July 1984; Redwood, 1984, p. 26).

Public disquiet over the De Lorean affair led to the enquiry by the House of Commons Select Committee. This important committee has the right of access to all relevant records and can call as witnesses all those involved in the decision. It issued its report in July 1984. The transcript of the Minutes of Evidence provides a useful source for the arguments made by the civil servants involved in justification of their decision. The Committee examined a number of different aspects of the affair including the monitoring of the project once it had started, but we will restrict our attention to the evidence pertinent to the original decision to fund the project.

ANALYSIS OF THE DOCUMENT

The structure of the text

The relevant evidence was presented to the Committee on 21 November 1983 and again, more briefly, on 23 January 1984. The Minutes of these sessions comprises questions by Members of the Committee and answers by the DOC and NIDA officials involved in the decision. Each question–answer pair is allocated a paragraph number in the report.

The text for analysis consists of 75 paragraphs of the Report, numbers 551–624 and 1425–8; this is the material focusing on the original decision. First the form of the questions asked needs to be considered since the justifications of the decision are in response to questions rather than a prepared, connected discourse. Thus the form of the questions will shape to some extent the kinds of account given. The 75 questions could be classified as follows: 30 questions called for a factual answer; 24 questions asked for a reason; 15 questions summarized statements and asked for confirmation; 5 questions asked for judgements on the action of another person or organization, while one was an invitation to continue a statement. Thus respondents were asked both to describe actions which they had taken and to provide reasons for those actions. In total, the text analysed comprised some 13 000 words.

The typical decision procedure adopted by the DOC when approached with a request for financial assistance would involve an assessment of the viability of the scheme, the likelihood of its success as a business, and second an analysis of the expected return in number of jobs created for the amount of money invested—a fairly explicit but confidential formula is used in this analysis. The Committee first investigated the adequacy of the DOC's assessment of the viability of the scheme, focusing on the haste with which this assessment was carried out. A careful reading of the document suggests that the DOC accounts for its procedures by first arguing that the decision to reach an agreement in line with the timetable demanded by De Lorean was the best one to make and then arguing that within this timescale their assessment was reasonably thorough.

However an analysis of justifications needs to go beyond this kind of interpretation with its risks of subjectivity and potential unreliability, and hence we applied to this account the procedure of empirical decision analysis (Gallhofer, Saris, and Melman, 1986; see also this volume). A number of techniques has been developed for the analysis of decisions from texts, including empirical decision analysis, cognitive mapping (Axelrod, 1976), and scenario analysis (Biel and Montgomery, 1986). We adopted the first method for three reasons: Gallhofer, Saris and Melman (1986) provide a manual for the technique including details of empirical studies of the technique's reliability and of a method for determining its validity; one of our theoretical interests is the role of expressed uncertainty in accounting for a decision, and EDA allows the incorporation of probabilistic statements (Gallhofer, Saris, and Melman, 1986, p. 97); we wish to relate this study to our research on the structure of arguments in justification, where decision trees are used to capture structure (Crozier, 1986). While our preference was for a demonstrably reliable technique that incorporates conditional and probabilistic language, any choice of a method imposes limitations, and, as will be seen, EDA makes it difficult to reflect argument structures where non-mutually exclusive outcomes lead from a course of action.

Adopting the procedure recommended for EDA, the text was scrutinized for references to alternative courses of action (A), for courses of action taken by De Lorean and other parties (AO), and for outcomes of all these courses of action (O). References to positive or negative values associated with these outcomes were coded (V +, V −), as were references to probabilistic links between actions and outcomes (p). The alternative that was chosen reflected the argument that in order to have a chance of the De Lorean project locating in Belfast then one would have to make a quick bid. The alternative courses of action identified in the text were renegotiating the bid and taking extra time for a more detailed assessment. Each of these alternatives is shown to lead to delay and to disadvantageous outcomes. A problem with representing these alternative courses of action is that they are interdependent: failing to make a rapid decision is an alternative in itself, but both renegotiating and making a further assessment also involve delay. The first comparison made in the text is between alternatives A1, making a rapid assessment, and A2, failing to make a bid quickly enough; the derived tree is presented in Figure 1a; subsequently in the text alternatives

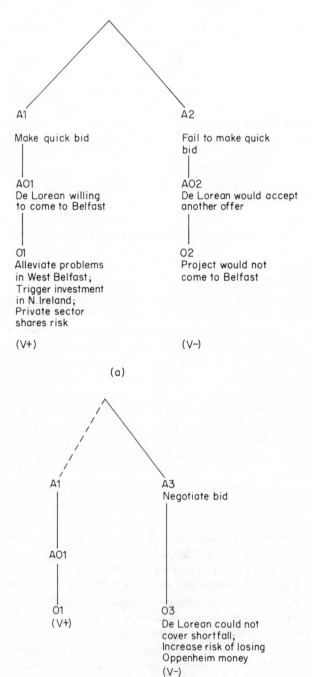

(a)

(b)

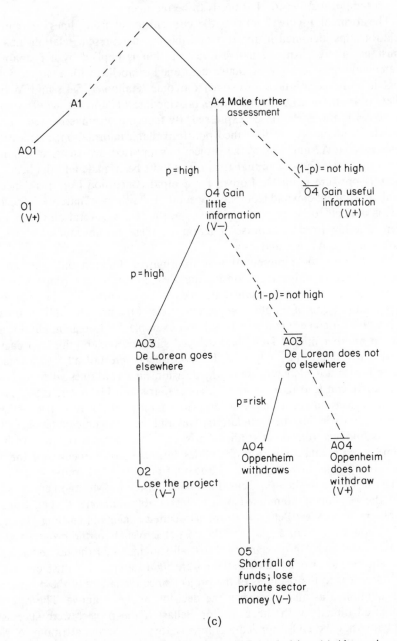

(c)

Fig. 1   Decision tree of argument justifying haste of the decision. (a) Alternatives one and two, (b) alternatives one and three, (c) alternatives one and four.

A3 and A4 are discussed; these are depicted in Figures 1b and c; i.e. the argument has a temporal structure that needs to be retained.

The form of Figure 1 follows the convention of using lines to represent relationships identified in the text and dashes to represent relationships that must be inferred. An alternative outcome that is implied by a probabilistic statement but is itself not explicitly mentioned is labelled with a bar to indicate that it is the negation of an explicit outcome (Gallhofer, Saris and Melman, 1986, p. 143). The EDA analysis does provide insights into the justification but some reservations should be expressed. By focusing on links between actions and their outcomes one fails to incorporate available information; e.g. the certain link between A2 and loss of the project is supported by extensive arguments concerning the knowledge that rival offers have been made and the belief that there is pressure upon De Lorean for a rapid conclusion from his American bankers, Oppenheim and Company. Second, the 'either–or' nature of a decision tree is difficult to match to the presence in the text of several outcomes being seen to follow from one course of action, i.e. these are not mutually exclusive outcomes (see A1, A3, and A4).

Nevertheless the representation is informative. Linking outcomes to one course of action rather than considering all their interrelationships is in itself a form of persuasive argument that needs to be captured. The justification is presented in terms of simplified representations of the problem: a large number of possible outcomes are not included. For example, De Lorean might not have chosen another offer if DOC had delayed since presumably his approach to Northern Ireland did imply that the rival offers were not all that attractive. There is also a tendency to frame the decisions as trivial ones where only one alternative can lead to a positive outcome (Saris and Gallhofer, 1984, classify this as a decision according to a reversed Simon rule). There is also omission of uncertainty in links between alternatives and their outcomes, a tendency that reflects findings from other studies (Saris and Gallhofer, 1984). Only A4 has a complex representation with probabilities, but here too the focus is on the high probability of negative outcomes following from a rejected course of action.

The justification shows a clear dominance structure (Montgomery, 1983) in that the account is dominated by one favourable outcome, that of bringing employment to West Belfast with the associated benefits of curbing violence.

We now turn to an analysis of the cost-effectiveness of the project and the DOC's assessment of its viability. First, all statements in the text referring to cost-effectiveness were identified; there were eight statements. Conspicuous here are references to the riskiness of the project since the failure of the project was not mentioned as an outcome in the decision analysed above. The risks are compared directly with the gains for Belfast if the project were successful, implying that the DOC applied a compensatory rule across attributes of risks and rewards. Normally the DOC would be expected to apply a conjunctive rule with the cost per job and the viability or riskiness of the project as attributes, and a project being approved if it fulfilled both criteria. Its critics have argued that in this case risk was neglected and only the number of jobs to be created was considered; there is an admission in the text that the usual criteria were relaxed but there is rejection of the criticism that the viability of the project was neglected. The remainder of the text deals with this question of viability.

The viability of the project

The committee focused on four areas of concern:

(a) the lack of a full engineering assessment of the scheme, particularly in the light of the DOC's inexperience in the motor industry;
(b) the neglect of the indications of risk that were apparent in the assessment they did carry out, including the McKinsey report;
(c) the lack of investigation into De Lorean himself;
(d) the lack of investigation into De Lorean's negotiations with the other interested agencies.

We identified 53 paragraphs in the text that were responses to these points of criticism. The discussion did not concern choices between courses of action and their consequences as much as the adequacy of procedures, and hence EDA was not an appropriate analytical tool. Close reading of the text suggests an argument structure: reasons are provided for one's assertions, and questions and criticisms are met by counter argument. We lack content-analysis methods to do justice to this kind of structure, although Biel and Montgomery (1986b) are developing a scheme for coding arguments in their study of Swedish energy policies. The scheme we adopted is a simpler version of theirs and involves two theoretically interesting categories: excuses (admitting that a procedure was inadquate but pointing to factors outside one's control) and justifications (asserting the correctness of procedures in the face of criticism). Additionally, a miscellaneous category is needed to code factual statements.

Coding was at the level of the individual response to a question. A small number of responses included more than one argument, making a total of 55 statements coded; in addition the reasons given in excuse or justification were noted. Results are presented in Table 1; such results are only preliminary since further work into refining the categories and exploring their reliability is needed. Classification of the arguments suggests (a) that responses are largely in terms of justifications in defence of procedures followed; (b) there is a suggestion of a shift in argument according to the particular criticisms made. There is a tendency to recognize the failure to carry out an engineering assessment; the principal excuse refers to lack of time, although justifications are also offered in that such assessment would have added little to what was already known. Elsewhere in the text excuses are rare; the most extensive set of justifications responds to the accusation that the risks identified in the McKinsey report were

Table 1   The viability of the project: frequency of excuses and justifications in response
to four kinds of criticisms

	Frequency of responses			
Criticisms	Excuses	Justifications	Miscellaneous	Total
Failure to provide engineering assessment	6	4	3	13
Failure to recognize risks	1	15	6	22
Failure to investigate De Lorean	0	4	2	6
Failure to investigate other bids	1	9	4	14
Total	8	32	15	55

ignored. This criticism is rejected on the grounds that McKinsey provided the most pessimistic evaluation of the project's viability ('the downside risk'), whereas there were other favourable evaluations by competent judges, including effective counterarguments by De Lorean. In addition attention was drawn to the difficulty of attracting sound projects to Northern Ireland.

GENERAL DISCUSSION

We should now like to consider more general issues arising out of the foregoing analysis of the De Lorean justification in the hope of making some points towards the development of a theory of the justification process. These issues arise out of two of our specific conclusions:

(a) To justify a decision in the sense of providing an account of unwanted consequences of a decision is to make an argument, and the structure of the account seems to be an argument structure in terms of making and defending assertions, appealing to the judgements of experts, etc.

(b) Specific sections of the argument refer to elements of a rational decision process; i.e. risks are evaluated and there seem to be trade-offs among absolute values of costs, benefits, and risks.

We need to pursue these implications further and to ask:

(a) What makes a good argument? That is to say, this justification takes place in a particular social context where there must be shared assumptions about the kinds of statements that are admissable and that can be accepted as an adequate justification of one's decision. It might be argued that this Committee has the brief of establishing the facts of the matter by asking factual questions, but it is clear from the transcript that arguments are offered in defence of the decision process rather than providing a straightfoward description of it.

(b) This leads to our second question: how does the decision-making process that emerges from the justification correspond to the actual decision-making process? Did the actual decision emerge as the result of the rational activity which is claimed? This question must be seen in the context of the large literature on organizational decision making which rejects the conceptualization of organizational decisions in terms of rational, individual decision processes (e.g. Weeks and Whimster, 1985).

We shall suggest that these two questions are in fact related; that providing a justification of a decision is to frame it in terms of a rational process that is in effect a construction; it need not bear any resemblance to the processes that led up to the decision. Accounts that provide accurate descriptions of the decision process do not necessarily make good justifications.

Good arguments

Our first approach to the argument structure was to devise a coding scheme that seemed to capture the statements of the text and that seem generalizable to other texts. However, this empirical procedure fails to capture the strategic dimensions of arguments, i.e. statements are combined in pursuit of some objectives and some overall grasp of what constitutes a good argument. This grasp allows participants to judge, for example, when a point has been adequately answered or when an argument has been carried. The questions of what constitutes a good argument and how arguments relate to rational decision processes are large ones that do not seem to have been directly addressed by psychologists. One might argue that there is no such thing as a good argument in the abstract since what seems sound to one person will appear weak to the adversary; however, presumably people on one side of a debate can rank-order possible arguments in terms of the effects they might be expected to have.

The most relevant literature would be that of persuasion and attitude change, but here the emphasis seems to be on human irrationality and less on the view that a person's attitude can be changed by the content of an argument. Research has shown that identical content can lead to different outcomes, depending on characteristics of the source of the message (its credibility, etc.) or its recipient (self-esteem, level of emotional involvement with the issue, etc.), or on the structure of the message, as in studies of order effects. Research on content has focused upon emotional content or on whether one side or more than one side of an argument should be presented. In the latter case the issue is complex, depending on a number of factors including the nature of the audience for the message. Evidence substantiating these assertions is reviewed by Triandis (1971), Burgoon and Bettinghaus (1980), and Perloff and Brock (1980).

Arguments have received most sustained attention from Perelman (Perelman and Olbrects-Tyteca, 1969; Perelman, 1979) who has defined argumentation as 'non-formal reasoning that aims at obtaining or reinforcing the adherence of an audience'. He stresses the relationship between the person making the argument and the audience; indeed it is the dependence of argument on the audience that distinguishes rhetoric from formal logic.

The De Lorean document records the arguments of a number of individual who are being questioned by those to whom ultimately they are responsible concerning the correctness of their procedures and the soundness of their judgement. Their arguments are developed within a question–answer framework subject to formal rules and conventions. Over and above its formal role in examining accounts the Committee had a wider political significance and there is a larger audience for the report including the mass media. All of these considerations influence the kind of argument in justification that can be offered. This leads us to assert that there can be no one-to-one correspondence between the account provided and the actual decision process since accounts can be expected to vary according to the social context of the justification and the nature of its audience. A rigourous test of this assertion will require material in addition to this particular document and an investigation of changes in argument with different audiences.

Organizational decisions

How are the decision processes of organizations to be described? One approach has been to work on the assumption that the decision could be treated as if it has been made by a single rational individual. The seminal contribution here is that of March and Simon (1958). They distinguish decisions that are routinized from those that call for problem-solving and search activities. For many if not most organizational decisions, knowledge of routines may be sufficient to predict actual decisions. March and Simon do attend to the structure of the organization; subunits may have conflicting goals and there are problems of division of labour and with communication, such as, for example, uncertainty absorption where information about uncertainty is lost in transmission through the organization.

Despite these concerns the thrust of this approach is on the impact upon organizational decisions of the rational processes of the individuals who are its members. This approach is common (Allison, 1971; Weeks and Whimster, 1985). Allison indicated the kind of inference that is characteristic of this approach: if an organization chose a particular alternative course of action then the organization must have had ends towards which the action constituted a maximizing means; the decision process can be reconstructed by assuming rationality. However, this has been criticized as neglecting the essential social nature of organizations, in particular, that the decision might reflect the structure of the organization or the balance of power relationships within it. Allison analysed the Cuban missile crisis of 1962 in terms of these three perspectives to demonstrate that while each contributed to an account of the decision process none offered a sufficient explanation. Table 2, which is developed from one provided by Allison (1971, p. 256), contrasts the three approaches in terms of the perspective they take upon the neglect of uncertainty, which has been shown to characterize many political decisions, and the extent to which the decision process can be reconstructed from a document.

Interpreting the decision described in a document as the outcome of a rational thought process leads one to assign neglect of uncertainty to cognitive processes. However, the other models offer alternative explanations, either in terms of information transmission between the subunits of the organization (March and Simon, 1958) or in terms of bargaining between power forces, where arguments that stress certain links between a course of action and its consequences will be more convincing and carry more weight. Organizational processes and power relationships are not normally revealed in documents that present accounts of

Table 2 Differences between three models of organizational decision making (table developed from one provided by Allison, 1971, p. 256)

	Models		
	Individual actor	Organizational process	Power relationships
Unit of analysis	Action as choice	Action as output	Action as political outcome
Decision a product of ...	Rational choice	Existing organizational programs	Bargaining
Source of neglect of uncertainty	Cognitive limitation/bias	Absorption in communication	Simple arguments
Can decision be inferred from document alone?	Yes	No	No

decision processes, and, as Allison showed, further information about the structure of an organization and its history of decision making is needed.

The De Lorean decision as an organizational process

The approach that we have taken to the De Lorean decision has essentially been that of the first model. We have used the account to set out tables that represent the alternative courses of action faced by the team responsible for the decision and in doing so have neglected (a) the temporal dimension of the decision, i.e. the decision may never have looked like that to the decision makers, and (b) we have treated the team as if it were a single individual with the decision as an outcome of its cognitions.

Yet this may be oversimplification of the process. First, several subunits of the organization were involved together with other organizations. Although these are identified in the document the hypothesis of the organizational process model, that a decision at time t can be predicted from the behaviour of the organization at times $t - 1, t - 2$, etc., needs to go beyond the account presented to the Committee. Similarly an analysis of the power structure in the organization would need to go beyond that account.

This can be demonstrated by considering information additional to that in the Committee Report. We can add two sources: a transcript of the Parliamentary Debate on the Report (*Hansard*, 1985); a journalistic reconstruction of the affair which was commended by the Committee (Fallon and Srodes, 1983). A detailed account of the decision will not be possible here, and indeed will need further information than is available in these sources, but we will make several points:

(a) The Report only gives a partial account of the decision process in that it excludes the deliberations of government ministers who were finally responsible for the decision. According to *Hansard* there were several meetings of relevant ministers in the crucial period from De Lorean's first contact (8 June 1978) and the final signing of the contract on 28 July 1978.

(b) It is clear from the relevant Minister's own statement to Parliament that he had to argue a case with ministerial colleagues for granting support to De Lorean, and that he had been a very enthusiastic advocate of this from the outset. Two points can be made here. First, this argument would be only one in a series of issues to do with Northern Ireland and, as Allison suggests in his Model III, part of an ongoing political bargaining process among ministers; second, there is a critical division of labour here, in that the minister is negotiating with his colleagues while it is the agency NIDA that is negotiating with De Lorean. However, NIDA's approach to the issue will be coloured by the realization that the minister is an advocate of one decision alternative (see, for example, Fallon and Srodes, 1983, p. 138).

(c) Again it is an oversimplification to conceive of one negotiating team. There are two agencies involved—NIDA and DOC—and a third agency, IDAC, with which the other two had a statutory duty to consult. In fact IDAC did not feel it could offer advice since it was dubious about the decision on commercial grounds but realized its wider political significance. While this action could have been interpreted as a warning sign, it is not seen as such in the justification, and in hindsight it had the effect of weakening the argument against the decision.

(d) Insight into the decision can be gained by restoring the temporal dimension and considering this alongside the divisions of labour involved. In early June NIDA was clearly impressed by the De Lorean reputation and documentation, and the political leaders could see an opportunity to 'do something' for Northern Ireland. When the conditional offer to De Lorean was made on 21 June 1978, it was on the understanding that De Lorean was putting up some $20 million including the Oppenheim money. Hence there was some parity in the contributions of the two sides and this $20 million can be seen to have had as much psychological as economic significance. However, on 26 June this American money was no longer available and De Lorean's representatives asked for further British money to compensate. While this could have radically changed the decision problem it does not seem to have been framed like that but rather was seen as a problem in its own right that was quickly resolved. We have already discussed the next potential change in the decision problem, the McKinsey Report of 18 July. What appears with hindsight to have been aberrations in the decision process can be interpreted as episodes in an ongoing process: given the ministerial initiatives that are prompted in early June and the commitment of the organization as a whole to one alternative it is problematic just what information could have been transmitted to radically alter the decision. Certainly the fresh information underlined the riskiness of the project but the minister in any case was already prepared to take a risky decision.

It could be argued that if the decision problem as it existed on, say, 18 July were set before the decision makers then they would have made a rather different appraisal of the situation than they made of the modified problem that they actually faced.

Argumentation and the decision process

We have examined at some length one political decision as it provides a very well documented example of the justification of a decision. Our examination suggests that we need to look further at the use of arguments. However, the relationship between arguments and decisions cannot be expected to be a straightforward one, in that (a) a decision that is made by an organization of any degree of complexity can be described at different levels and (b) the form of an argument can be expected to vary with a large number of factors including the objectives of the person making the argument, that person's conceptualization of the audience, the aspect of the decision that has been called into question, and the actual decision outcome.

Nevertheless, we offer the following generalizations which draw upon social psychological studies of providing accounts, the notion that dominance structures are easy to justify, and our own analyses of political arguments:

(a) While occasionally political leaders may focus on one overriding problem, usually they face many issues simultaneously where they have to persuade more than one individual or organization and where their actions and statements are available for inspection by many audiences. All these result in pressures for the simplest argument that is acceptable. While the elements in any decision are complex, decisions have to be made, communicated, and justified, and this leaves no room for complex messages to be transmitted. The simplest argument is that there is no alternative to the course of action that has been recommended.

(b) This argument will be unacceptable for certain kinds of audiences and particularly when one is called upon to justify a decision. In this case one has to select the simplest argument that will show that one has acted correctly. In the case of routine decisions it may be enough to show that the correct procedures have been followed. However, in the case of decision problems (following the distinction made by March and Simon, 1958) this will not be sufficient. Here the criterion will be that of rationality. As Montgomery (1983) has proposed, the simplest argument here will relate to a dominance structure; alternative courses of action can be introduced but it is shown that these are dominated by one's own action. If this is not acceptable then one may have to go on to demonstrate a more refined principle such as maximization of expected utility.

In making these assertions we are proposing:

(a) that these are arguments intended to achieve certain effects and they do not necessarily relate to decision processes;

(b) that arguments will be framed in these terms, i.e. it is not acceptable to justify your decision in terms of some heuristic ('that is how we always make such decisions'), even if that is how decisions are often made and that is how decision makers may often describe their activity in private! Neither is it acceptable to describe the organizational or political process that led up to the decision since this is not sufficient to establish rationality;

(c) that the key variable is the reference to non-chosen alternatives since arguments will vary in terms of how these are framed. We predict a systematic relationship between nature of audience, need to justify, and reference to rejected alternatives.

These generalizations may have heuristic value in directing research into the neglected area of the justification of decisions.

REFERENCES

Allison, G. T. (1971). *Essence of Decision. Explaining the Cuban Missile Crisis*, Little, Brown and Company, Boston.
Austin, J. L. (1961). *Philosophical Papers*, Oxford University Press, London.
Axelrod, R. (1976). *Structure of Decision: The Cognitive Maps of Political Elites*, Princeton University Press, Princeton, N.J.
Biel, A., and Montgomery, H. (1986a). Scenarios in energy planning. In B. Brehmer, H. Jungermann, P. Lourens, and G. Sevón (Eds), *New Directions in Research on Decision Making*, North-Holland, Amsterdam.
Biel, A., and Montgomery, H. (1986b). Paper presented at the European Group for Process Studies of Decision Making, Göteborg.
Burgoon, M., and Bettinghaus, E. P. (1980). Persuasive message strategies. In M.E. Roloff and G. R. Miller (Eds), *Persuasion: New Directions in Theory and Research*, Sage Publications, London.
Crozier, W. R. (1986). Paper presented at the European Group for Process Studies of Decision Making, Göteborg.
Fallon, I., and Srodes, J. (1983). *De Lorean: The Rise and Fall of a Dream Maker*, Hamish Hamilton, London.
Fischhoff, B. (1980). For those condemned to study the past: reflections on historical judgment. In R. Shweder and D. W. Fiske (Eds), *New Directions for Methodology of Behavioral Science: Fallible Judgment in Behavioral Research*, Jossey-Bass, San Francisco, Calif.
Gallhofer, I. N., Saris, W. E., and Melman, M. (1986). *Different Text Analysis Procedures for the Study of Decision Making*, Sociometric Research Foundation, Amsterdam.
Hansard (1985). House of Commons Official Report. Parliamentary Debates (Hansard), Vol. 78, No. 108, Wednesday 1 May 1985. HMSO, London.
Hogarth, R. M. (1980). *Judgement and Choice*, Wiley, New York.
House of Commons (1984). Twenty-fifth Report from the Committee of Public Accounts. Session 1983–4. Financial Assistance to De Lorean Motor Cars Ltd. HMSO, London.
March, J. G., and Simon, H.A. (1958). *Organisations*, Wiley, New York.
Montgomery, H. (1983). Decision rules and the search for a dominance structure: towards a process model of decision making. In P. Humphreys, O. Svenson, and A. Vari (Eds), *Analysing and Aiding Decision Processes*, North-Holland, Amsterdam.
Nisbett, R., and Wilson, T. (1977). Telling more than we can know: verbal reports on mental processes, *Psychological Review*, **84**, 231–59.
Perelman, C. (1979). *The New Rhetoric and the Humanities*, D. Reidel, Dordrecht, Holland.
Perelman, C., and Olbrects-Tyteca, L. (1969). *The New Rhetoric: A Treatise on Argumentation*, University of Notre Dame Press, London.
Perloff, R. M., and Brock, T. C. (1980). 'And thinking makes it so': cognitive responses to persuasion. In M. E. Roloff and G. R. Miller (Eds), *Persuasion: New Directions in Theory and Research*, Sage Publications, London.

Redwood, J. (1984). *Going for Broke ... Gambling with Taxpayers' Money,* Blackwell, Oxford.

Saris, W. E., and Gallhofer, I. N. (1984). Formulation of real life decisions: a study of foreign policy decisions. In K. Borcherding, B. Brehmer, C. Vlek, and W. Wagenaar (Eds), *Research Perspectives on Decision Making under Uncertainty,* North-Holland, Amsterdam.

Scott, M. B., and Lyman, S. (1968). Accounts, *American Sociological Review,* **33,** 46–62.

Semin, G. R., and Manstead, A. S. R. (1983). *The Accountability of Conduct,* Blackwell, Oxford.

Shepard, R. N. (1964). On subjectively optimum selections among multi-attribute alternatives. In M. W. Shelley and G. L. Bryan (Eds), *Human Judgments and Optimality,* Wiley, New York.

Slovic, P. (1975). Choice between equally valued alternatives, *Journal of Experimental Psychology: Human Perception and Performance,* **1,** 280–7.

Svenson, O. (1979). Process descriptions of decision making, *Organizational Behavior and Human Performance,* **23,** 86—112.

Triandis, H. C. (1971). *Attitude and Attitude Change,* Wiley, New York.

Weeks, D., and Whimster, D. (1985). Contexted decision making: a socio-organizational perspective. In G. Wright (Ed.), *Behavioral Decision Making,* Plenum, New York.

17

Decision trees and decision rules in politics: The empirical decision analysis procedure

IRMTRAUD N. GALLHOFER

and

WILLEM E. SARIS

INTRODUCTION

Large numbers of primary documents are available in which political decision makers explain their choices. Examples of such documents include minutes of governmental meetings, coded telegrams from embassies, reports from various governmental agencies.

There are several problems in analysing such texts in order to arrive at a description of the decision maker's argumentation. First, there is the problem of choosing the concepts one should use. Second, the problem arises as to whether different readers (coders) of a document using the same concepts obtain the same results (coder reliability). Third, how can one assess whether or not the coding instrument measures what it is intended to measure? Fourth, given a reliable representation of the argumentation, which hypotheses should be made in order to describe the choice rule used by the decision maker?

In a long-term study, the authors of this paper have tackled these problems while developing the empirical decision analysis (EDA) procedure (Gallhofer, 1978; Gallhofer and Saris, 1979a, 1979b, 1979c, 1982, 1988). The theoretical framework of the approach is decision theory as it was developed through

Process and Structure in Human Decision Making
Edited by H. Montgomery and O. Svenson. © 1989 John Wiley & Sons Ltd

collaboration between statisticians and experimental psychologists (Edwards, 1961; Fishburn, 1964; Keeney and Raiffa, 1976). Although Edwards was still optimistic in 1961 about the usefulness of the subjective expected utility (SEU) model, the so-called rational or analytic choice model, Simon (1957) had already proposed models for bounded rationality. Later studies (e.g. Tversky, 1969; Slovic, 1975; Montgomery, 1977; Huber, 1982; Larichev *et al.*, 1980) confirmed that the choices of human decision makers were not in agreement with the SEU model but rather followed a number of other rules. For an overview of these rules we refer to Svenson (1979) and Huber (1982). The EDA procedure has been developed to describe decision rules used by decision makers.

In presenting this method, we shall first describe the coding instructions, then the results of the reliability studies will be discussed, and subsequently the research methods and results will be presented, including an application.

CODING INSTRUCTIONS

The purpose of the content analysis is to derive a decision maker's decision tree on the basis of his/her argumentation.

DECISION TREES

In the present context a decision tree gives an overview of the argumentation derived from the written protocol. Figure 1 gives an example of a decision tree. This decision tree relates to a telegram from a Dutch official in Indonesia to the Foreign Minister in The Hague in 1947. The document discusses the possibilities of maintaining law and order in Indonesia.

A decision tree consists of a chronological sequence of the actions (A) available to the decision maker, the possible actions of the opponent(s) (AO)—if present—and the possible outcomes (O) for the decision maker. The subjective values or utilities (U) of the possible outcomes (O) as well as the subjective probabilities (P) of the actions of the opponent(s) and the outcomes are also indicated in the diagram.

Figure 1 illustrates a decision maker who has a choice between two strategies or courses of action. By 'strategy' we mean a program of action that might be adopted by the decision maker. Grammatically it frequently consists of a set of imperative clauses which may be modified by conditional phrases (see also Fishburn, 1964, p. 23). Figure 1 shows two strategies which can be paraphrased as follows:

Strategy 1.   Take a strong military action. If severe sanctions occur lavish the

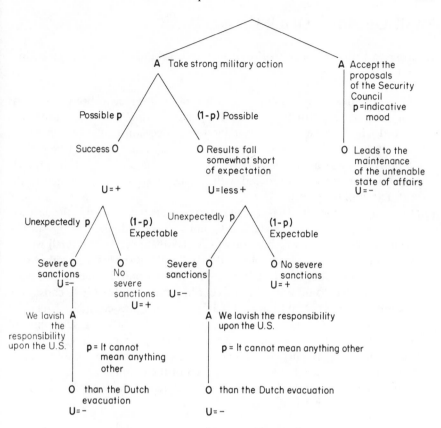

where strategy I reads: Take a strong military action. If severe sanctions occur lavish the
        responsibility on the United States. Otherwise nothing else has to be done
and strategy 2 reads: Accept the proposal of the Security Council

Fig. 1 Example of a decision tree.

responsibility on the United States. Otherwise nothing else has to
be done.

Strategy 2.   Accept the proposal of the Security Council.

This example shows that the simplest form of a strategy (strategy 2) consists of
a single action of the decision maker.

Based on the utilities assigned to the various outcomes and the probabilities
of occurrence of the outcomes and the actions of the opponent(s)—which actually
do not accur in the example of Figure 1—the decision maker can decide which
strategy should be chosen.

TASK OF THE CODERS

In order to help the coders perform their task adequately, we split it up into several steps:

(a) The coder has to read the document carefully in order to become familiar with the general structure of the discourse. During this stage he/she will record which strategies are available to the decision maker, which course of action is preferred, and which are the major paragraphs where these courses of action are elaborated. After having acquired this primary information he/she can proceed with the next step which is devoted to the extraction of concepts.

(b) In order to extract the decision theoretic concepts represented in the decision tree, one must first specify the coding units. As recording units (the specific segment of text into which a concept is classified; see Holsti 1969) we use grammatical units such as noun and/or verb phrases. This means that they can vary, depending on the concept. The context unit, i.e. the largest body of text that has to be searched for recording units (Holsti 1969), consists of a complete sentence. Within each paragraph that was considered relevant to the argumentation at the previous stage one starts by screening all sentences, regardless of whether decision-making concepts are present or not. If they are present, the sentence is broken down into recording units and, finally, a concept is assigned to each of these units.

In order to illustrate this coding step we present the following sentence, which is the context unit:

> In the case where an action against Djocjakarta might, however unexpectedly, provoke severe sanctions, so that the Netherlands have to give way, then as a last resort we can lavish the responsibility upon the United States.

It will now be broken down by bracket notation in noun/verb phrase components to which concepts are assigned:

> (O:In the case where (A:an action against Djocjakarta) might (P:however unexpectedly) provoke (U:severe sanctions))
> (A:so that the Netherlands have to give way, then as a last resort we can lavish the responsibility upon the United States)

This example illustrates a possible coding. It consists of two main verb/noun phrase recoding units. The first unit is considered as an outcome (O) concept and the second as an action (A) concept. In the outcome (O) three other concepts are embedded, i.e. an action (A) concept, a probability (P) concept and a utility (U) concept.

(c) After having extracted the concepts for each relevant paragraph, one starts to construct decision trees based on the concepts that have been found. First, partial trees are made, relating to specific paragraphs. Then these partial trees, containing interrelated argumentations (e.g. referring to the same action), are combined into larger structures. Finally, the entire argumentation—consisting of all actions available to the decision maker—is represented in an overview diagram (see Figure 1).

Further details on this approach can be found in Gallhofer and Saris (1986, Appendix 3), where all the coding steps are illustrated by an example.

ASSESSMENT OF THE CODING RELIABILITY

Since a highly reliable instrument is a prerequisite for the validity of the procedure, it is necessary to investigate the inter-and intracoder agreements. Several reliability studies have been undertaken by the authors (Gallhofer, 1978; Gallhofer and Saris, 1979a–c, 1988) and satisfactory results were obtained. The reliability of the assignment of concepts was studied in the following way. First coders individually coded several documents. Then they were grouped in pairs, compared their results, and, where differences occurred, they tried to arrive at a common solution. After some time they repeated this procedure. In this way we were able to use individual and group codings for the computation of the inter- and intracoder reliability.

CONCEPT RELIABILITY

For the reliability of the concept assignment we needed an *association measure for nominal data*. We selected Scott's π. It is defined as the ratio of the above chance agreement (Krippendorff, 1970, p. 144). If P_0 is the observed proportion of agreement and P_e the expected proportion of agreement then

$$\pi = \frac{P_0 - P_e}{1 - P_e}$$

The numerator is a measure of the above-chance agreement observed and the denominator is a measure of the above-chance agreement maximally possible:

$$P_0 = \frac{1}{n} \sum n_{ii}$$

where n is the total number of codings and n_{ii} is the number of codings that is assigned to concept i by both coders. The proportion of expected agreement is defined by

$$P_e = \frac{1}{n^2} \sum \left(\frac{n_{i.} + n_{.i}}{2} \right)^2$$

where $n_{i.}$ is the frequency with which concept i is used by the first coder and

$n_{.i}$ is the frequency by which concept i is used by the second coder. When the level of agreement equals chance expectancy, the value of π is zero; if perfect, it is one, and if less than can be expected by chance, its value becomes negative.

The agreement scores of the inter- and intracoder reliability for the assignment of concepts at the individual level were all > 0.8, which was judged satisfactory. Since the agreement scores of the group codings did not increase the reliability significantly (Gallhofer, 1978), our conclusion is that this step could just as well be performed at the individual level. Nevertheless, for the further analysis, those results were used upon which two coders agreed.

DECISION TREE RELIABILITY

For the assessment of the coding reliability of the construction of decision trees individual and group data for both partial and overview trees—the latter present the entire argumentation (see Figure 1)—were available. For an agreement measure an *ad hoc* measure was used, constructed for this purpose. The denominator of the agreement coefficient consists of the sum of the maximum number of branches for each node in the tree structure made by either of the coders. The numerator presents the sum of the branches which are indentical for both coders, i.e. with respect to the number of branches and their concepts. The agreement measure is thus the ratio between the sum of the identical branches and the sum of the maximum number of branches:

$$M = \frac{\text{number of identical branches}}{\text{maximum number of branches}}$$

It can take on values ranging from 0 to 1. For an illustration of the computation we refer to Gallhofer and Saris (1979c).

The results of the first reliability study showed that the construction of partial trees could be satisfactorily performed. The median agreement at the individual level was 1.0. The agreement with respect to the construction of overview diagrams, however, proved to be unsatisfactory, both at the individual and group levels. The agreement scores ranged between 0.3 and 0.7. In order to improve the procedure, the following steps were undertaken:

(a) It was decided to use pairs of coders who first coded the texts independently and then produced a joint coding. In this way they could correct each other's mistakes.
(b) The instruction was changed. In the earlier study, coders concentrated too much on details at the beginning. In the new instruction they first had to become familiar with the general structure of the document and then study the details.
(c) A procedure for the selection of good coders was developed. A detailed new

reliability study (Gallhofer and Saris, 1988) showed that thanks to these improvements the construction of overview diagrams can be done almost perfectly, which means that the procedure is repeatable.

With respect to the selection of good coders some further explanation seems to be in order. We use a standard coding for a decision tree derived by the joint coding of a group of four coders. The coders first constructed the tree individually, then came together, in groups of two, producing a joint coding, and finally came together in a group of four to obtain the final coding. Since the individual agreement scores of the four coders with the standard coding are known, one can assess the score for good individual codings. In this case it should be > 0.8. This score is the minimum criterion when selecting new coders.

In the following we summarize the results obtained by the coders trained according to the new instructions. Of the six coders who took part in this research (Gallhofer and Saris, 1988), four arrived at an agreement greater than 0.8. with the standard coding. The remaining two coders achieved an agreement of between 0.6. and 0.8. Given these results, the latter two were not selected to take part in the further codings. The four good coders then coded 71 documents individually and achieved the following intercoder reliability: for 36 texts the scores were between 0.95 and 1.0; for 20 texts the agreement ranged between 0.8 and 0.95; for 8 texts the agreement was between 0.7 and 0.8; and for only 7 texts it ranged between 0.6 and 0.7. Taking into account that the group codings are used for the analysis, one may assume that the agreement is almost perfect.

ASSESSMENT OF VALIDITY

Since it is often very difficult to find independent evidence to corroborate results obtained by analyses based on textual data, frequently one has to rely on indirect or partial evidence to get an indication of whether or not the instrument measures what it is intended to measure. In the case of results obtained by the EDA procedure one can make use of indirect evidence. One can, for example assess whether or not the instrument works. Figure 2 summarizes our validation design.

This figure shows that the decision maker has a structure of the decision problem in his/her mind, i.e. he/she perceives available actions and possible outcomes. Besides evaluating these outcomes a strategy is chosen using a choice rule. This process is latent and can not be perceived by the researcher. The researcher has, on the one hand, parts of the text produced by the author, which relate to the structure of the decision (i.e. the decision tree), and, on the other hand, another distinct part of the text where the decision maker indicates which strategy is chosen. By coding the first part of the text a derivation of the decision structure, i.e. a decision tree, is obtained. By coding the second part of the text an indication of the chosen strategy is obtained.

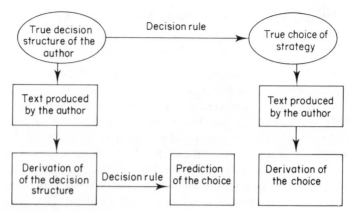

Fig. 2   Validation of the EDA procedure. Characteristics indicated with circular forms refer to unobserved characteristics.

On the basis of the decision structure we can arrive at a prediction of the choice by using a decision rule. If the predictions of the choices agree closely to the measured choices, one can be more assured that the instrument is measuring what it is supposed to measure.

In order to predict the choices, one needs, besides decision trees, decision rules that specify how human beings choose. In the second part of this chapter, the usefulness of this approach will be illustrated.

AN APPLICATION OF THE EDA PROCEDURE

The purpose of this study was to predict the use of decision rules based on the argumentation provided by the decision makers, relating to Dutch foreign policy. We start with a discussion of the decision rules found in our study. Hypotheses are formulated with respect to the use of the different rules. Then the data are discussed, followed by the results, and conclusions are drawn.

DECISION RULES

In the literature many different decision rules are proposed (e.g. Simon, 1957; Svenson, 1979; Vlek and Wagenaar, 1979). In the following we shall only summarize the decision rules which were detected in our sample and indicate what type of information is necessary to conclude that they have been used.

The *subjective expected utility (SEU) model* states that a decision maker should choose the strategy with the highest expected utility. The expected utility of a strategy is defined as a composite function of the utilities of the outcomes and their probabilities:

$$EU(S_j) = \sum_{i=1}^{k} p_{ij} U_{ij}$$

where EU (S_j) indicates the expected utility of strategy j, p_{ij} the probability of the occurrence of outcome i under strategy j, and U_{ij} the utility of outcome i under strategy j.

From the above it is clear that, in order to test the fit of this model, the verbal probability and utility statements must at least indicate a rank ordering and preferably a size. The rank-ordered statements still have to be quantified. We call statements that can be quantified *intensity statements*. Thus, in order to test the fit of this model probabilities and utilities with intensities are required.

The *risk-avoiding rules* have been developed previously by the authors (Gallhofer and Saris, 1979a, 1979b). The choice rule consists of selecting the strategy with the highest probability of positive outcomes or, which amounts to the same thing since the sum of the probabilities is assumed to be one, of selecting the strategy with the lowest probability of negative outcomes.

The risk-avoiding rules can be expressed more formally as follows:

if $p_{-i} < p_{-j}$ then S_i is chosen

or equivalently,

if $p_{+i} > p_{+j}$ then S_i is chosen

where p_{-i}, p_{-j} are the probabilities of negative outcomes under strategy i or j; p_{+i}, p_{+j} are the probabilities of positive outcomes under strategy i or j.

In order to test the fit of these rules only probabilities with intensities have to be indicated.

The *dominance, lexicographic, and addition of utilities rules* have in common that the several aspects or dimensions of outcomes, which are considered certain, must be used systematically across strategies.

The *dominance rule* states that the strategy that should be selected is better than the other(s) on at least one dimension and not worse than the other strategy (-ies) on the remaining aspects.

The *lexicographic rule* suggests first rank-ordering the aspects in importance and then selecting the strategy that is most attractive with respect to the most important attribute. When applying this rule to the data an additional verbal statement about the indication of the most important aspect is required.

The choice rule of the *addition of utilities rule* suggests summing up the utilities of each aspect per strategy and then selecting the strategy with the highest total value. In order to test this rule an indication of overall utilities per strategy is required.

From the above it is clear that intensities of utilities are necessary in order to test the fit of one of these rules.

The last two rules, i.e. *Simon's satisficing rule* (Simon, 1957, p.248) and the *reversed Simon rule*, specify the following choice rules. *Simon's rule* suggests selecting the (first) strategy detected that leads to satisfactory outcomes only. The *reversed Simon rule*, which has been developed by the authors to cover political situations for which no satisfactory strategy was available, consists of excluding all the strategies that lead with certainty to negative outcomes only, as long as there is another strategy which might lead to a positive result.

No intensities of probabilities and utilities are required to test the fit of these rules. Table 1 summarizes the four classes of decision rules based on the required information about probabilities and utilities. So far we have only indicated that the relationship between the information and the decision rules in Table 1 is necessary but not sufficient. This means, for instance, that the risk-avoiding rules can never be applied without knowledge about the intensities of probabilities. On the other hand, all the available information need not always be used. A decision maker could, for example, use Simon's rule whether or not he/she had provided information with respect to intensities of utilities or probabilities, or both.

Table 1 Relationship between decision rules and the precision of the information about utilities and probabilities

	Utilities with intensities	Utilities without intensities
Probabilities with intensities	SEU model I	Risk-avoiding rules II
Probabilities without intensities	Dominance rule Lexicographic rule Addition of utilities rule III	Simon's rule Reversed Simon rule IV

HYPOTHESIS WITH RESPECT TO THE USE OF DECISION RULES

Although the decision rules are formulated in statements which indicate what should be done in order to determine a choice, their function in descriptive studies is different. In such studies the rules should represent the formal description of an argument presented by a decision maker. This means that they will represent the link between the description of the decision problem and the choice made. The specification of an argument by a decision maker consists of two steps:

(a) The selection of components that are necessary to formulate the decision problem, i.e. the strategies, outcomes, potential aspects, and uncertainty. This activity is called *structuring*.
(b) The *evaluation* of the outcomes and the probabilities constitutes the second activity.

Having structured the situation and evaluated the probabilities and utilities, the decision maker completes his/her argument and draws a conclusion. Given the function of the evaluation in the formulation of the argument, we can specify our hypothesis:

> The information with respect to utilities and probabilities is not only a necessary but also a sufficient condition for the use of a specific decision rule to describe the outcome.

This hypothesis suggests that we expect to find an approximately one-to-one relationship between the formulation of the decision problem by the decision maker and the decision rule used. In practice, this means that given the information with respect to the utilities and probabilities, a rule will exist which is just complex enough to require this information and then we should be able to predict the final choice. This is a useful postulate because in this study we found that the decision makers very seldom explicitly mentioned the rule used to derive the choice. This is in contrast to think-aloud experiments, because there subjects do not usually have to define the decision problem as it is presented to them (see Payne, 1976; Svenson, 1979; Huber, 1982).

DATA

Dutch foreign policy decisions in the period 1900 to 1955 were studied. The documents we used consisted of primary material, such as the minutes of the meetings of the Dutch Council of Ministers, coded telegrams from advisers abroad to the Government and reports from several government agencies. The selection of the period 1900 to 1955 was determined by the fact that classified material was available under the condition that it was used for pure scientific purposes.

DATA COLLECTION

When collecting the raw data of the decision cases, the following problems were encountered:

(a) The total number of foreign policy decisions during 1900 and 1955 is unknown because the various state offices did not keep systematic inventories of all the decisions made in their departments.

(b) When all available means are used to gather as complete an inventory of decisions as possible, the possibility still exists that some cases will be omitted, as the records may be non-existent or inappropriate because they do not contain arguments with respect to strategies.

In order to eliminate these problems as much as possible, the population of foreign policy decisions during 1900 and 1955 was defined as follows. Only those decisions were registered which are described in historical or political studies in such a manner that one can assume that documents exist which might contain arguments concerning strategy choices.

With respect to the selection of historico-political studies from which we drew our raw data, we first used handbooks and reference books in order to get an overview of the existing literature. Thereafter, the most recent studies of historical periods were consulted and complementary material was gathered from diaries and memoirs of concerned officials. In this way we collected 136 decision clusters from which we drew a sample of 50 clusters. Our sample covers a great variety of political topics such as the maintenance of Dutch neutrality during World War I, decisions during the economic crisis in the 1930s, the decolonization of Indonesia, the European integration in the 1950s, etc. For each cluster, all the decision documents available in the archives of the Council of Ministers, the Department of Foreign Affairs, and some private archives of decision makers were collected. Altogether we obtained a number of 235 different decisions for analysis.

QUALITY OF THE INFORMATION PROVIDED

Table 1 shows that some decision rules require utility and probability statements with intensities (class I models), others only probability statements with intensities (class II models) or only utility statements with intensities (class III models), and the last group (class IV models) requires no intensities at all.

By *intensity statements of utilities* or *probabilities* we mean verbal statements that indicate a size or a rank-ordering. In fact, metric information is sometimes required, but as we are studying texts in natural language, one can assume that the above-specified intensity statements are translations of numerical information into ordinary language. In the following the variety of statements will be briefly illustrated by examples:

(a) *Utilities with intensities* indicate a rank ordering or size, e.g. 'this is better than ...', 'this is the best outcome', etc.
(b) *Utilities without intensities* consist of expressions that only indicate whether some outcome is positively or negatively evaluated, e.g. 'advantage', 'disadvantage', 'loss', etc.
(c) *Probabilities with intensities* are statements like 'the chance is very high...' or 'the probability is lower if this strategy is used ...', etc.
(d) *Probabilities without intensities* consist of expressions like 'possible', 'uncertain', 'it could happen', or certainties indicated in the indicative mood like 'this happens', etc.

DETERMINATION OF THE DECISION RULE USED

Given the probability and utility statements used by the decision makers, the decision problem can be classified into one of the four classes specified in Table 1. One then applies the rule(s) of the class to the data and determines which strategy should be chosen. Finally, one compares the strategy obtained by a specific decision rule of the appropriate class with the strategy actually chosen by the decision maker. If the strategies are identical we say that the rule fits or explains the choice. If this is not so, the model cannot explain the choice.

In the following we illustrate the determination of the decision rule used by an example. Figure 3 presents the decision tree, i.e. the overview of the argumentation.

The first step which will be undertaken is to reduce the data again in a table. Table 2 presents this reduction. Table 2 shows that all the intermediate outcomes of the decision tree leading to a final branch are summarized together. In this way one obtains outcomes for S_1 and for S_2. These outcomes can be divided into several aspects, i.e. the success or failure of the military action, whether or not sanctions could occur, and whether or not the Dutch have to evacuate. The table also indicates the evaluations of the various aspects $U(a_i)$. Then the probabilities of the occurrence of the outcomes are summarized. In order to arrive at such a summary one has to take the 'products' of the verbal probability statements leading to a specific final outcome. Taking, for example, the combinations of branches that lead to 'no severe sanctions' under S_1, the probability of O_2 and O_4 (Table 2) is 'possible * unexpectable'. Knowing that the product of the probabilities cannot be greater than the smallest probability one has to search for this one. It would be 'unexpectable'. However, 'possible' does not indicate an intensity and therefore the probability of getting 'no severe sanctions' can only be considered as 'uncertain'. The determination of the other probabilities is similar. With respect to S_2 the probability is 'certain'. The verbal statement relating to this probability also contains no intensity.

Regarding the subjective utilities, Table 2 also shows that the only exception

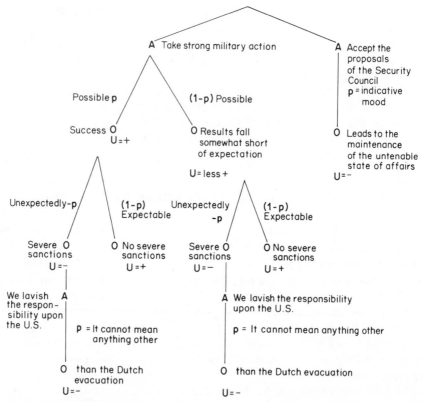

Fig. 3   Example of a decision tree.

is the statement 'the results fall somewhat short of expectation'. However, since the remaining utilities are not indicated by rank orderings or intensities, this single piece of information cannot be used.

In order to *determine the decision rule*, one must first establish the appropriate class of decision rules (see Table 1) based on the information about utilities and probabilities summarized in Table 2. When examining Table 2 it is clear that the decision maker used probabilities and utilities without intensities.

Since the outcomes can be split into aspects one has also to check whether they are used systematically across strategies. Table 2 shows, for example, that O_4 and O_2 (S_1) do not contain a_3 and that O_5 (S_2) only consists of a_3. Thus the decision maker did not systematically use the same outcomes. One can therefore conclude that class IV (Table 1) is appropriate. In this class two decision rules are mentioned. The first is Simon's rule, which states that one has to search until one finds a strategy that only leads to satisfactory outcomes. This choice obtained by the rule does not coincide with the actual choice (S_1)

Table 2 Summary of the argumentation

Strategies	Outcomes				
	O_1	O_2	O_3	O_4	O_5
	a_1:success	a_1:success	a_1:less success	a_1:less success	—
	a_2:sanctions	a_2:no sanctions	a_2:sanctions	a_2:no sanctions	—
	a_3:Dutch evacuation	—	a_3:Dutch evacuation	—	a_3:Dutch evacuation
S_1*	$U(a_1)$: + $U(a_2)$: − $U(a_3)$: − p = possible	$U(a_1)$: + $U(a_2)$: + p = possible	$U(a_1)$: less + $U(a_2)$: − $U(a_3)$: − p = possible	$U(a_1)$: less + $U(a_2)$: + p = possible	
S_2					$U(a_3)$: − p = certain

where * indicates the chosen strategy and a_i aspect i of one outcome.
S_1 reads: take a strong military action and if sanctions occur lavish the responsibility on the United States. Otherwise nothing else has to be done.
S_2 reads: accept the proposal of the Security Council.

since the strategy does not lead with certainty to satisfactory outcomes only. The second is the reversed Simon rule, which states that one has to reject all strategies that lead with certainty to unsatisfactory outcomes while there exists a strategy where satisfactory outcomes are also possible. According to this rule S_1 should be chosen. This rule coincides with the actual choice and it fits the data. Given this result we decided that the *reversed Simon rule* is the rule that can explain the choice.

RESULTS

Table 3 indicates the total number of decision situations in which the different types of information are specified. It shows that the decision makers tried to avoid complicated descriptions, using intensity statements of utilities and probabilities at the same time (class I models). This class occurred three times. The rules using intensities of probabilities (class II models) occurred more frequently than the rules using intensities of utilities (class III models). Decision rules that did not require intensities at all occurred most frequently (class IV models).

Furthermore, Table 3 relates to our hypothesis, which states that we expect

Table 3 Prediction of the fitting decision rules on the basis of the measurement level of the information

Information about utilities and probabilities	Classes of decision rules	Correct prediction of the decision rule	No fitting decision rule available	Total
Probabilities with intensities and utilities with intensities	I SEU model	2	1	3
Probabilities with intensities and utilities without intensities	II Risk-avoiding	70	1	71
Probabilities without intensities and utilities with intensities	III Dominance, lexicographic rules, etc.	46	3	49
Probabilities and utilities without intensities	IV Simon, reversed Simon rules	109	3	112
Total		227	8	235

an approximately one-to-one relationship between the formulation of the decision problem by the decision maker and the decision rule used. The table shows that the decision rules that used all the information available could almost always describe the choice. Only in 8 of the 235 cases was no decision rule found in the appropriate class which could describe the choice. Our hypothesis is thus confirmed.

VALIDITY OF THE INSTRUMENT

Referring to Figure 2, we can state that in 227 of the 235 cases we could predict, based on the derivation of the decision structure, a choice by means of a decision rule of the appropriate class. The derivation of the actual choice of the decision maker is also obtained by coding another part of text which indicated the choice of strategy. In 227 cases the predicted choices coincided with the derivation of the choice.Therefore, we can conclude that we have a good indication that the

EDA approach measures what it is intended to measure, namely the true decision structures of the decision makers.

CONCLUSIONS

The study showed that only seven decision rules could predict the choices relating to a great variety of political topics and situations. These findings present strong evidence that these rules are the rules of argumentation the decision makers were assumed to apply. We state *assumed* since rules never were specified explicitly in the documents.

As was indicated above, the formulation of the argument consisted of two steps, i.e. first, the problem was structured and, second, the utilities and probabilities were evaluated. The choice then followed automatically, according to the decision makers. This means that they assumed that their audience knew which rule to apply. Results of a subsequent study (Saris and Gallhofer, 1984), where the effects of situational, personal, and functional characteristics of decision makers on their formulation of the problem were investigated and proved to be almost absent, even suggest that decision makers use these rules quite arbitrarily. We therefore also prefer to speak about *rules of argumentation* instead of decision rules, since they do not represent thought processes.

Table 3 showed that the most frequently used rules were the most simple ones. Decision makers thus also tried to resolve problems in this way even when they were on the brink of war.

When suggesting further research with the EDA procedure, systematic studies on data of other nations could be extremely valuable. In this way one could answer the question as to whether or not the use of these rules can be corroborated cross-nationally. In this respect it might also be interesting to have evidence on whether or not great powers decide in a more sophisticated way in situations where vital interests are at stake.

Given the decision trees, relating to a great variety of cases, the systematic study of the relevant aspects considered by the decision makers involved could clarify a variety of questions: e.g. whether or not the aspects they consider are dependent on the departmental affiliation of the decision maker. For instance, the Minister of Finance might have a preference for financial aspects, while his colleague in Foreign Affairs might concentrate on international ones, etc.

Another interesting question to study would be to investigate under which conditions individuals will be convinced of the necessity to consider other aspects they had previously overlooked or rejected. It is obvious that for such an investigation cases must be available in which several decision makers discuss a particular problem cross time. An analysis of this last question might also reveal some characteristics of collective decision making.

Finally, on the basis of answers to the above-mentioned questions decision aids could be developed which will often turn out to have the structure of a *multiattribute subjective utility model* (class I, Table 1). This very complex model, which considers all kinds of value trade-offs and combines with probabilities, can only be handled, in our opinion, by means of decision aids. Its advantage would be that decision makers could improve the quality of their decisions.

REFERENCES

Edwards, W. (1961). Behavioral decision theory, *Annual Review of Psychology*, **12**, 473–98.
Fishburn, P. C. (1964). *Decision and Value Theory*, Wiley, New York.
Gallhofer, I. N. (1978). Coders' reliability in the study of decision making concepts, replications in time and across topics, *Methoden en Data Nieuwsbrief van de Sociaal-Wetenschappelijke Sectie van de VVS, MDN*, **1**, 58–74.
Gallhofer, I. N., and Saris, W. E. (1979a). The decision of the Dutch Council of Ministers and the Military Commander-in-Chief relating to the reduction of armed forces in Autumn 1916, *Acta Politica*, **1**, 95–105.
Gallhofer, I. N., and Saris, W. E. (1979b). Strategy choices of foreign policy decision makers: The Netherlands 1914, *Journal of Conflict Resolution*, **23**, 425–45.
Gallhofer, I. N., and Saris, W. E. (1979c). An analysis of the argumentation of decision makers using decision trees, *Quality and Quantity*, **13**, 411–30.
Gallhofer, I. N., and Saris, W. E. (1982). A decision theoretical analysis of decisions of the Dutch Government with respect to Indonesia, *Quality and Quantity*, **16**, 313–44.
Gallhofer, I. N., and Saris, W. E. (1983). A decision theoretical analysis of decisions of the Dutch Government in exile during World War II, *Historical Social Research, Quantum Information*, **26**, 3–17.
Gallhofer, I. N., and Saris, W. E. (1986). Appendix 3: An illustration of the Empirical Decision Analysis procedure. In I. N. Gallhofer, W. E. Saris, and M. Melman (Eds) *Different Text Analysis Procedures for the Study of Decision Making*, Sociometric Research Foundation, Amsterdam, pp. 141–152.
Gallhofer, I. N., and Saris, W. E. (1988). A coding procedure for empirical research of political decision-making. In Willem E. Saris and Irmtraud N. Gallhofer (Eds)., *Sociometric Research, Data Collection and Scaling*, Vol. 1, Macmillan, London, pp. 51–68.
Holsti, O. R., (1969). *Content Analysis for the Social Sciences and Humanities*, Addison Wesley, Reading, Mass.
Huber, O. (1979). Intransitive Präferenzen and Strategien für Multidimensionele Entscheidungen: Gewichtete-Präferenzen-Mengen-Strategie und Differenz-Strategie, *Zeitschrift für Experimentele und Angewandte Psychologie*, **26**, 72–93.
Huber, O. (1982). *Entscheiden als Problemlösen*, Huber, Wien-Stuttgart-München.
Keeney, R. L., and Raiffa, H. (1976). *Decisions with Multiple Objectives: Preferences and Value Trade-offs*, Wiley, New York.
Krippendorff, K. (1970). Bivariate agreement coefficients for reliability of data. In E. F. Borgatta and G. W. Bohrnstedt (Eds), *Sociological Methodology*, Jossey Bass, San Francisco, Calif., pp. 139–50.
Larichev, O. I. *et al.* (1980). Modelling multiattribute information processing strategies in a binary decision task, *Organizational Behavior and Human Performance*, **26**, 278–91.
Montgomery, H. (1977). A study of intransitive preferences, using a think-aloud procedure, In H. Jungermann and G. de Zeeuw (Eds), *Decision Making and Change in Human Affairs*, Reidel, Dordrecht.

Payne, J. W. (1976). Task complexity and contingent processing in decision making: an information search and protocol analysis, *Organizational Behavior and Human Performance*, **16**, 366–87.
Saris, W. E., and Gallhofer, I. N. (1984). Formulation of real life decisions: a study of foreign policy decisions, *Acta Psychologica*, **56**, 247–65.
Simon, H. A. (1957). A behavioral model of rational choice. In *Models of Man, Social and Rational*, Wiley, New York, pp. 135–52.
Slovic, P. (1975). Choice between equal valued alternatives. *Journal of Experimental Psychology, Human Perception and Performance*, **1**, 280–7.
Svenson, O. (1979). Process descriptions of decision making, *Organizational Behavior and Human Performance*, **23**, 86–112.
Tversky, A. (1969). Intransitivity of preferences, *Psychological Review*, **76**, 31–48.
Vlek, Ch., and Wagenaar, W. A. (1979). Judgement and decision under uncertainty. In J. A. Michon, E. G. J. Eijkman, and L. F. W. de Klenk. (Eds), *Handbook of Psychonomics*, Vol. II, North-Holland, Amsterdam, pp. 253–345.

Author index

Subject index